CW01021989

Journey to Freedom Series

DYING
TO
LIVE!

Commendations and
Testimonies

JOURNEY
TO FREEDOM

"If you are serious about wanting to experience the deep truths of God in your life, then this is possibly the most relevant and pertinent tool of ministry I have discovered. It is insightful, challenging, and informative. I heartily endorse this tool of transformation. And now I challenge you to read it and prepare for change!"
Alistair P Petrie *Executive Director – Partnership Ministries*

"It is an inexpressible relief and joy to discover daily teaching from the Word of God which embraces the breadth of Christian teaching, and whose depth, by the convicting and instructing power of the Holy Spirit, reaches the nooks and crannies of the reader's heart. This comprehensive teaching about the ways, works and words of the living God, always invites us deeper into intimacy with Him. It is personal and practical, pastoral and prophetic, encouraging and educating, appealing and revealing. It is Christ-centred, Holy Spirit empowered and inspired. I love it! I need it! I'm going to use it! So should you!"
Stuart McAlpine *Pastor, Christ Our Shepherd Church, Capitol Hill, Washington D C*

"The church is starving through lack of teaching that connects us to Christ and builds our foundation in Him. This is why I am so thrilled with *Journey to Freedom*. It is a marvellous discipleship tool that can inspire you in your walk with God and help you overcome every personal struggle. I hope you can make this part of your daily devotions. It is strong meat that boosts your spiritual diet!"
J Lee Grady *Director, The Mordecai Project and former Editor, Charisma Magazine*

"Down-to-earth lessons in the reality of our lives, with desperately needed spiritual answers. They teach us how to apply the blood, cross and resurrection of our Lord Jesus Christ to transform us from weakness to strength, incapacity to capability, misery to blessedness."
John Sandford *Co-Founder of Elijah House Ministries*

"*Journey to Freedom* presents an amazing array of information that is at once biblical, practical and comprehensive. Discipleship is generally a lost art in the church today. So, to find a guide like this, covering the simplest truths of the faith to the deepest and most profound is like discovering buried treasure – simply outstanding!"
David Kyle Foster *Director, Mastering Life Ministries, Franklin, TN and Producer of Pure Passion TV Channel*

"What an incredible opportunity for the body of Christ to help people grow into strong, mature Christians. Simple, understandable and yet profound teaching that anyone interested in finding fullness in the Lord can easily access. The materials are presented in a practical way with opportunity for personal application. An incredible opportunity to learn the ways of the Lord."
Ruth Ruibal *President, Julio C. Ruibal Ministries, Colombia*

"Consecutive, practical Bible teaching in a straightforward and understandable way – pastoral in content and personal in application. It is designed to engage us where it finds us but not to leave us as we are. It will stimulate the mind; stir the emotions; strengthen the will; and nourish the spirit. My concern is not just to commend it to you, but to plead with you to take a look for yourself with a view to making a new discipleship commitment to our Lord Jesus."
Rev Jim Graham *Former Pastor of Gold Hill Baptist Church and Director of External Ministries.*

"As I read through the teachings, I was drawn into the spiritual journey toward wholeness that is offered by *Journey to Freedom*. Peter Horrobin's insights into God's purpose in creating each of us are powerful and he is anointed with God's desire to call us to lives that are healed of sin and its consequences. I was reminded of the scripture *'And do not be conformed to this world, but be transformed by the renewing of your mind, so that you may prove what the will of God is, that which is good and acceptable and perfect'* (Romans 12:2)."
Rev Peter Tsukahira *Co-Founder and Director, Or Ha Carmel Ministry Centre, Haifa, Israel*

TESTIMONIES
from some of those who applied the *Journey to Freedom* teaching in their lives when first published on-line as Ellel 365.

"I weep with gratitude for what God has done for me."

"Ellel 365 has changed my life forever. These past twelve months have been the most fulfilling and exciting experience I have had in my walk with the Lord."

"My relationship with God is going from strength to strength – I just love it."

"Ellel 365 has been a lifeline – it held me safe while Father God touched the broken places."

"I so long for everyone to experience what I'm now experiencing."

"Ellel 365 is the most important thing I've ever done – it's reality!"

"Ellel 365 has been truly LIFE TRANSFORMING –
and I still have a way to go!"

*"In faith, honesty and obedience my heavy burden was lifted,
I was set free – what joy!"*

**"The relief from the hold of sin was wonderful –
worth every pain and all the tears I've shed!"**

*"Now I know I have a FATHER in heaven. The lie of the enemy
has been broken."*

**"The teaching is extraordinary and beautiful. It all makes perfect
sense. I'm amazed at the things I am learning – I wish I'd had this
when I first became a Christian."**

"Thank you from the bottom of my very grateful heart!"

"My formerly derailed destiny in life is being put back on the fast track!"

"This journey becomes more exciting every day. I have dealt with so
many issues in my own life."

**"Ellel 365 is challenging and provoking – God is using it to wonderfully
transform my life."**

"Inspired and inspirational. The teaching is astounding and has opened
up a whole new experience for me in my Christian journey."

*"I now believe I have a destiny and a future which I didn't have before – miracles
DO happen!"*

"Excellent and brilliant foundational teaching for every Christian."

Book 6

Journey to Freedom Series

Personal Transformation – One Step at a Time

DYING TO LIVE!

Peter Horrobin
Founder of Ellel Ministries

Understanding the Gospel and Living it Out

Sovereign World

Published by
Sovereign World Ltd
Ellel Grange
Bay Horse
Lancaster
Lancashire LA2 0HN

www.sovereignworld.com
Twitter: @sovereignworld
Facebook: www.facebook.com/sovereignworld

Published September 2019
Copyright © 2019 Peter Horrobin

The right of Peter Horrobin to be identified as author of this work
has been asserted by him in accordance with the
Copyright, Designs and Patents Act 1988.

All rights reserved.
No part of this publication may be reproduced, stored in a retrieval system,
or transmitted in any form or by any means, electronic, mechanical,
photocopying or otherwise, without the prior
written permission of the publisher.

ISBN 978-1-85240-770-4 (Printed edition)
ISBN 978-1 85240-775-9 (Kindle edition)
ISBN 978-1-85240-780-3 (E-pub edition)

All Scripture quotations, unless otherwise indicated, are taken from the
Holy Bible, New International Version®, NIV®. Copyright ©1973, 1978,
1984, 2011 by Biblica, Inc.™ Used by permission of Zondervan.
All rights reserved worldwide. www.zondervan.com.
The "NIV" and "New International Version" are trademarks registered
in the United States Patent and Trademark Office by Biblica, Inc.™

British Library Cataloguing-in-Publication Data
A catalogue record for this book is available from the British Library.

Cover designs by Paul Stanier of Zaccmedia
www.zaccmedia.com

Printed in Great Britain by Bell & Bain Ltd, Glasgow

CONTENTS

Stage 3 – The Passion and Death of Jesus (2)   99

"Jesus' words of forgiveness to the Roman soldiers echo down the years of time as a constant challenge to those who think they have an excuse to be unforgiving."

Stage 4 – Resurrection Life!   141

"Christianity would be nonsense were it not for the resurrection. It is still nonsense to those who choose not to believe!"

Stage 5 – The Great Commission for the Body of Christ

"The Great Commission must have been the most under-staffed and under-funded, but most successful, campaign in world history. Two thousand years later it is still meeting its goal!"

Stage 6 – Pentecost – Power for the Church

"The experience of Pentecost changed 120 fearful followers of Jesus into a band of fearless saints! The church without the Holy Spirit is like a car without gas – useless and going nowhere."

Stage 7 – The Church Expands its Horizons

"Fire cannot be contained within an inflammable container. It will always break out. The Holy Spirit is the fire in believers – He will always burn His way out into the hearts of others!"

Stage 8 – He's Coming Back!   315

"A world that disbelieves the first coming of Jesus has no reason to either fear or welcome the second coming – until it happens!"

Now Read On...   363

PREFACE TO JOURNEY TO FREEDOM, BOOK 6

Welcome to Book 6 of our *Journey to Freedom*. This book contains the teaching that enables us to make sense of the whole of Scripture, from Genesis to Revelation! What happened in Jerusalem all those years ago has been changing lives ever since.

Jesus' ministry began in Nazareth after He returned from His wilderness experience of being tempted by the devil. From that moment on, as Jesus progressed from Nazareth to Calvary, He taught the truth about the Kingdom of God, healed the sick and set the captives free. We saw in Book 5 how these three brief years were the three most productive years of any person's life in all of history. But they were also years of preparation for the suffering that was to come. They were years of popularity as the sick and hurting sought Him out and discovered the reality of His love, power and authority, but they were also years in which the lengthening shadow of the cross hung over His life.

The Pharisees and all the religious authorities hated Him. Jealous of His power and His popularity, they began to plot His death – not knowing that in so doing they were preparing to kill the very Son of God, who would become the most perfect sacrifice for the sin of the whole world.

In Book 6 of our *Journey to Freedom* we are going to 'walk with Jesus' into Jerusalem and watch what happens every step of the way from Bethany to Calvary. Then we will stand with the women at the tomb in utter amazement, as Jesus is raised from the dead. And then see how Jesus prepares the disciples – and the church through all the ages – to take the Gospel of the Kingdom of God to all the corners of the world in the power of the Holy Spirit.

This is the most heart-breaking yet thrilling story that has ever been told! How can it be that God's love should be so great that He would allow His Son to suffer in abject agony so that the likes of you and me can know Him and inherit eternal life? One day in heaven we will see the wounds of His love in His hands and worship Him!

How I pray that, as you read these stages of our journey, God will so impact your heart with these extraordinary truths that you will never be the same again – transformed by the power of His love and empowered to serve Him for the rest of your days.

And finally, we will rejoice together in anticipation of the fact that, not only did Jesus come to die for our sins, but He is coming back again for those who are His own – those who have been redeemed and set free! There is a triumph day awaiting the saints as they look forward to the light of a glorious new day dawning. Yes, it will be a day of judgement for those who have rejected Him and His love – but it will be a glorious day for those who are alive 'in Christ' for evermore. We have a lot to look forward to.

It may be that you are reading this book without having seen or read the earlier books in the series. I have, therefore, copied much of the *Preface* to Book 1 below, which is relevant to all the books in the series. But, may I encourage you to also read the earlier books, and ensure that you have a solid Christian foundation in your life.

FROM THE PREFACE TO BOOK 1

In over 30 years of ministry, I have witnessed first-hand, and on many occasions, how the Lord has brought deep healing, restoration and freedom to even the most hurting and broken of people. *Journey to Freedom* contains the life-transforming keys that God has given us in His Word, which will enable you to enjoy personal transformation and freedom, one step at a time.

The original edition of *Journey to Freedom* was published on-line under the title *Ellel 365* – providing a whole year's teaching and training in *365* daily units. While thousands of people have enjoyed reading the lessons of *Ellel 365* on-line, there is still a large body of people who prefer the enjoyment of being able to hold a traditional book in their hands. These volumes, therefore, have been produced in response to popular demand.

This is a journey through which God can transform your life one step at a time, as you understand and apply each chapter's scriptural teaching. I don't write these words lightly – I believe them with every part of my being. I KNOW God changes people's lives, I have seen it happen! I KNOW He brings healing and freedom to those who are struggling. I KNOW God is interested in every detail of our lives. I KNOW He wants to set us free from the holds of the enemy. And I KNOW He wants to see you living in the destiny He has prepared for you.

We serve a truly awesome God who is as real and active today as He was in all the stories we read in the Bible (Hebrews 13:8). We have seen many set free from long term physical and psychological conditions, addictions and generational curses. Deep wounds of abuse and rejection have been healed by our gentle Father God. Identities that have been crushed, and sometimes burdened with guilt and shame, have been restored and relationships have been healed and repaired.

People have been healed from the consequences of deep traumas. Wounds have been touched by the Lord and the holds of the enemy have been broken. The fruits of bitterness have melted away through love and forgiveness. Debilitating fears have been discarded and replaced with courage and trust – so many beautiful stories of life-transformation, by a God who cares passionately for you and for me.

STRONG AND LASTING FOUNDATIONS

All buildings need strong and lasting foundations. In a similar way our lives need to have strong and lasting spiritual foundations. We will then be able to enter into the calling and destiny that God has reserved for each one of us. *Journey to Freedom* will help you establish such foundations as a preparation for all that God has for you in the rest of your life.

I am excited and envisioned about the faith journey we're embarking on together. A wealth of vital material is available to you. And you will be able to make this journey at the pace that is just right for you, with the freedom to move on from one chapter to the next whenever you feel ready.

It may be tempting to flick through the book and dip into later chapters, especially on subjects you have a special interest in, but you can't construct a safe building without all the foundations being in place. And the foundations which will be built into your life through the early chapters of *Journey to Freedom* could be of critical importance to you. The most genuine and lasting works of personal transformation that I have witnessed, have usually come as part of such an ongoing pilgrimage with the Lord. This is how the Holy Spirit normally works in our lives in order to establish godly order – one step at a time.

For many of us the struggles in our lives aren't going to be fixed in a day. We may cry out "Heal me, Lord", but for most of us God doesn't heal us dramatically or through an instant transformation. He heals us by carefully and tenderly working deep in our hearts, in the hidden areas that we may have tried so hard to ignore or discard. When our Heavenly Father brings His truth into our innermost being, He establishes those strong and lasting foundations, through which He brings stability, deep healing and wholeness.

Many of the people I meet and have prayed with, have come to our Centres because of the unwelcome fruit they see in their lives, such as depression, relationship breakdown, sicknesses, financial crisis or ruin, insomnia, addictions, pornography or obesity and many more different problems that Christians can struggle with. This causes them to cry out to the Lord for healing of the symptoms, but the real problems usually go a whole lot deeper.

What is the real cry of their heart? It is things like sadness, despair, fear, anxiety, sense of failure and unworthiness. It's feeling guilty and unfulfilled. It's anger, loneliness, the cold wall of self-protection, inner brokenness, hopelessness and lack of identity. It's not having a reason to live.

As a human being I may be an expert at covering up my struggles. I may try and function normally and ignore the inner limping which has become part of my everyday life. But the Lord longs to reach those places and repair damage which can be lying in deep areas of our heart; not just deal with the fruit seen on the surface – the problems I'm struggling with today.

Jesus said, *"'If the Son sets you free, you will be free indeed'"* (John 8:36). Unless He heals the foundation of our lives, we can never really become the people He created us to be and enjoy the blessing of being that person!

TRUTH AND REALITY

On each stage of this journey, as you read and take in one chapter at a time, I believe the Lord will be building new foundations of truth and revelation into your heart.

Journey to Freedom isn't a Bible study aimed at making us more knowledgeable Christians – the heart of this journey is to learn how to apply the truths of God's word and His character deep into our own being. Then He can transform the hidden depths of who we are into the beautiful creation He intended us to be. It's all for His glory and not for ours. My prayer is that by the enabling power of the Holy Spirit you will have the courage and the willingness to allow the Lord to shine His truth into every area of your being.

It's so easy to hide the true motives of our hearts, and even to deceive ourselves! But it's only as we are real before the One who created us, that we can fully allow Him to make that essential difference to our lives.   Psalm 51:6 (NKJV) says *'You desire truth in the inward parts, and in the hidden part you will make me to know wisdom'*, and Jesus Himself said, *"'Then you will know the truth, and the truth will set you free'"* (John 8:32).

So, if you've not already done so, may I encourage you to commit your life afresh to the Lord and give Him permission to shine His light of truth deep into your heart:

Father God, thank You so much for who You are, for Your love and for Your desire to restore my life, so that I can walk in the destiny prepared for me from the very beginning. I pray that You will show me the areas where I have been hurt and need healing. Help me to see the places where I have got it wrong and need forgiveness and restoration. Help me to give You first place in every area of my being as I learn how to apply the truth of Your Word in my life. I invite you to be Lord of every area of my being. In Jesus' name, Amen

ON A PRACTICAL NOTE

The original *Ellel 365* programme contained five teachings each week, followed on the sixth day by a review of all that had been covered in the previous five days and, on the seventh day, there was a devotional reading to round off the week.

The structure of the original material has been retained in this printed version of *Journey to Freedom*, so that you can follow the same weekly pattern through a whole year. Alternatively, you may prefer to work through the books at your own speed, either slower or faster, to suit your own personal situation. Each week's teaching of the original Ellel 365 is now referred to as a *'Stage'* in this book form of *Journey to Freedom*.

Whatever reading pattern you choose, may I encourage you to persevere. Some of the most profound testimonies from *Ellel 365* were from people who did just that, and at the end of the journey were totally amazed at all that God had done. I passionately believe in the God of miracles – but I also recognise that some miracles take place over a period of time! And when I see now, the extraordinary transformation that God has wrought, one step at a time, I stand amazed at the way the God of miracles has been at work.

I would love to hear what God does in your life on your own *Journey to Freedom*. You can share your testimony by writing to me at peter. horrobin@ellel.org. I will look forward to hearing from you.

Peter Horrobin
Ellel Grange
September 2019

STAGE 1

Facing Reality – Jesus Enters Jerusalem

"When Jesus entered Jerusalem, the crowds welcomed Him. But that was before they discovered His journey would pass by Calvary."

JESUS ANOINTED AT BETHANY

Having looked at the healing ministry of Jesus (in Book 5 of *Journey to Freedom*), we are now turning our attention to the events surrounding Jesus' death and resurrection, and what we can learn from them.

Six days before the Passover celebrations, as Jesus was on his way up to Jerusalem, a thanksgiving meal was given in Bethany *'in honour of Jesus'* (John 12:2), hosted by Simon the Leper (Mark 14:3). Jesus and His disciples were probably staying in the home of Lazarus, Mary and Martha, and Simon will have been one of their neighbours. As we saw in Book 5 (of *Journey to Freedom*), Lazarus and his sisters were probably Jesus' closest friends, outside the immediate circle of His own family and the friends and family of His disciples. They were very special to Jesus and Lazarus had been the subject of one of His previous miracles, when He raised him from the dead.

When John was writing his Gospel many years later, and telling of the amazing miracle of Lazarus' resurrection from the dead, he identified Lazarus' sister, Mary, as *'the same one who poured perfume on the Lord and wiped his feet with her hair'* (John 11:2). Mary had become very well known for what she did. Even Jesus said that *"'wherever the Gospel is preached throughout the world, what she has done will also be told, in memory of her'"* (Mark 14:9).

Mary was a very sensitive woman who loved to sit at the feet of the Saviour – much to the frustration of Martha who always seemed to end up doing the chores! This thanksgiving dinner, in honour of Jesus, wasn't going to be an exception to what had become the usual order of things – Martha was serving and Mary stayed close to the Master.

MARY'S ACT OF SELFLESS DEVOTION

Nard was probably the most expensive perfume of the day. It was distilled from oil, only found in the roots of a plant that grew in the foothills of the Himalayas. Traders would bring the roots on the well-worn trade routes from the East and sell their goods in the more lucrative markets of the West. *'A pint of pure nard'* (John 12:3) would have cost a small fortune to buy.

Matthew and Mark tell us that the oil had been kept in an alabaster flask – another sign of its preciousness. Mark and John tell us that it was worth at least a year's wages (Mark 14:5 and John 12:5). It was undoubtedly exceedingly valuable. The Scriptures tell us nothing of how Mary acquired the perfume, only how she used it.

At some stage during the meal Mary broke the alabaster jar containing the nard and began to pour it over Jesus. Mark says she poured it over His head (Mark 14:3) and John tells us she poured it over His feet and then wiped His feet with her hair. A pint of nard is a lot of perfume and there would have been more than enough to have poured it over both His head and His feet for *'the house was filled with the fragrance of the perfume'* (John 12:3).

There was no question of Mary using just a little of the perfume as a token gesture and keeping the rest for herself. This was an act of utterly selfless devotion in which she used all she had, of the most valuable thing she possessed, to demonstrate to those present, and to all who would read about her act for the rest of time, her understanding of just who Jesus was.

Nard was one of those precious perfumes, referred to also in the Song of Solomon, which hallmarks the completion of a relationship between a bride and her bridegroom. But there is absolutely nothing anywhere in the Scripture to suggest that the relationship Mary had with Jesus was of a personal or intimate nature. The pouring out of the oil in a public place, as opposed to in the privacy of a private room, speaks of a totally different form of relationship than that between a man and a woman in a private expression of their human love.

To fully understand this dimension of what was happening, we need to see how Paul described the church, the Body of Christ, as being the Bride of Christ. He says the relationship between Christ and the church, like the relationship between a husband and a wife, *'is a profound mystery'* (Ephesians 5:32). John, in the book of Revelation picks up the imagery of a Bridegroom and a Bride when he describes a moment that is yet to be when Jesus, the Lamb of God, celebrates *'the wedding supper of the Lamb'* (Revelation 19:9) with His bride (the church) who *'has made herself ready'* (Revelation 19:7).

When Mary used a pint of nard to anoint Jesus, I believe she had been led by the Holy Spirit to carry out a prophetic act of enormous significance, through which God was saying to the world that the events in Jerusalem that were soon to follow would be the first steps towards a time that is still to come, when Jesus would one day be the Bridegroom at a glorious wedding and how *'blessed are those who are invited'* (Revelation 19:9). But the only way that the Bridegroom would be able to take His Bride to Himself would be through walking the path of death and resurrection, and for this reason Jesus referred to her act of devotion as a preparation for His burial.

THE CRITICS RISE UP!

Whenever anyone walks in obedience to Jesus with acts of selfless love and devotion, there will always be those who rise up to criticise – especially if money has been spent in a way that others would consider wasteful! The moment the nard was poured out there were those there with 'their pocket calculators', working out that the oil would have cost at least a year's wages – an enormous sum of money. Not surprisingly, the complaints were led by Judas Iscariot, the treasurer for the disciples, who wanted to know *'why this perfume [wasn't] sold and the money given to the poor?'* (John 12:5).

Sadly, John tells us, that Judas *'did not say this because he cared about the poor, but because he was a thief; and as keeper of the money bag, he used to help himself to what was put in it'* (John 12:6). Judas was annoyed that a substantial donation wasn't being put into the disciples' money bag, from which he could have helped himself whenever he had a personal need! He had no interest in the poor – only in himself.

Even today, there are people who use the lame and the crippled to beg for donations, most of which goes to the 'Judas' who controls them. A similar principle operates when pimps encourage young girls into prostitution, to make money for themselves. As far as Judas was concerned, the poor were a good excuse to collect money on their behalf, from which he could steal a supply to meet his personal needs. What a terrible indictment of the state of Judas' heart – even before he was offered the bribe of thirty pieces of silver to personally betray Jesus into the hands of the authorities. His heart was already corrupted. Mary's critics *'rebuked her harshly'* (Mark 14:5).

JESUS' RESPONSE

When Jesus jumped to her defence, He didn't disagree with their assessment of the value of the perfume, but He carefully explained why what she had done was a very precious and beautiful thing. He said:

'The poor you will always have with you, and you can help them any time you want. But you will not always have me. She did what she could. She poured perfume on my body beforehand to prepare for my burial' (Mark 14:7-8).

Mary had poured out an anointing of precious oil on Jesus at a time when He was able to be blessed by receiving it. Mary correctly read the situation. Jesus was about to enter the most critical and dangerous season of His life. What He would do in the next few days would pave the way for all who believe and trust in Him to be redeemed out of the hand of the enemy and enter into a glorious renewed relationship with Father God. The marriage supper of the Lamb could never happen without the sacrifice of the Lamb of God for the sins of the world. The Bridegroom could never have the Bride without the sacrifice of love that Calvary would represent.

SACRIFICIAL LOVE

Mary may not have known exactly what was going to happen in the next few days, but in her spirit she knew that this was the time to pour out her best for the One who had done so much for her, her brother and her sister. What she did was a profoundly prophetic act. It was out of a heart of gratitude that she worshipped Jesus with everything she was and everything she had.

Such extravagant sacrificial love is rare, but in the history of Christian Missions, it is the lives that have been unconditionally laid down for the Lord that have been used by Him to produce the most fruit. Those lives have, as it were, been a sweet-smelling perfume that has blessed the heart of God in much the same way as Mary's use of her precious nard was such a blessing to Jesus.

We may not own any perfume that is worth a whole year's salary or be in possession of any serious wealth at all. But our very lives can be like a sweet-smelling savour – a fragrant offering to the Lord, the fruit of which rises to the throne of grace like incense (2 Corinthians 2:15).

I often talk about another Mary, whose life was just this – a sweet-smelling savour to the Lord. Mary Slessor was a Scottish lass who, as a young girl, was captivated by a vision to serve God in Calabar, on the slave coast of West Africa. Her vision was finally fulfilled at the age of 29 and for forty years her life was laid down for the Lord in one of the most hostile regions of the world. Without fear she confronted disease, cheated death on many occasions and little by little changed the face of the region. Her courage and her faith in God brought enormous fruit for the Kingdom of God. Hers was a life of 'pure nard', utterly precious and poured out for the Saviour whom she loved so much – just like her namesake of two thousand years previously.

Each one of us has a life, which has the potential to be like the nard in an alabaster jar. It is utterly precious to the Lord and, as we pour it out, we will bring joy and blessing to the face of the Saviour.

THE FINAL ACT

The tragedy of this extraordinary story is that for Judas it was the last straw. He couldn't bear any longer to stand by and see such foolish things happening. It was the end as far as he was concerned. So he 'went to *the chief priests to betray Jesus to them. They were delighted to hear this and promised to give him money. So he watched for an opportunity to hand him over'* (Mark 14:10-11).

If Judas wasn't now going to get his hands on some money by robbing the disciples' purse, he might as well go where he knew he would be rewarded well. And so Judas began to put his feet on the pathway of betrayal – a pathway which he would never leave.

We can all look at Judas and say we would never have done what he did – and I pray that truly is the case. But let's each of us search our hearts and see if there is any way in which we have been robbing God of time, our tithes, our donations, our gifts or our abilities. Then we need to put right anything the Lord shows us, ask for His forgiveness and once more let our lives be poured out like nard in the service of the King.

SUMMARY

When Mary poured out her alabaster bottle of pure nard on the head and feet of Jesus, it was a prophetic act of preparation for Jesus, in anticipation of His death and burial. Mary's love for and devotion to Jesus were such that she wanted to give of her very best for Him. Immediately, however, the critics rose up in anger, citing the needs of the poor as the reason for their anger, but in reality they were angry that they couldn't have a share of what the oil was worth for themselves. When we lay our lives down for the Lord, they become like sweet-smelling incense arising to the throne of God.

PRAYER

Thank You, Lord, for the amazing example of Mary's sacrificial love for Jesus. Help me, Lord, to lay my very best before You, so that my whole life will be a blessing to Jesus and be as incense rising before the throne of God. In Jesus' name, Amen.

THE TRIUMPHAL ENTRY TO JERUSALEM

I recently visited the famous Kruger National Park, in South Africa, an area as big as Wales and teeming with wild life in its natural environment. We had many wonderful experiences and a couple of very interesting, and potentially frightening ones, quite close together. The first of these involved a leopard and an elephant, and in the second we had to reverse up a hill to escape from two rhinos who had no intention of getting out of our way! For a short time, it was a little frightening and we were glad when the rhinos went off the road into the bush.

There were six of us in the vehicle that day. However, later, when we were talking about what had happened, we found that we couldn't agree on the exact order in which the different events had happened, even though they were very fresh in our memory. All of us had been affected in different ways by what we had seen and experienced, and our emotions and our memories got a bit jumbled as a result! We all agreed on what we had seen, but we couldn't remember exactly the order in which things had happened.

That in no way invalidated the memories we all had, but it did help me to understand why sometimes in the different Gospel accounts, things can be presented by the writers in a different sequence of events. Exciting happenings that affect our emotions can also distort our memories. And this problem was made even more difficult for Matthew, Mark, Luke and John by the fact that, by the time they finally wrote their accounts of the life and death of Jesus, at least twenty to thirty years had passed.

The triumphal entry of Jesus into Jerusalem is one example of this. Both Matthew and Mark record it as having taken place well before the time when Jesus was anointed by Mary in Bethany (Matthew 21:1-9 and Mark 11:1-11), whereas Luke and John say it happened afterwards (Luke 19:28-44 and John 12:12-19). Does it matter? Not at all! What matters is that it really did happen, and all four Gospel writers were united in describing what occurred.

Sometimes critics of Christianity use these minor 'discrepancies' to try and discredit the Word of God. My experience in the game park has done the reverse! The minor variations in describing what happened only serve to validate the truth of Scripture, as events that were seen through the eyes and ears of different writers.

JESUS – THE POPULAR HERO

A lot of people would have been to see Jesus and Lazarus at the thanksgiving meal held at the home of Simon the Leper (John 12:9). The raising of Lazarus from the dead was an outstanding miracle – news of which would have travelled the length and breadth of the land in no time. You can imagine the women chatting at the well as they drew water; the men as they met in the market square about their daily business; and even the children as they played and learned together; there would have been only one topic of conversation – Lazarus! He's alive!

"Do you know, he'd been dead four days?"
"Yes, and there was quite a smell when he came shuffling out of the tomb in his grave clothes!"
"Who did it, I wonder?"
"What's his name?"

"Jesus – the one who fed five thousand people with just a handful of food – that was quite a miracle, too."

"Where's he from, did you say?"

"Nazareth?"

"Nazareth – never heard of anything good coming from that place, have you?"

And so the chat would have gone on, until not many people in the land would have been unaware of who Jesus was, where He was from and what He had done. And many of them, it seems, had come to Bethany, to catch a glimpse of both Jesus and the 'miracle man' Lazarus. And this was Passover time as well, so – *'the great crowd that had come for the Feast heard that Jesus was on his way to Jerusalem'* (John 12:12).

By now, Jesus was famous. He was a popular hero with the people, if not with the religious authorities who considered Him to be their enemy, because *'many of the Jews were going over to Jesus and putting their faith in him'* (John 12:11). So when word got about that He was on His way from Bethany to Jerusalem for the Feast, the crowds were out in force. When they got to the Mount of Olives:

'Jesus sent two of his disciples, saying to them, "Go to the village ahead of you, and as you enter it, you will find a colt tied there, which no-one has ever ridden. Untie it and bring it here. If anyone asks you, 'Why are you untying it?' tell him, 'The Lord needs it'" (Luke 19:30-31).

And that's exactly what happened.

The detail with which the prophetic Scriptures of the Old Testament are fulfilled in the New Testament, is quite remarkable. Hundreds of years earlier, Zechariah had prophesied, *'Do not be afraid, O Daughter of Zion; see, your king is coming, seated on a donkey's colt'* (Zechariah 9:9). Jesus couldn't have entered Jerusalem in a humbler way – riding on the colt of a donkey. He did nothing to elevate Himself by coming in a carriage or chariot, and there was no fine horse, just the most humble animal on the planet for Him to ride on, a simple donkey.

Nineteen hundred years later, towards the end of the First World War, Jerusalem fell into the hands of the British and their Allies. The city had been under Turkish Muslim control for over 400 years. The Commander of the Allied Forces, General Sir Edward Allenby, led the entry into the city as a Christian, on the first day of the Jewish feast of Hanukkah in December 1917.

Allenby was an accomplished horseman and it would have made sense for him to have ridden triumphantly into the city. But outside the Jaffa gate, he dismounted and entered on foot because, he said, Jesus entered on a donkey and he wasn't prepared to enter in a more elevated way than his Lord and Master!

In Christian work it can be so tempting to want to take glory to oneself and to elevate oneself higher than Jesus would have done. The lesson of General Allenby is an important one for all of us who have any form of public ministry. Jesus is the one who humbled Himself and if we want Him to lift us up, then we, too, must humble ourselves.

HOSANNA! HOSANNA!

So Jesus entered Jerusalem riding on the colt of a donkey. *'Many people, because they had heard that he had given this miraculous sign [the raising of Lazarus] went out to meet him'* (John 12:18). By the time He reached the gates of the city, therefore, there were crowds of people greeting Him in the traditional way, by waving the branches of palm trees, but what they were shouting was new. The people who recognised who He was, and knew the Old Testament Scriptures, started the chant, which was taken up by the shouting crowds:

- *'Blessed is he who comes in the name of the Lord!'* (John 12:13 and Psalm 118:26)
- *'Blessed is the King of Israel!'* (John 12:13)
- *'Blessed is the coming kingdom of our father David!'* (Mark 11:10)
- *'Peace in heaven and glory in the highest'* (Luke 19:38)
- *'Hosanna in the highest!'* (Mark 11:10)

What they were shouting were the words of welcome to the Messiah of the Jews, and words which were in direct fulfilment of prophecy. However, *'at first his disciples did not understand all this. Only after Jesus was glorified did they realise that these things had been written about Him'* (John 12:16). But as far as the Chief Priests and the Pharisees were concerned this was a disaster and they *'said to one another, "See, this is getting us nowhere. Look how the whole world has gone after Him!"'* (John 12:19).

Crowds can be dangerous. It's amazing how a mood can sweep across a lot of people and suddenly a crowd dynamic takes over. Jesus was wise enough to know that, just because a great crowd of people had welcomed Him into the city of Jerusalem, it didn't mean that they were all wanting to follow and obey Him. Most of the people were wanting a figurehead Messiah, who could do miracles and who would free them from the Romans. What Jesus was offering them, however, was something very different, and that sadly most people wouldn't want because it would involve the submission of their will to the Godly authority of Jesus in their lives. And that's a price that most people weren't willing to pay!

WALK IN THE LIGHT

When He'd entered Jerusalem and some of the crowd were still gathered together, Jesus warned them that the time was coming soon when He would be lifted up to die (John 12:31-33). Referring to Himself as the Light, Jesus then told them, *'"You are going to have the light just a little while longer. Walk while you have the light, before darkness overtakes you. The man who walks in the dark does not know where he is going. Put your trust in the light while you have it, so that you may become sons of light"'* (John 12:35-36).

The advice that Jesus gave to the crowds on that day in Jerusalem, is no different from the teaching John gave to his readers at the beginning of his Gospel when he said, *'In him was life, and that life was the light of men. The light shines in the darkness, but the darkness has not understood it'* (John 1:5). Jesus is *'the true light that gives light to every man coming into the world'* (John 1:9). And the advice I would give you today, as we pursue our *Journey to Freedom* is still the same – walk in the light that only Jesus can give. He truly is the Light of the World.

The crowds who were waving their palm branches and shouting *'Hosanna!'* melted away to almost nothing just a little while later. Tragically, many of these would be the same people who, only a few days later, were shouting for the release of Barabbas. The fact that people today may be part of a large congregation, singing songs of worship, and maybe even waving their arms in the air, doesn't necessarily mean that they're walking in the Light of the truth of Jesus Christ.

To walk in the Light requires walking in obedience, out of love. And none of us will know how long we have on earth to walk in the light, before we're called home to participate in the joys of heaven. It's only those who have become the *'sons (and daughters) of light'* (John 12:36) who have such a prospect. And only they are able to be a light for others, so that in the darkness of the world, everyone will have a chance to see the Light shining and choose whether or not to walk in it! So often it is the way we live our lives *(in the Light)* rather than the words we speak, that touches others who are still living in the darkness!

SUMMARY

The crowds who had heard about Lazarus were keen to follow Jesus and see both Him and Lazarus. By the time Jesus entered Jerusalem on the colt of a donkey, there was a large crowd of people waving palm branches and shouting 'Blessed is He who comes in the name of the Lord'. But being part of a shouting crowd is not the same as walking in the Light in loving obedience. Having entered Jerusalem Jesus told the people around him that He wouldn't be there much longer, and how important it was that they should chose to walk in the Light before the darkness overtook them. Even today we need to heed the same advice.

PRAYER

Thank You, Lord, that You chose to enter the city of Jerusalem in humility. Knowing that You resist the proud, help me, Lord, to always want to walk in Your ways, so that when I face temptation, I will always have the courage to say No to the enemy and Yes to the One who is the true Light who came into the world. In Jesus' name, Amen.

Stage 1, Chapter 3

JESUS WASHES HIS DISCIPLES' FEET

In any book there are often certain passages of writing that epitomise the whole story. Every page of the book may be important in its own way, but some sections have a way of expressing the heart of what the writer was trying to say. I sometimes listen to 'condensed books' being read on the radio as I'm driving along our motorways. What's read is only a fraction of the whole, but somehow or other, the abridged version has caught the essence of the whole.

I wouldn't, of course, want to pick out any sections of the Word of God and say they are any more important than others. However, the first few verses of John 13 seem to epitomise perfectly how the heart of God for the heart of man was demonstrated in Jesus' words and actions during his brief life here on earth.

It was, however, only John, of the four Gospel writers, who was most sensitive to the spiritual significance of everything he witnessed. It was he who recorded the moment when Jesus carried out a symbolic and prophetic act which would impact the whole of true Christianity for the rest of time. Any version of Christianity that leaves out the significance of what it meant for Jesus to wash the feet of His disciples is, at best, a distortion of the truth. **For what Jesus did, on that never to be forgotten night in Jerusalem, is central to the nature and character of who He is and is the essence of salvation itself – God, on bended knee, serving those He came to save.**

PREPARING FOR PASSOVER

This Passover was undoubtedly going to be the most important one of Jesus' life. It was His last and it not only had to be memorable, but through it He wanted to establish a regular expression of worship and relationship between man and God that would last for the rest of time until He came again. Jesus had a lot still to teach His disciples.

Mark tells us how He had already prepared a place for them to meet and gave them a sign that would lead them to the building:

> 'On the first day of the Feast of Unleavened Bread, when it was customary to sacrifice the Passover lamb, Jesus' disciples asked him, "Where do you want us to go and make preparations for you to eat the Passover?"
>
> 'So he sent two of his disciples, telling them, "Go into the city, and a man carrying a jar of water will meet you. Follow him. Say to the owner of the house he enters, 'The Teacher asks: where is my guest room, where I may eat the Passover with my disciples?' He will show you a large upper room, furnished and ready. Make preparations for us there.'" (Mark 14:13-15).

We are told nothing of the identity of the man with the water jar (the sign) and my suspicion is that it was an angel whom God used to direct the disciples to the upper room, where they were to hold this highly significant meal. There are many incidents in Christian history where angels have appeared as human beings, acting as God's special agents in particular situations.

In Genesis 18 we are told of three men who visited Abraham, telling him that Sarah would have a baby by the following year. In the next chapter they are described as angels, when two of them left and went towards Sodom. There are many stories, from more recent years, of angels appearing in human form, intervening on behalf of God in the affairs of men. I know of several such instances in the missionary history of my own family.

In the next chapter of our *Journey to Freedom* we will take a careful look at the other events in what has become known as the 'Last Supper', but today we are focussing solely on the incident at the beginning of the meal, which only John tells us about, when Jesus washed the disciples' feet.

DIVINE LOVE EXPRESSED IN HUMAN FORM

It was as if every moment of Jesus' final Passover meal was divinely orchestrated. Firstly He had been anointed, almost as a preparation, by Mary at Bethany. Then His Messianic status had been acclaimed by the people as they welcomed, with waving palm branches, the One who had come in the name of the Lord. And now, with all the details in place for the celebration of the Passover Feast *'the time had come for him to leave this world and go to the Father. Having loved his own who were in the world, he now showed them the full extent of his love'* (John 13:1).

If you or I had known that we were about to leave our disciples behind and, after our death, return to be with Father God in heaven, I wonder what we would have done to show them the full extent of our love? Perhaps we would have had a sack of unique presents hidden in the room, with something special as a permanent memento for each. Perhaps we would also have added a personal prophetic word appropriate for each disciple.

Maybe, however, because of our own misplaced sense of importance, we would have taken the top space at the table and let the disciples serve us with all the best things, as a farewell gesture. After all, if we were going to lay down our lives for them, this would be the least we would expect and deserve by way of appreciation!

Once again, Jesus blew apart every possible scenario that you or I might imagine in His desire to show them *'the full extent of His love'*. It's no surprise that the Scripture says of God that *'my thoughts are not your thoughts, neither are your ways my ways'* (Isaiah 55:8).

John tells us that the evening meal was being served – and that *'the devil had already prompted Judas Iscariot, son of Simon, to betray Jesus'* (John 13:2). Jesus knew that *'the Father had put all things under his power'* (John

13:3), so whatever happened from now on was totally within the will of Jesus. He was not being controlled by His Father, pulling the strings of His life. The angels were not forcing Him to do one thing or another. Everything He did was His own free-will choice – even to release Judas to do what Satan had already put into his heart was within the will of Jesus. But He wasn't going to stand in the way of any of the purposes of God.

Quite suddenly, Jesus got up from the meal:

'took off his outer clothing and wrapped a towel around his waist. After that he poured water into a basin and began to wash his disciples' feet, drying them with the towel that was wrapped around him' (John 13:4-5).

Even Judas was in the circle of disciples whose feet were washed by Jesus!

There was no way in which Jesus was going to use this final Passover Feast to do anything but teach, by example. He wanted to show His followers how to love one another, by serving them even in the most menial of tasks. The streets of Jerusalem were dusty and dirty. It wasn't possible to walk on them without one's feet getting dirty – foot washing was an essential part of the domestic routine. It was a job for the servants to do.

It must have been a shocking moment for the disciples, when they suddenly realised that Jesus was taking upon Himself the role of a servant. His act was turning upside down every convention of the day. The One who should have had His feet washed by others, was on His knees washing the feet of those who served Him as disciples!

BUT WHAT ABOUT PETER?

All was going well until Jesus came to Peter! By now we've come to expect that Peter's reactions would be different from everyone else's. For example, it was only Peter who jumped out of the boat to walk towards Jesus on the water. It was only Peter who realised who Jesus really was when he blurted out *'"You are the Christ, the Son of the living God"'* (Matthew 16:16). And here, it was only Peter who let his real feelings be known as he objected to Jesus washing their feet. He had no intention of letting Jesus wash *his* feet and told Jesus so. Perhaps it was pride that was riding high in Peter's emotions when he said, *"'You shall never wash my feet'"* (John 13:8). Whatever the reason for his response, it was not the right answer!

In His reply to Peter, Jesus began to teach about what He was doing. He may have been washing their physical feet, but there were spiritual lessons to be learned as well. Jesus answered Peter by saying *"'Unless I wash you, you have no part with me'"* (John 13:8) and Peter suddenly realised that he had got his responses very wrong. Now he wanted Jesus to wash everything – from top to toe – *"'not just my feet but my hands and my feet as well!'"* (John 13:9).

But once again he got it wrong! He had gone from the one extreme of not wanting his feet to be washed by Jesus, to the other extreme of wanting everything to be washed – and both responses were wrong! I really feel sorry for Peter sometimes. He tries so hard to get it right, but always seems to end up misreading the situation. Jesus told Him that *"'a person who has had a bath needs only to wash his feet; his whole body is clean. And you are clean, though not every one of you'"* (John 13:10) – this latter comment referred to Judas Iscariot.

LET ME EXPLAIN

The spiritual messages of this whole episode are two-fold:

1. **Serve One Another**

    Jesus humbled himself and served those who one might expect should have been serving him.

    > *'"Now that I, your Lord and Teacher, have washed your feet, you also should wash one another's feet. I have set you an example that you should do as I have done for you'"* (John 13:14-15).

    If Jesus, the very Son of God, our Lord and Master, can get down on His knees and wash the feet of His disciples, none of us have any excuse for lording it over others and demanding that they serve us!

    The very word 'minister' means 'serve'. However, sometimes in the church the impression is given that, when someone becomes a minister, they have a right to be served. What Jesus did totally undermines that perspective and reverses it. **For it is only as we serve others that they will truly discover what it's like to be loved. And that's what Jesus was doing when He washed the disciples' feet – He was showing them how much He loved them. At the same time He was teaching them and us that when people receive love from us, then they will also be receiving love from the One who taught us how to love.**

2. **Having a Bath and Washing Your Feet!**
    When Jesus told Peter that he'd already had a bath and only needed his feet to be washed, He wasn't talking about Peter's physical cleanliness. Jesus was saying to the disciples that they were already spiritually clean – and had had a good bath. They were cleansed from the filth of their sinful condition. In John 15:3 Jesus told them, *"You are already clean because of the word I have spoken to you."* This is the same cleansing that we receive through faith in Jesus when we are first born again of the Spirit of God – our sins are forgiven and we are cleansed through the application of the blood of Jesus to our lives.

But Jesus still told Peter that he need his feet washed – and that *"unless I wash you, you have no part with me"* (John 13:8). By this Jesus was making it very clear that life is a journey. As Christians we can all still sin and make wrong choices. Therefore, unless we are constantly coming to Jesus with the dirt in our lives and asking for forgiveness and cleansing (foot-washing), we will accumulate dirt and become more and more separated from Him. Not letting Him into the dirt is the same as not making Him Lord of every area of our life. Christians do sin – and in order to continue on their pilgrimage of faith they need forgiveness and cleansing.

The other day I did some digging in our garden. The soil where I live is very heavy with clay and, when I came back to the house, I suddenly realised the weight of my boots with all the clay that coated them. Fiona, my wife, would not have been blessed if I'd tried to enter the house without removing them first and cleaning my feet! In a very similar way, when we try to enter the presence of the Lord, when our feet are heavy

JESUS WASHES HIS DISCIPLES' FEET

with the spiritual dirt of where we have been walking, then the words of Jesus to Peter suddenly become relevant to us: *"unless I wash you, you have no part with me"* (John 13:8).

In his first letter John returns to this theme of regularly being cleansed when he states the wonderful truth that, for believers, there is forgiveness for sin and cleansing from the consequences of sin (1 John 1:9). And when Paul gave instructions to the Body of Christ about how to remember Jesus in the communion service, he made it clear that confession, forgiveness and cleansing from sin are important stages in our personal preparation for receiving the elements of bread and wine as we remember the death and resurrection of Jesus (1 Corinthians 11:27-32).

AN EXAMPLE TO FOLLOW

There is no greater example for us to follow, than the example of Jesus. He is our Master and Lord and so, as we choose to live our lives following Him in simple trust and obedience, we will discover that we can keep our feet clean as we run the race of life, journeying with Him every step of the way. And if for any reason we do sin, praise God for 1 John 1:9 which says, *'If we confess our sins, he is faithful and just and will forgive us our sins and purify us from all unrighteousness.'*

SUMMARY

Jesus surprised and shocked His disciples by beginning their Passover celebration by washing their feet. In so doing He was humbling Himself and giving us an example of how we, as members of the Body of Christ, should love and serve each other. But He was also showing us that through our faith in Him we have been made clean from all the dirt of sin. However, we still need to come to Him on a daily basis to have our feet washed and cleansed - so that the effects of walking in a sinful world can constantly be removed from us.

PRAYER

Thank You, Jesus, for Your amazing example of how we should love and serve one another in the family of God. Help us never to elevate ourselves in a manner unworthy of our calling. Thank You, Lord, for making us clean when we first came to You and for wanting to cleanse us from the consequences of getting dirty on our daily walk - so that where we have placed our feet in sinful things we can be forgiven and cleansed. In Jesus' name, Amen.

Stage 1, Chapter 4

THE LAST SUPPER

THE LAST SUPPER

When Jesus washed the feet of His disciples, He made a profound, prophetic statement to the Body of Christ for the whole of time. He was showing us that the Kingdom of God is built through serving one another in humility, not by self-elevation or pride.

The washing of the disciples' feet was one form of serving others, but what Jesus was about to do was to turn the whole Passover celebration into a dramatic, prophetic illustration of the greatest act of service the world has ever known – either before or after Jesus came. There can be no higher form of sacrificial service than the Creator of the Universe laying down His human life, in order to serve and to save all those who believe in Him.

THE PASSOVER

The instructions for celebrating the Passover meal were laid down by God in the Old Covenant. It was to be a thanksgiving meal for the Jews, through which every generation would have cause to remember the extraordinary way in which God had liberated the children of Israel from the tormenting hands of the Egyptians, under the leadership of Moses and Aaron (Exodus 12:3-14).

God sent many, many plagues on the land of Egypt in an attempt to break down Pharaoh's resistance to letting the Israelites go, but none of them resulted in their freedom. No matter how often God told him to let His people go, Pharaoh consistently hardened his heart and said no (Exodus 7-10). So, God planned one final plague (Exodus 11).

This plague was a judgement on the whole of Egypt. News of God's intentions was given to Pharaoh by Moses. God said that the firstborn of every family, from the highest to the lowest in the country, would die when the Lord passed through the land. Pharaoh could never say that he hadn't been warned. '*"Then you will know", said Moses, "that the* L*ORD makes a distinction between Egypt and Israel"'* (Exodus 11:7). Provided the Israelites did what God told them to do by way of preparation, the plague of death would only affect the Egyptians and not touch any of God's people. Obedience was the key to salvation!

God not only told Moses what to say to Pharaoh, but He also gave instructions to Moses to prepare the Israelites for this great deliverance. They were to take a sacrificial lamb, slaughter it and place some of its blood '*on the sides and tops of the door frames*' (Exodus 12:7) of every home where they were dwelling and were gathered together in obedience to God's instructions. That night was to be one of death and deliverance. It would bring death to the Egyptians but deliverance for the people of God.

Moses explained to the Israelites that the blood on the door frames would be a sign they were inside so that when God saw the blood He would '*pass over*' them. God told them that:

'*No destructive plague will touch you when I strike Egypt. This is a day you are to commemorate; for the generations to come, you are to celebrate it as a festival to the* L*ORD, a lasting ordinance*' (Exodus 12:13-14).

The Israelites did everything that the Lord had commanded them to do in preparation for this night of deliverance, and:

'*at midnight the* L*ORD* *struck down all the firstborn in Egypt, from the firstborn of Pharaoh … there was loud wailing in Egypt for there was not a house without someone dead. During the night, Pharaoh summoned Moses and Aaron and said, "Up! Leave my people, you and the Israelites! Go, worship the* L*ORD* *as you requested"'* (Exodus 12:29-31).

So it was that '*because the* L*ORD* *kept vigil that night to bring them out of Egypt,'* all the Israelites were instructed by the Lord '*to keep vigil to honour the* L*ORD* *for the generations to come'* (Exodus 12:42). As a result, the Passover celebrations became central to the Jewish people's cycle of worship throughout their history.

About two thousand years ago a small group of Israelite descendants were doing just that, keeping vigil on Passover night in an Upper Room in Jerusalem. That's why Jesus and His disciples were gathered together – they were living out their history in thanksgiving to God for their deliverance.

It was the night on which the Passover lamb would be sacrificed as part of the celebrations of the Feast. But all the participants, except One, had no idea that, during this particular Passover celebration, one of their number would actually become the Passover Lamb. Jesus, the Lamb of God, would die and His blood would be shed, not just to set Jewish people free from spiritual Egypt, but so that all the world's peoples would know that God had prepared a mighty deliverance for them, from the hands of the enemy of God.

Such is the power of the blood of Jesus that death can have no claim on the person whose sin is covered by the sacrificial blood of the Passover Lamb. The '*angel of death'* has to pass over those whose names are written in *the 'Lamb's Book of Life'* (Revelation 21:27), because their sins are covered by the blood of Jesus (Revelation 20:15).

Lewis Jones[1] powerfully expressed this in his hymn – a hymn which has stood the test of time, and has long been a favourite of those who love the Lord Jesus for what He did for them on the cross:

Would you be free from your burden of sin?
There's power in the blood, power in the blood;
Would you o'er evil a victory win?
There's wonderful power in the blood.

Refrain:
There is power, power, wonder working power
In the blood of the Lamb;
There is power, power, wonder working power
In the precious blood of the Lamb.

At the beginning of His ministry, John the Baptist had pointed Jesus out to his own disciples when he said, *"'Look, the Lamb of God, who takes away the sin of the world!'"* (John 1:29). It was at Passover time, when everyone was celebrating the deliverance of the Israelites from Egypt, that Jesus was preparing Himself to fulfil John's prophetic word and suffer and die. He would die not just for the descendants of Israel, but for all the descendants of Adam, including you and me.

JESUS SHARES THE BREAD AND THE WINE

And so the last Passover meal that Jesus would share with His disciples began, as they gave thanks for God's mighty deliverance of the Israelites from the Egyptians all those years ago. Jesus told them how much He had been looking forward to sharing this particular Passover with His disciples for, He said, *"'I will not eat it again until it finds fulfilment in the Kingdom of God'"* (Luke 22:16). He meant He wouldn't eat it again until the final fulfilment of this mighty deliverance, when He would come again. He would then claim as His own all the people who truly come to God through Him, and He would establish the Kingdom of God as an eternal Kingdom.

But at that time, when their eyes were not yet fully opened to see all that was coming to pass in their presence, the disciples must have struggled to understand the meaning of all that He was saying. They were hearing the words, but they didn't yet understand the significance of everything that was happening around them.

Then Jesus took some *'bread, gave thanks and broke it, and gave it to them, saying, "This is my body given for you; do this in remembrance of me"'* (Luke 22:19). Jesus was showing the disciples that, just as He had broken the bread and given some of it to each of them, His body was about to be broken for all who would receive Him. In this simple act

He was also telling the disciples how, after He had gone, they and all believers should remember Him until He comes again.

'Then he took the cup, gave thanks, and offered it to them, saying, "Drink from it, all of you. This is my blood of the new covenant, which is poured out for many for the forgiveness of sins"' (Matthew 26:28).

Under the terms of the Old Covenant, the blood of animals was poured out as a symbolic and prophetic act, when people confessed their sins and asked God for forgiveness.

The blood of the animals could never actually deal with sin but, every time an animal sacrifice took place, it was a prophetic picture of the only sacrifice, that was yet to come, that would actually deal with sin. The faith of those who truly repented of the sins they were confessing, would be credited to them for righteousness – like a down-payment on the full blessing that was yet to come.

When talking about the men and women of faith from the Old Testament times, the writer of the Hebrews made it clear that their faith had been sufficient for the restoration of their relationship with God, but he also said:

*'These were all commended for their faith, yet none of them received what had been promised. God had planned **something better** for us, so that only together with us would they be made perfect'* (Hebrews 11:39-40) (emphasis added).

The sacrifice of the Lamb of God would, once and for all, be the key to dealing with the eternal consequence of sin for all those who had lived before Jesus came, but died 'in faith', and for all those who 'in faith' would subsequently trust Jesus for their salvation.

When Jesus gathered with His disciples for the Last Supper, the promise of *'something better'*, was about to be fulfilled. Somebody who was totally sinless was about to die for the sins of the people. Death could only hold those who were born under the curse of sin in bondage but, as Jesus was sinless, He could not be held in bondage by the curse of sin. So, as Jesus said, His shed blood would become the blood of the New Covenant (Mark 14:24), replacing the blood of sacrificed animals and establishing for all time a means of grace, through which sins could be forgiven and the door of heaven opened for all those who have faith in Him.

All of that was implicit when Jesus broke the bread and drank the cup and said to the disciples *'this is my body'* and *'this is my blood'* (Mark 14:22-24). With these words Jesus instituted what has become known as the 'Communion Service', the 'Eucharist' or the 'Lord's Supper'. Through it members of the Body of Christ continually give thanks to God for their deliverance from spiritual Egypt, just as the Jews at Passover time give thanks for their deliverance from physical Egypt. Passover celebrations were intended by God to be a parable to the Jews. They speak of what their Messiah would do in bringing the most amazing deliverance of all time to the whole world through the Jews, and how He would release those with faith in Him into the freedom of eternity.

As believers in Jesus, or Yeshua as He is always called by Messianic believers, we don't celebrate Communion only once a year, as was laid down in the Old Covenant for the celebration of the Passover. No, whenever believers are gathered together to remember what Jesus did for us, through the breaking of bread and the sharing of the cup together, we have opportunity for fellowship, thanksgiving, confession, repentance, healing and deliverance around the table of the Lord.

THE HAND OF THE BETRAYER

One of the most shocking facts of the Gospel accounts, however, is also contained within the narrative of this Passover with Jesus. For, tragically, the events of the Last Supper also illustrate that it was possible for someone to spend three years in close fellowship with Jesus, doing the same things as the other disciples, even using Jesus' delegated authority to pray for healing and cast out demons, and yet not be in relationship with Him. I'm reminded of what Jesus said of people like this in Matthew 7:21, *'"Not everyone who says to me, 'Lord, Lord,' will enter the kingdom of heaven, but only he who does the will of my Father who is in heaven."'* Judas was undoubtedly one of the people referred to in this verse.

I find it amazing and fascinating to see how even the smallest details of the events surrounding the death and resurrection of Jesus are the subject of Old Testament prophecies. The Psalmist couldn't have known the significance of what he was saying when he wrote *'even my close friend, whom I trusted, he who shared my bread, has lifted up his heel against me'* (Psalm 41:9). Jesus identifies this Scripture, in John 13:18, as referring to Himself and the one who would betray Him, the one who *'would lift up his heel'* against Jesus.

A betrayer is almost always someone who knows you well. It is their very familiarity with you that enables them to get close and take advantage of their close relationship. Sometimes a betrayer can 'seem to be faithful and loyal,' even for many years, but all the time the reality is that their hearts are not with you and, in the secret place of their heart, they're planning how to use their close relationship with you to undermine your integrity and destroy your name or your reputation or, even, trap you physically. An act of betrayal is an act of evil intent.

No wonder the Scripture says that *'as soon as Judas took the bread'* which Jesus had dipped in the dish, *'Satan entered into Him'* (John 13:27). When we listen to the voice of the enemy, and then make a free-will choice to serve him, through obedience to him, he's given access to our lives. Then, when we sin, we give the enemy a foothold into our lives, resulting in the need for deliverance from an evil spirit (see Ephesians 4:27). In Judas' case it wasn't just an evil spirit who occupied him as a result of his evil choice; it was Satan himself, the prince of demons, who came and entered Judas at that moment. This was an assignment that Satan had no intention of delegating to a less senior devil!

It's no wonder that Jesus was *'troubled in His spirit'* when He told them, *"I tell you the truth, one of you is going to betray me"* (John 13:21). He knew what would happen to Judas, when he carried out the desire that had been lodged in his heart by the enemy. The response of the disciples to Jesus' shocking words was to be expected. They had no idea what or who Jesus was talking about – and no doubt each one was desperate to know who it was. They certainly didn't want to think that any one of them was going to be guilty of betraying their Lord and Master – and yet, that's what Jesus had said was about to happen.

One of the disciples appears to have had an even closer relationship with Jesus than the other. In his anxiety to find out who the betrayer would be, *'Simon Peter motioned to this disciple and said, "Ask him*

PERSONAL NOTES

which one he means"' (John 13:24). In reply, Jesus didn't mention his name, but said:

> 'It is the one to whom I will give this piece of bread when I have dipped it in the dish. Then, dipping the piece of bread, he gave it to Judas Iscariot, son of Simon. As soon as Judas took the bread, Satan entered him' (John 13:26-27).

THANKS BE TO GOD – THERE IS LIFE AFTER SIN!

We will continue to look at the tragic story of Judas Iscariot when we cover the betrayal of Jesus in the Garden of Gethsemane, but for now let's dwell on the fact that there was a 'betrayer' among the twelve and ask ourselves the hardest question of all: Have we ever betrayed Jesus by giving the impression that we were serving Him whilst really harbouring in our hearts a desire to sin against Him? Before you begin to wait on Him for His answer, let's own the fact that this is something we've all done for 'all have sinned and fall short of the glory of God' (Romans 3:23).

For me, one of the greatest miracles of the story of salvation is that Jesus still loves us, even when our hearts have been far from Him and we've behaved like 'the prodigal son'. As we prepare ourselves to look more closely at the cross, and everything it means to believers who love the Lord, let's ask Him to show us our hearts as they really are – not so that we can collapse into spiritual depression under the strain of guilt, but so that we can rise from our knees knowing the forgiveness of our wonderful Saviour, who loves us so much. He was willing to become our Passover Lamb, so that for the rest of time and all of eternity the enemy's hold on our destiny would be broken. Hallelujah! What a Saviour!!

SUMMARY

The Passover celebration, which we know as the Last Supper, is the moment when Jesus declared to His disciples that His body would be broken and His blood would be shed for all peoples. John the Baptist's prophecy that Jesus was 'the Lamb of God who would take away the sin of the world' was about to be fulfilled. The Last Supper was also, however, the moment when Jesus' betrayer was revealed to all the disciples, and the events that would lead to Calvary began to unfold before all their eyes.

PRAYER

I'm so grateful, Jesus, that You were willing to become the Passover Lamb for me, so that the angel of death would have any hold over me in eternity. Help me, Lord, to always live in the reality of what You've done for me. When I share the bread and the wine of Communion at Your table, please help me to use those times to examine my heart, so that any seeds of betrayal in me may be dealt with. I love You, Lord Jesus. Thank You so much for being obedient to what Father God asked You to do for me. In Jesus' name, Amen

---

1 Public domain

Stage 1, Chapter 5

JESUS PRAYS IN THE GARDEN

After Jesus had shared the bread and the wine with His disciples, Judas left them to carry out the terrible act of betrayal that Satan had put into his heart and which he had agreed to do. It must have been a moment of personal devastation for Jesus as He saw one of the twelve, whom He had loved and nurtured for three years, going away to do this evil thing. John put it simply and dramatically; *'as soon as Judas had taken the bread, he went out. And it was night'* (John 13:30).

For Judas, night had come in two ways – yes, the sun had gone down, but I believe John was making a much more profound comment than telling us what time it was! He was saying that night had come to Judas and he would never see the light of Christ again. He had entered eternal darkness.

The events of the Last Supper weren't yet over, however, for Jesus went on to talk to His disciples about where He was going. He said, *'"Where I am going, you cannot follow now, but you will follow later"'* (John 13:36), meaning that He was soon going to die but they would all die at a later stage and then they would be able to join Him.

PERSONAL NOTES

Peter, of course, wasn't happy that Jesus was going somewhere without him. He wanted to go with Him there and then, even it meant that he too had to die. In typical Peter fashion he said, *"'Lord, why can't I follow you now? I will lay down my life for you'"* (John 13:37). Jesus replied in words that Peter couldn't possibly have believed to be true, *"'Will you really lay down your life for me? I tell you the truth, before the cockerel crows, you will disown me three times'"* (John 13:38). Later we will see how this prophecy was fulfilled, when we look at how Peter had to face the truth about himself.

GETHSEMANE

From the Upper Room, where Jesus had celebrated the Passover with His disciples, Jesus then went to the Mount of Olives to pray. Luke tells us that this is where He went 'as usual' (Luke 22:39). It was familiar ground, and Matthew and Mark identify exactly where on the Mount of Olives He went – the Garden of Gethsemane.

Jesus knew that time was of the essence. Judas had already gone to betray Him. It wouldn't be long before Jesus' accusers would find where He was. After all, Judas had been there many times before, and knew exactly where Jesus would have gone to pray. Most of the disciples stayed near the entrance to the Garden, while Jesus went on a little further. *'He took Peter, James and John along with him'* (Mark 14:33) and in a rare demonstration of His humanity *'he began to be deeply distressed and troubled. "My soul is overwhelmed with sorrow to the point of death," he said to them, "Stay here and keep watch"'* (Mark 14:33-34).

He then left Peter, James and John and went a little further into the Garden, whereupon He fell to the ground and, in agony of soul, poured out His heart to His Father. He looked on all that was going to happen in the next few hours. He likened the events He was facing to a cup that He had to drink, and cried out to God, *"'Abba, Father, everything is possible for you. Take this cup from me. Yet not what I will but what you will'"* (Mark 14:36).

This was one of those moments when heaven was silent. Jesus had expressed His willingness to *'drink the cup'* but was also looking to God to see if He had an alternative solution to man's sin problem. Everyone knew how Abraham had been willing to sacrifice his son, Isaac, but that at the last minute God provided an alternative sacrifice – a ram caught in a thicket – and Abraham didn't have to sacrifice his son after all. Perhaps Jesus was thinking that something similar might happen again. But heaven was silent, and Jesus knew the answer from Father God was "No".

This silent 'No' must have impacted Jesus a great deal and we can only marvel at His willing response to drink the cup that had been put before Him.

JESUS' PRAYER

While all the Gospel writers record the fact that Jesus prayed in Gethsemane, Matthew, Mark and John also tell us that the disciples, including Peter, James and John, fell asleep as they waited for Jesus to finish praying! It's only John who tells us what Jesus prayed (John 17).

Most commentators believe that it was John himself, who was *'the disciple whom Jesus loved'* (John 21:20), and perhaps there was a special moment of conversation between John and Jesus, possibly after the resurrection, when Jesus shared with him the details of His private prayer in the Garden. No-one knows for sure why only John recorded these precious details, but the content of Jesus' prayer tells us so much about His selfless heart and how much He cared for those whom God had sent Him to save.

The prayer is divided into three sections:

- Firstly Jesus prayed about His own personal situation as His life was drawing to a close.
- Then He prayed for His disciples.
- Finally He prayed for all believers who would come to know Him through the witness of the disciples.

JESUS PRAYS FOR HIMSELF

When I was a child my Dad had a huge magnifying glass. I loved going out in the garden on a sunny day with the magnifying glass and some old newspapers. I would then use the magnifying glass to focus the sun's rays on to one spot on the paper and watch, as it quickly went brown, began to smoke and, finally, burst into flames. I was fascinated by what I was learning about the power that can be released through focussing the rays of the sun.

In this opening part of His Gethsemane prayer Jesus is bringing the whole of His life and mission into focus and highlighting the reason why He had come to earth. It was *'that he might give eternal life'* to all those whom Father God had given Him (John 17:2). It's as if Jesus is saying that the fire of God has made it possible for the heart of man to be ignited with the gift of eternal life when His love is focussed on us!

Jesus is looking forward to returning to heaven and is asking that His Father would glorify Himself through glorifying the Son (John 17:1 and 5). This is exactly what happened a few days later when the Father raised Jesus from the dead – great glory was given to God through what happened to the Son. Jesus' prayer was answered.

Jesus also said that He had brought glory to the Father *'on earth by completing the work'* that He had been given to do (John 17:4). (Jesus had already previously told His disciples that, if they bore fruit as His disciples, they would bring glory to the Father - John 15.)

It's the same for us. When God shows us what He wants us to do and we do it, it brings glory to the Father (John 15:8). **What an exciting and encouraging challenge to be able to bring glory to God, simply by walking in His ways and doing the things that He has asked us to do!** For, as we walk in obedience and bring glory to the Father, He rejoices to bless us with His Spirit.

We can take great comfort from the fact that Jesus prayed for himself. This wasn't a selfish act but a real cry from His heart, just as we often need to cry out to God for ourselves in times of desperation. When we face trials it is good to model our response on Jesus' praying that God will empower us to do His work, regardless of the pain and help us to focus on what will be gained from it for God's glory and not for selfish ends.

JESUS PRAYS FOR HIS DISCIPLES

In the second part of His prayer Jesus turns His attention to praying for the disciples who were given to Him by the Father (John 17:6). When Jesus was praying this prayer, His whole mission rested in the hands and hearts of the eleven who were left. Everything He had lived for, everything He was about to die for, and, after He had returned to heaven, the whole future of God's Mission Earth project was depending on them. They were an ordinary bunch of men, fragile and fearful and, in the case of Thomas, full of doubts! But Jesus had handpicked them and He trusted them to be obedient.

No wonder Jesus devoted such a lot of time to praying for them on His last night on earth before His day of destiny. He told the Father how the disciples had believed the teaching He had given them (John 17:7-8), and that as a result they were now believers who were *'not of the world'* (John 17:16), just as Jesus was not of the world.

Like Jesus they were *in* the world but now, having believed in Him and received eternal life from the Father, they were no longer *of* the world. And that is the situation of every born-again believer – we're still in the world but, because we're now in a restored relationship with Father God, we're no longer under the control of the god of this world, and so **we're no longer of (or belonging to) the world.**

However, since we still live in the world, we're still vulnerable to the attacks of the evil one. In His prayer Jesus said that, while He was on earth, He'd protected His disciples and kept them safe (by the power of the Name that He'd been given). It was as if Jesus was reporting back to His Father with the results of His mission so far and said that *'"None has been lost, except the one doomed to destruction so that Scripture would be fulfilled"'* (John 17:12).

But now the disciples were going to be on their own in the world since this is where they had to be to fulfil their mission. Jesus therefore asked the Father to *'"protect them from the evil one"'* (John 17:15). He asked the Father would *'"Sanctify them by the truth"'* (John 17:17). Through living a holy life, according to the truth of God, they would be protected from the evil one.

Jesus said that He had sent His disciples into the world. Just as He had been protected from the enemy through His personal sanctification and continued commitment to holiness, He prayed that the disciples, too, would know the blessing and protection that comes from living a holy life. And this is a principle that is absolutely vital for each one of us as we journey with the Lord along our personal road of faith. *Journey to Freedom* is just one possible tool to help us map out a strategy for both godly living and protection from the enemy.

Jesus' prayer for His disciples reveals the heart and strategy of God for holiness and protection. If we don't do things that give the enemy rights in our lives (unholy, unsanctified things, ie sin), then we'll remain under the covering and protection of God – a sanctified life is a protected life.

I personally take great encouragement from this amazing prayer. If Jesus cared enough about His disciples to pray for them on the night before He died, it tells me that He cares enough to pray for all believers who want to be disciples. Do you remember that Jesus told Peter *'"Satan has asked to sift you as wheat."'* But then He told Peter, *'"But, I have prayed for you that your faith may not fail"'* (Luke 22:31-32).

What an encouragement that must have been for Peter – knowing that Jesus was aware of the testing times he was going to face, and that Jesus had prayed for him in advance. These are important lessons – if Jesus prayed for Peter when he was under test, be assured that Jesus has also prayed for you. This means if you turn to Him when you are facing a trial, you'll reap the benefit of His prayer for protection from the enemy.

JESUS PRAYS FOR ALL BELIEVERS

Finally, Jesus opens up His praying to include everyone who will eventually come to faith through the message preached by the first disciples (John 17:20). Unquestionably this means on the night before He died Jesus prayed for you and me! In particular He prayed that believers would be in unity with the Father – just as Jesus and the Father are one – and that they would be in unity with each other.

Throughout the history of Ellel Ministries, denomination has never been an issue, even though denominational allegiance has been the biggest source of division in the Body of Christ for hundreds of years. In all our years of ministering healing and discipleship to people all over the world, there haven't been divisive denominational issues within the ministry – even though our teams all come from many different churches.

I believe the reason for this is that the teaching on all our Retreats, Training Courses, Schools and Conferences does not divert from the foundational message of salvation, as contained within Scripture from Genesis to Revelation, and through which God brings healing to His people. If we departed from that I believe there would be division and disunity, and I don't believe we would be seeing the same amount of fruit across the world.

In the Psalms, God says that *'where the brethren dwell together in unity, He commands a blessing'* (Psalm 133). That also means that where the brethren dwell together in disunity then the enemy is given rights – not to bless, but to bring his disruption, and even cursing, into our personal lives and churches. No wonder Jesus prayed that *'"all of them may be one, Father, just as you are in me and I am in you"'* (John 17:21).

It's so special that this prayer of Jesus was preserved for us by the Holy Spirit. For, even though we are told that Jesus never ceases to intercede for us in heaven (Hebrews 7:25), the fact that we have a record of His prayer here on earth, gives us tremendous encouragement to believe and know that He truly is also praying for us now from His place in glory. The evidence of what He did on earth is the assurance of what He's still doing for us in heaven.

THE FINAL PRAYER

The final part of Jesus' prayer is so special and profound that I can do no better than simply quote it here for you to read and absorb into your lives. This is what Jesus prayed for YOU!

'"Father, I want those you have given me to be with me where I am, and to see my glory, the glory you have given me because you loved me before the creation of the world. Righteous Father, though the world does not know you, I know you, and they know that you have sent me. I have made you known to them and will continue to make you known in order that the love you have for me may be in them and that I myself may be in them"' (John 17:24-26).

Remember:

- Jesus wants us to be with Him in glory – what a prospect for us to look forward to! There are no exceptions to this prayer, everyone is included who has come to faith in Jesus Christ and is trusting Him for their salvation!
- Jesus wants us to see His glory!

- Jesus wants the love the Father has for Him to be in us!
- Jesus wants to be in us and live with us day by day for the rest of our lives!

SUMMARY

Jesus' prayer in Gethsemane was the last extended prayer time that He was to have before His crucifixion. He knew that the time was quickly coming when His betrayer would find Him, and it was vital that He used this time to prepare Himself for what was to come. He prayed for the disciples, who would be the pioneers of the church, founded after the resurrection, and He prayed for all believers for the whole of time who would respond to the message of the disciples.

PRAYER

Thank You, Lord, for the prayers You made while You were on earth for your disciples and for all believers. I'm so blessed and encouraged to know that You prayed for me the night before You died, and that this prayer speaks of how You're continuing to pray for me from Your place in glory at the right hand of the Father. Help me, Lord, never to forget that You love me so much that You want to show me Your glory in heaven. Help me to live for You in such a way that I never lose sight of the wonderful blessings that await those who die in You. In Jesus' name, Amen

STAGE 2

The Passion and Death of Jesus (1)

"Jesus suffered terribly, physically. But His greatest heartache was feeling forsaken when the sin of mankind separated Him from His Father."

JESUS' BETRAYAL AND JUDAS' DEATH

We are closing in on the central events of the Gospel story and seeing what special personal lessons we can learn from all that happened to Jesus during the final day of His life on earth, and at and after His crucifixion! This is the heart of the Christian message, and it's absolutely vital that we fully comprehend what was going on when Jesus died, when He was buried, and when He was raised again from the dead.

This is the most dramatic sequence of events in the whole of human history and is unrepeatable. These events divide history, and the passing of time has been measured from them for two thousand years! But first we must catch up with the tragic event that occurred in the middle of the Last Supper – the betrayal of Jesus by Judas.

TRUST AND BETRAYAL

It's a sad fact that betrayal and trust go hand in hand! It's only possible to betray people who trust you. The pain of betrayal is felt by those who trusted someone, and later discovered that person to be untrustworthy.

PERSONAL NOTES

PERSONAL NOTES

The Psalmist unwittingly prophesied the betrayal of the Messiah and set his words in the context of trust when he wrote, *'even my close friend, whom I trusted, he who shared my bread, has lifted up his heel against me'* (Psalm 41:9).

God spoke through Jeremiah the sad facts of many family situations when He said, *'Your brothers, your own family, even they have betrayed you; they have raised a loud cry against you. Do not trust them, even though they speak well of you'* (Jeremiah 12:6). It's so tragic to see the betrayal of trust within a family or marriage leading to the complete breakdown of all personal relationships. And people will sometimes use the cruel tactic of betrayal, using lies and half-truths to destroy someone's reputation. In doing this they are seeking to elevate themselves by pulling that other person down.

All the best spy stories include characters who build up a relationship of trust with 'the enemy' so that they can discover important information and relay it back to their home country. And the giving away or selling of sensitive business information by supposedly 'trusted employees' can be of vital significance to a business competitor.

Everyone knows what it means to 'be a Judas' – because what Judas did to Jesus has entered into the cultures of people throughout the world. His name is known the world over as being synonymous with treachery and betrayal of a close friend. The name Judas will never feature in the lists of popular boys' names. Who would want their children to go through life carrying such a name?

THE BETRAYER

When Jesus gave the bread to Judas at the Last Supper, both knew what would happen next (John 13:26-30). Judas had already made his plans, and when he left the Passover meal he went straight to those with whom he had already made an agreement.

'The chief priests and the teachers of the law were looking for some way to get rid of Jesus, for they were afraid of the people' (Luke 22:2). They were afraid that Jesus' popularity would destroy their platform of power. It was vital for them to get rid of Jesus before the momentum behind this rabbi from Nazareth reached an uncontrollable level.

Judas may have had many weaknesses, as we all have, but he had one besetting sin which controlled him – financial greed. This was obvious on the day Mary blessed Jesus by pouring her pint of pure nard over Him. Judas was horrified that something of such value should be just poured away like this. He'd wanted to sell the oil, put the money in the bag as donations for the poor and then probably help himself whenever he had a personal need (John 12:4-6).

On more than one occasion I have known of church treasurers who used the trust given to them to handle the finances of the church as an opportunity for their own financial gain. On one occasion a treasurer with an addiction to gambling was found to have been systematically removing cash from the offering plates and using it to bet on the horses! The bigger the offering, the easier it was for him to help himself to money without anyone else knowing! By the time his sin was exposed tens of thousands of pounds of the Lord's money had been wasted on his addiction.

Stealing money that belongs to the Lord is a serious offence, as Ananias and Sapphira discovered when they tried to conceal some of the proceeds of the sale of a field that everyone else believed they had given wholly to the Lord. The judgement of God on them was swift and exemplary (Acts 5:1-11) – both of them died because of what they had done.

Unresolved sinful desires in the core of our being will always lead to the practice of other sins to feed the habit. Uncontrolled addictions lead to committing other since to get what is needed to feed the addiction. The most common modern day example is when somebody who's on drugs and can't afford to pay for their habit, then starts stealing money, or goods they can sell, to pay for the drugs. Deception and lies are always part of the cover up. Violence, disease and premature death are often the tragic side-effects of trying to resolve secret sinful desires by feeding them, instead of getting help to overcome them.

Satan took advantage of Judas' secret desire for money to use him as a pawn in the divine game of chess that was being played out on the streets of Jerusalem at this Passover time.

Judas knew what the chief priests wanted. He also knew that the death of Jesus was inevitable because Jesus had already told them He was going up to Jerusalem to die (John 12:23-26). Maybe Judas thought he wouldn't be doing anything terribly wrong if he helped the chief priests out by giving them a way of solving their problem!

Maybe, in the inner working of his mind, Judas calculated that Jesus was inevitably going to die, so he might as well make some personal profit out of the process. The chief priests would be glad of his help and any money that changed hands would all be his – none of it would have to go into the bag. He might have thought he wasn't influencing the end-result, but just smoothing the process. Maybe he assumed that, since it was going to happen anyway, he couldn't be held responsible for the part he played. He might even have thought he was helping Jesus with what He had to do.

Of course, it's all speculation about what was actually going on in Judas' mind. But I've had experience of helping people examine what thought processes they went through when they were contemplating something sinful. It's easy for people to rationalise something that's wrong with totally deceived thinking.

One man rationalised he could take a mistress on the grounds that it made him happy and that his happiness would make him a better husband to his wife and a better father to his children!

I once met a pastor who rationalised his acts of adultery by saying that every time he made love to this particular woman it helped her to be healed! It's interesting that, when we want something badly (as Judas wanted the money), we can justify our actions in our own minds. Yet, as Judas discovered, sin is sin and there are no excuses for sin.

However it was that Judas justified his behaviour to himself he went out of the Passover meal and got on with the job. And so it was, that:

'Judas went to the chief priests and the officers of the temple guard and discussed with them how he might betray Jesus. They were delighted and agreed to give him money. He consented and watched for an opportunity to hand Jesus over to them when no crowd was present' (Luke 22:4-6).

Matthew tells us that *'they counted out for him thirty silver coins'* (Matthew 26:15).

The price was now agreed. Judas knew what profit he was going to make out of the arrangement. It must have seemed like a good deal to Judas, to be paid for doing something that was going to happen anyway. I wonder at which point the remorse and the guilt began to register in his mind and play on his conscience?

There may be some of you reading these notes who know there have been times in your life when you have lived a lie – given the impression of living a godly life, but secretly have been harbouring something very ungodly in your thinking or your behaviour.

Before we move on and see what happened to Judas I want you to know that even though what you've done may look like a betrayal of Jesus, **there's nothing you've done that's so awful it's put you beyond the mercy and forgiveness of God.**

So if, for any reason, you're now aware of the Holy Spirit pricking your conscience, be encouraged. It's not because the Lord wants to condemn you – **the judgement and punishment for your sin has already been carried by Jesus.** He wants you to know that even betrayal can be forgiven and even those who've turned their back on Jesus can be restored – as we will find out when we read about what happened to Peter.

THE BETRAYAL

Jesus had gone with His disciples from the Passover meal to pray in the Garden of Gethsemane on the Mount of Olives. When He'd finished praying, He left the Garden to head back to Jerusalem. John tells us that they'd crossed the Kidron valley and had reached a familiar olive grove where Jesus often met with His disciples. Both Gethsemane and the olive grove were places Judas knew well (John 18:1-2). They were off the beaten track and away from the crowds – ideal places for Jesus to be arrested without there being the possibility of a huge crowd also being present. It was also late at night, or very early morning – a time when most people would be asleep.

'So Judas came to the grove, guiding a detachment of soldiers and some officials from the chief priests and Pharisees. They were carrying torches, lanterns and weapons' (John 18:3).

'Now the betrayer had arranged a signal with them: "the one I kiss is the man; arrest him and lead him away under guard." Going at once to Jesus, Judas said, "Rabbi!" and kissed Him' (Mark 14:44-45).

'Jesus replied, "Friend, do what you came for." Then the men stepped forward, seized Jesus and arrested him' (Matthew 26:50).

PERSONAL NOTES

At this Peter drew out a sword and cut off the ear of Malchus, the servant of the High Priest. Jesus healed the man's ear (Luke 22:51) and rebuked Peter for using such a weapon and telling him that those who use swords will die by the sword! He also said that if He needed to defend Himself, He could call on His '"*Father and he will at once put at my disposal more than twelve legions of angels!*"' (Matthew 26:53). But, He said, if He did that '"*how then would the Scriptures be fulfilled?*"' (Matthew 26:54). And His final word to Peter at that time, as recorded by John, was '"*Shall I not drink the cup the Father has given me?*"' (John 18:11).

Jesus had already asked His Father if the cup He was drinking could be taken from Him (Luke 22:42) and it was clear that the Father's will was that He should drink it. Jesus intended to go through with the mission that had been planned in heaven, so that the children of men might be redeemed and able to partake of heaven's glory.

As the events of the night unfolded Jesus was intensely aware of both the Scriptures and His own destiny. He knew what the Father had asked Him to do. He had His own free will and if He wished to abort the mission and call on the angels to rescue Him, then He could do so. However, because of His love for you and for me, Jesus did not resist His arrest. He was determined to fulfil His own prophetic word, recorded by John, '"*For God so loved the world that he gave his one and only Son, that whoever believes in him shall not perish but have eternal life*"' (John 3:16). This was what He'd promised and this was what He would fulfil.

THE END OF THE BETRAYER

A little later in the story, after it became clear that they were going to put Jesus to death, Judas:

'*was seized with remorse and returned the thirty silver coins to the chief priests and the elders. "I have sinned," he said, "for I have betrayed innocent blood*"' (Matthew 27:3-4).

His guilt weighed heavily upon him. He wasn't coming back to God in repentance and asking for forgiveness, but he was wishing he hadn't put himself in the position of having done such a terrible thing.

There's a huge difference between repentance and remorse – 'remorse' is realising the consequences of sin, 'repentance' is wanting to turn from the sin and ask for forgiveness. Many people in prison are filled with remorse because they're now in prison and unable to live their lives freely. They wish they hadn't done whatever it was they were being punished for or, at least, that they'd been clever enough not to get caught. For the repentant sinner, however, there is hope; for the one who's only filled with remorse, there's no hope.

Remorse is regret for the human consequences of what's been done. That remorse can only lead to repentance if the Holy Spirit brings conviction of the sin that was committed against God. Remorse is soulish, repentance is spiritual.

When people have been tempted by Satan into some form of sin, they soon discover that Satan has no sympathy for them in the mess their sin has created. He cruelly uses people and then disowns them. That's exactly what the chief priests did with Judas. Once they'd used him for what they wanted, they had no further interest in him and said, '"*What is that to us. That's your responsibility!*"' (Matthew 27:4).

The Scripture then records the outworking of remorse that's without repentance in the life of Judas. His was now a life without hope and so he '*threw the money into the temple and left. Then he went away and hanged himself*' (Matthew 27:5). Because this money was now blood money, or cursed money, the chief priests couldn't put it in the temple treasury, so they bought the potter's field and created a place of burial for foreigners out of it. It became known as the '*Field of Blood*' (Matthew 27:8).

And so a tragic life came to its end – a life that had been lived so close to the Saviour. But Judas had never fully appreciated the love the Saviour had in His heart for sinners such as him. His desire had always been to use Jesus for His own ends – the earthly benefits he longed for became the curse which brought about his own untimely end.

THE JOY OF HOPE

Oh how I pray, as I write the final words of this section that, any who are reading this and trying to walk close to the Saviour, but whose motive for being there is to serve themselves and not the Lord, will cry out to God that the convicting power of the Holy Spirit of God will come upon them. And then that a spirit of repentance will consume their heart and that, while it may now seem like night, there will be joy in the morning (Psalm 30:5).

As David said, following His own terrible betrayal of God, *'The sacrifices of GOD are a broken spirit; a broken and a contrite heart, O GOD, you will not despise'* (Psalm 51:17). There's no-one beyond the redeeming love of God. While there's yet time, come to Him. These are the words of Jesus:

"'I am the bread of life. He who comes to me will never go hungry, and he who believes in me will never be thirsty... and whoever comes to me I will never drive away'" (John 6:35-37). Let the joy of the Lord be your strength, as you rejoice in the forgiveness God gives to those who are humble and repentant of heart. **And remember that includes you, whatever the enemy may try and say to you to the contrary!**

SUMMARY

After the Passover meal, Judas left to meet the chief priests and to seal the arrangement he had with them to deliver Jesus into their hands. They didn't want this to happen when there were crowds of people, so Judas led the soldiers to the place where Jesus always went to pray on the Mount of Olives. There, Judas greeted Jesus with a kiss and immediately the soldiers knew who it was they were to arrest. Later, when Judas realised that they were actually going to kill Jesus, he was filled with remorse, threw down the thirty silver coins he had been paid and went out and hanged himself. Judas was filled with remorse but he wasn't repentant and without repentance there can't be any remission of sins (Luke 24:47).

PRAYER

It's hard to believe, Lord, that someone could walk with You for three years and still not understand how much You loved them, and then choose to betray You. Help me, Lord, to always be aware of those times when Satan might tempt me to walk away from You, or even do things that would be an act of betrayal. I never want to leave Your side or betray Your love. Thank You so much, Lord, that even though You were betrayed, You still chose to die for mankind because of Your love for the human race. I'm so grateful, Lord, that I'm included in Your family. In Jesus' name, Amen.

JESUS BEFORE THE SANHEDRIN

The chief priests sent many people with Judas to arrest Jesus. There was quite a crowd there to see Jesus taken into custody, as if He were a criminal leading a rebellion. He'd been teaching every day in the temple courts and no-one had arrested Him there. Jesus told the crowd, *"'this has all taken place that the writings of the prophets might be fulfilled'"* (Matthew 26:56).

Every time Jesus made a statement like this it was giving people an opportunity, especially the chief priests, to re-consider their involvement in what was happening. For if what they were doing to Jesus really had been foretold by the prophets, then they were the generation who were guilty of rejecting God's salvation, brought to mankind by the Messiah of God. But in the eyes of the chief priests they were protecting the religious system, which gave them status and credibility, and in so doing they thought they were protecting God! They were rejecting the Truth in order to defend their version of what they wanted truth to be. This is the core of what has become known as being 'pharisaical' – meaning 'behaving like the Pharisees'.

And so it is, that in every generation there are those for whom obedience to religion has become more important than their relationship with God and their obedience to Him. God's heart cries out against religious practices which have become separated from the reality of truly knowing Him. For example, when He spoke through Isaiah, He said:

> '"I cannot bear your evil assemblies ... your festivals ... have become a burden to me ... even if you offer many prayers I will not listen ... come now, let us reason together ... if you are willing and obedient, you will eat the best from the land"' (Isaiah 1:14-19).

So, it wasn't the first time that their commitment to religion had put the chief priests and the Pharisees on a collision course with God. And now they had arrested God's Son, believing they were protecting God's work!

At that moment *'all the disciples deserted him and fled'* (Matthew 26:56) probably in fear of also being taken prisoner. Yes, even Peter left Him. Jesus was totally alone as He was arrested and taken by the hands of cruel men into Jerusalem to face, first, the former High Priest, Annas, and then His chief antagonist, Caiaphas, the High Priest in office.

THE JEWISH AUTHORITIES

The chief priests considered themselves to be the guardians of the orthodox truth. They were the custodians and interpreters of the law of Moses and they were the enforcers of the hundreds of rules and regulations to which relationship with God had been reduced by generations of rabbis and lawyers. The High Priest carried the ultimate spiritual authority in the land and acted as the senior religious officer in charge of the Sanhedrin.

The Sanhedrin not only exercised religious authority but acted as a court with considerable powers to enforce civil and criminal law. But it did not have the authority to order the death penalty without the approval of the Roman procurator. At the time of Jesus' trial, the Roman Procurator was Pontius Pilate. If they were to enforce their intention of having Jesus sentenced to death, then they would have to have the authorisation of Pilate.

Throughout the period of Roman occupation of Israel the High Priest's appointment had to have the sanction of Rome and he was, therefore, a puppet of the Romans. This arrangement was a trade-off between the Romans and the Jews. The Romans did not want a local religion to be used as a force for sedition or rebellion against the occupying forces. But they knew that if they attempted to suppress the religion of the people, they would provoke constant rebellion against the Romans. Compromise was reached by the Romans retaining the right to appoint the High Priest and the High Priest, now controlled by the Romans, knowing that his tenure in office would only continue if he satisfied his Roman masters. It was an uneasy arrangement, but it seemed to work.

The newly formed province of Judaea came under direct Roman rule in AD 6. The first High Priest to be appointed by the occupying powers was Annas, a young man, only 27 years of age. But in AD 15 he was deposed by the Procurator for going beyond his powers and carrying out the death penalty without Roman approval. Even though he'd been deposed, as a former High Priest he was still a very powerful figure in the Sanhedrin.

In AD 18 Caiaphas, the son-in-law of Annas was appointed as High Priest. He ruled the Sanhedrin as the highest religious and legal authority in the land for almost twenty years and was the High Priest who had approved the payment of thirty silver coins to Judas, in exchange for a peaceful arrest of the man known as Jesus of Nazareth.

Because of what had happened to Annas, Caiaphas had to be careful to protect his Rome-approved position. Whilst he would aggressively enforce religious justice in the land, he knew that the Romans would be watching him carefully. He didn't want to suffer the same fate as his father-in-law and be dismissed from office. So, his biggest problem in respect of Jesus would be to make a charge against Jesus stick, so that His offence would be seen to be a crime punishable by death under both Jewish and Roman law. Caiaphas was determined to get rid of Jesus, but without the co-operation of Rome he couldn't do it.

The respect that was given to Annas, as the former High Priest, is clearly expressed within the Scripture for, when Jesus had been arrested and taken into Jerusalem, the first person He was taken to stand in front of was Annas (John 18:12-13). Caiaphas needed Annas' opinion in order to help him prepare the case for putting before the Romans.

Annas *'questioned Jesus about his disciples and his teaching'* (John 18:19). In His reply Jesus simply told him that He had always taught openly in the synagogues or at the temple where everyone could hear Him. *'"Ask those who heard me. Surely they know what I said"'* (John 18:21). This response provoked a physical attack on Jesus as he was truck on the face by one of the officials, to which Jesus replied, *'"If I said something wrong, testify as to what is wrong. But if I spoke the truth, why did you strike me?"'* (John 18:23). There was of course no reply to Jesus' question and, still bound, He was now sent to Caiaphas, the current High Priest.

BEFORE CAIAPHAS

By the time Jesus was delivered to Caiaphas for questioning, not only was the High Priest there waiting, but the teachers of the law and the elders were already assembled as well. *'The chief priests and the whole Sanhedrin were looking for false evidence against Jesus so that they could put him to death'* (Matthew 26:59). It is a sad fact that when people have already made up their mind about something, and only want to justify their own position, they lose interest in the truth. By then the truth is dangerous to them, for it might remove the grounds for their arguments.

The authorities knew that Jesus had power and authority that was greater than theirs and they also knew that, unless they dealt with Him swiftly, the people would probably rise up in support of Him. They had ceased to be interested in the truth and were only interested in getting rid of someone who was now a serious threat to their own status.

I've seen on several occasions what happens when truth, integrity and morality get in the way of a person's soulish objectives. Truth is compromised, integrity is temporarily irrelevant, and morality is suspended for the sake of what is considered a higher objective. Even people in an office as important as the High Priest can be tempted to compromise themselves in order to protect their position and save their own face.

It's hard to believe how the appointed defenders of orthodox beliefs according to the law of Moses could consciously be looking for false witnesses, when the ninth commandment says so clearly, *'You shall not give false testimony against your neighbour'* (Exodus 20:16). No doubt the Sanhedrin excused itself on a technicality by saying that Jesus wasn't their neighbour, but I don't think that argument will be sustainable on the Day of Judgement when we are all called to give account of ourselves before the throne of God! (Matthew 12:36). The chief priests were consciously implicating many people in their sin by encouraging them to break the Ten Commandments.

But even though many false witnesses came forward, they couldn't find any whose statements would agree with each other (Mark 14:56), so their evidence would not carry any weight with the Roman authorities. Unless the Romans could be convinced about the validity of the case, the chief priests were not going to be able to achieve their objective. Time was passing and the chief priests were desperate to get this matter settled before the Sabbath. They only had the day that was now beginning to dawn to reach their goal, the death of Jesus of Nazareth.

JESUS REMAINS SILENT

The way Jesus handled the false accusations that were brought against Him was to remain silent. He did not feel any need to defend Himself against lies, just as Isaiah had foreseen:

'he was oppressed and afflicted, yet he did not open his mouth; he was led like a lamb to the slaughter, and as a sheep before her shearers is silent, so he did not open his mouth' (Isaiah 53:7).

This goes right against our natural instinct to defend ourselves, and I know this well, from our own experiences in ministry.

On one occasion, the Ellel leaders went away for a day to pray about how we should respond to some of the things that were being said. But it was as if God was not hearing the cry of our heart when we were asking Him what to do. In truth, we only wanted His answer about how to deal with our accusers – and God wasn't answering our prayers! Then, right at the end of the day, one of our number sensed God was asking us a question: "What have I asked you to do?" Our only response to this question was to remember the Scripture that God gave us at the beginning of our ministry, Luke 9:11, which talks about welcoming the people, proclaiming the Kingdom and healing those in need.

That was our calling and as we joined together in prayer at the end of the day we all knew that God had spoken – we must leave any accusers for God to deal with, and we must simply get on with what He has asked us to do for the hurting and broken lambs whom He was sending to our doors. It was the best advice we could ever have been given and over time we saw God deal with such situations in His way.

TELL US WHO YOU ARE!

The High Priest was getting agitated with Jesus (Matthew 26:62), so he challenged Jesus under oath: '*"Tell us if you are the Christ, the Son of God"*' (Matthew 26:63). Up till now all the accusations against Him had been false, but now Caiaphas was speaking the truth and Jesus was free to respond in the affirmative: '*"Yes, it is as you say"*' (Matthew 26:64). Jesus then went on to speak of His return: '*"But I say to you all, in the future you will see the Son of Man sitting at the right hand of the Mighty One and coming on the clouds of heaven"*' (Matthew 26:64).

Caiaphas was incensed. As far as he and the assembled gathering of lawyers and elders were concerned this was all they needed to hear. For a man, who wasn't God, to claim to be God, was a clear act of blasphemy for which, under the Mosaic law, the only punishment was death. The problem was, if the one making such a claim really was God, then Jesus would be innocent – a possibility that didn't seem to occur to the authorities that night, while they were intent on carrying out their desire! It's certainly true that evil intent blinds the spiritual eyes and deadens the conscience.

When Caiaphas asked all the officers who'd heard Jesus what they thought, they all agreed: '*"He is worthy of death"*' (Matthew 26:66). Then they taunted Him with their jibes and '*spat in his face and struck him with their fists. Others slapped him and said, "Prophesy to us, Christ. Who hit you?"*' (Matthew 26:67-68).

They had their evidence and now they wanted to get the sentence carried out, but without Pilate's help their hands were tied. So:

'*very early in the morning, the chief priests, with the elders, the teachers of the law and the whole Sanhedrin, reached a decision. They bound Jesus and led him away and handed him over to Pilate*' (Mark 15:1).

But when the chief priests presented Jesus to Pilate a subtle interpretation of what Jesus had said was introduced by them. They told Pilate that He was a king – and that would definitely get Pilate's attention. Rome didn't want another king causing disruption in the province!

A QUESTION

It's easy to read through this sequence of events, leading up to Jesus being presented to Pilate, and only see the chief priests in the bad light they deserve. But let's ask ourselves an honest question, "Have we ever twisted the truth in order to gain an advantage over someone? Have we ever told lies about someone in order to elevate ourselves by pushing them down?"

It's easy to condemn others, but it's also easy to forget sometimes that we can be just as guilty of the same things. As we consider what was happening to Jesus through these final days of His life and work on earth, let's use the opportunity to spend time with God asking ourselves the hard questions, and then put right anything the Lord shows us about ourselves.

SUMMARY

The chief priests now had a clear agenda. They wanted to get Jesus out of the way and have Him killed before the Sabbath. After Judas had betrayed Jesus into their hands, they needed to gather evidence against Him, but the testimony of those who brought false witness against Him didn't agree. But when Jesus acknowledged that He was the Christ, the Son of God, they believed they had enough evidence to put before Pilate. For without Pilate's help they couldn't carry out the death sentence.

PRAYER

Thank You, Lord, for teaching us so much by the way You responded to those who accused You falsely. Help me to remember these lessons whenever I am put under test by those who don't know or love You. Please give me Your wisdom at all times, so that my life and witness will always be acceptable to You. Show me, Lord, any times when I have behaved wrongly by wanting to accuse people of things they weren't guilty of for my own advantage, then show me what to do to put them right. In Jesus' name, Amen.

PETER'S DENIALS

PERSONAL NOTES

We will return to look at what happened to Jesus when He was taken to Pontius Pilate. For now it's vital to see what was happening to Peter whilst Jesus was before Annas and Caiaphas. This blot on Peter's journey of faith is of great importance to each one of us on our own personal journey.

It would be nice to sweep this story under the carpet and pretend it didn't happen, but that would encourage people to escape into self-deception and unreality. For whether we like it or not, there's something of Peter in every single one of us!

There are many ways of telling a story. When it could reflect badly upon ourselves it's amazing how adept we become at telling it in such a way that the real truth gets hidden and we even blame others for our mistakes! In modern political language it's called 'spin'. When politicians want to tell the people some bad news, they'll always try and dress it up in language that puts the best possible light on things. They want to minimise damage to their reputation by 'spinning' a story which camouflages the truth!

PERSONAL NOTES

The Bible, however, doesn't contain any spin. It tells the story exactly as it is. God doesn't make any effort to cover up the mess so that people will be impressed with the success of the mankind experiment. He lets the consequences of man's free-will choices be clearly seen by everyone.

I'm sure that if you or I were thinking about what to put in the Bible, we wouldn't have included Cain's murder of his brother Abel, or the Israelites worshipping a golden calf – even though God had just brought them safely across the Red Sea. We wouldn't have included King David's adultery with Bathsheba, or Jonah's rebellion against the instructions of God. We wouldn't have included the passages of Scripture we're now going to look at about the lies of Peter and his betrayal of Jesus, just when Jesus was in greatest need.

I WILL NEVER DISOWN YOU!

Jesus had been warning the disciples for some time that He was going up to Jerusalem for the Feast of Passover, and that He would die there. While the disciples had never been given a reason to disbelieve anything Jesus said, they hadn't really believed or grasped the significance of His words. Even after Jesus told them that one of their number would betray Him, and Judas had left to do the deed, they didn't accept the reality of what He'd said.

As they were leaving the Upper Room, where they had celebrated the Feast, Jesus reminded them of the prophecy that said, *'I will strike the shepherd, and the sheep of the flock will be scattered'* (Matthew 26:31 and Zechariah 13:7). Jesus clearly saw Himself as the Shepherd and, by implication, the disciples were, therefore, the flock who would be scattered. Immediately Peter jumped to his own defence – no-one was going to include him among a bunch of people who would desert his Master. *'"Even if all fall away on account of you, I never will"'* (Matthew 26:33), he declared.

You can almost sense the gentle shaking of His head, and the understanding look with which Jesus said to Peter, *'"I tell you the truth, this very night, before the cock crows, you will disown me three times"'* (Matthew 26:34). Peter was even more stirred up by the words of Jesus. Almost angry, he replied with yet more fervour, *'"Even if I have to die with you, I will never disown you"'* (Matthew 26:35). And all the other disciples agreed with their spokesman, Peter. And so the scene was set. Jesus, followed by His brave disciples, who said they would never leave Him, set out for the first test of their allegiance in the Garden of Gethsemane.

In one simple and devastating sentence Matthew described what happened when Judas arrived at the Garden with the officers of the temple guard and a large crowd sent by the chief priests and the elders with swords and clubs (Matthew 26:47). We are told, *'then all the disciples deserted him and fled'* (Matthew 26:56). Only a few hours separated their vow to be committed to follow Jesus, even if it meant death, from their fleeing in fear as they deserted their Lord and Master. And Jesus, now in the hands of cruel men, was left to walk alone to His destiny in the city of Jerusalem.

YOU WILL DISOWN ME THREE TIMES

Even though the disciples had fled from the scene – at least far enough to be out of immediate danger – they couldn't ignore what was happening. I imagine them creeping along behind the crowd, far enough from the action to be safe, but as close as they dared get to where Jesus was.

One of the disciples, the Gospels don't tell us which one, was known to the High Priest, so Peter, attached himself to him and they *'went with Jesus into the high priest's courtyard, but Peter had to wait outside, at the door'* (John 18:15-16) while the other disciple got permission, spoke to the girl on the door and brought Peter inside as well. There's no doubt about Peter's motives or intentions – he wanted to get as close as he possibly could to Jesus in His hour of need.

But as he was entering the courtyard, the girl on the door challenged him with a simple question, *'"You aren't one of his disciples, are you?"'* (John 18:17). At this, Peter panicked. All his bravado disappeared into thin air and, instead of answering this young girl honestly with the truth, fear took over and his lips spoke out a lie, as he said, *'"I am not"'* (John 18:17).

There are two circumstances in which a lie is often the first thing that comes into our head. Firstly, when we have done something wrong and we try to escape the consequences by denying our involvement in whatever it was. Secondly, when to admit the truth, even when we're not doing anything wrong, could be costly or dangerous.

Peter wasn't doing anything wrong. He had permission to enter the

PERSONAL NOTES

High Priest's courtyard. The girl was only asking a question out of her own curiosity. But fear grabbed Peter's heart and, instead of owning the fact that, yes, he was a disciple of Jesus, he preferred to disown any association he had or might have had with Jesus.

A HEART EXAMINATION!

Before we shake our heads in disbelief that someone as close to Jesus as Peter could not only have fled when Jesus was arrested, but was now also telling lies to disassociate himself from any relationship with Him, let's examine our own hearts. We need to ask ourselves some hard questions!

Have we ever told lies in order to try and avoid punishment? Have we ever not told the whole truth, in order to try and minimise our sinfulness? Have we ever been afraid of what people would think of us, if they knew just how committed we were to following Jesus? Have we avoided situations that would make us vulnerable, where we would have to own up to what we believed?

We may have to admit that we've failed Jesus in this way, because the carnal nature from which sinful choices originate always wants to defend itself against being found out. I remember having done something wrong when I was a child but denying it. I didn't want to be punished for what I'd done, and rather than own up to it, I kept on saying "it wasn't me", even though I knew it was.

Before we move on, let's ask the Lord to help us see ourselves as He sees us, so that we can face reality about ourselves and the things we've tried to keep hidden. Sadly, if we tell a lie often enough we can even begin to believe it ourselves and, after a period of time, this self-deception will become the false reality we live in. There may be times when we need to allow others in the Body of Christ, whom we trust, to help us recognise any 'artificial reality' in which we are living? The way out of self-deception is honesty, humility and willingness to submit to others in authority over us, and to be accountable to them.

MORE LIES

If we tell one lie and get away with it, falsehood enters our reality; in order to defend ourselves against further accusations, we then have to tell more lies. We have to 'prove' that the first lie we told was the truth. If, having, told one lie, which was believed, we then tell the truth the next time round, then it becomes obvious to people that on one of those occasions we weren't telling the truth. So, once one lie has been told and believed, the only way to maintain consistency is to keep on telling more lies. We have to protect ourselves from being found out about the first lie.

This is the exact situation Peter found himself in. He'd already lied to the girl on the gate. Now someone else, was also warming himself by the fire where Peter was standing with the other disciple. This person said the same thing to Peter as the girl on the gate had done, and he was now caught in a trap of his own making (John 18:25). He'd lied once and now he had to lie again, in order to keep up the charade of not having been one of Jesus' disciples.

Finally, as the people heard him talking with the other disciple, one of them said, '"s*urely you are one of them, for your accent gives you away"*' (Matthew 26:73). It's a fact that when people are telling a lie, they often raise their voice, shout, swear and even lose their temper, especially if someone persists in trying to get them to own up to the situation. Peter was no exception to this universal 'law' – when people shout the loudest, the likelihood is that they're not telling the truth!

And so Peter, this big man, the natural leader among the twelve disciples, lost his composure and *'he began to call down curses upon himself and he swore to them, "I don't know the man"'* (Matthew 26:74). And all of this was happening within a few yards of where Jesus was being questioned, first by Annas, and then by Caiaphas, the High Priest.

The man who had vowed he would never leave Jesus, or betray him, was now out of control. And at that very moment *'a cock crowed'* (Matthew 26:74) and *'Peter remembered the word that Jesus had spoken: "Before the cock crows, you will disown me three times." And he went outside and wept bitterly'* (Matthew 26:75).

Suddenly Peter had to face the truth about himself. He was consumed with remorse as he saw himself, not as the leader whom Jesus could depend on, but as the broken man who was no better than the weakest of men. He wept bitterly as he tried to come to terms with what he'd done. Despite all his protestations of loyalty and faithfulness he'd fallen badly at the very first challenge to his commitment to the Lord. He was a broken man who'd suddenly discovered that he was incapable of following Jesus in his own strength.

A LIFE DIVIDED IN TWO

There is absolutely no doubting how much Peter loved Jesus, and how much he wanted to serve him. But as long as he was going to do it in his own strength, he was always going to fail. This is a place that we must all come to, sooner or later. For if we're trying to run the race of life and build the Kingdom of God in soulish determination, we'll never fulfil our destiny.

It's only when we discover our own weakness and inability to 'fix it' that we can start leaning on Him to strengthen us and discover what the apostle Paul also had to discover for himself. God had to say to him:

'My grace is sufficient for you, for my power is made perfect in weakness. Therefore I will boast all the more gladly about my weaknesses, so that Christ's power may rest on me' (2 Corinthians 12:9).

No-one knows the depth of pain and personal anguish that Peter must have gone through in the hours that followed his own betrayal of Jesus. There was Jesus, in the terrible agony of His suffering and Peter had no way of showing Him any love or comfort. He had no opportunity, even, of saying sorry to Him.

But God, in His mercy, hadn't forgotten Peter. All that Jesus had invested in training this 'wild stallion' of a man wouldn't be wasted. He was to become a leader of men. The time would come when Jesus would help Peter to get his life back on track.

Peter's life was divided in two. There was his life before he betrayed Jesus, and his life after he was restored. In between, Peter must have endured intense pain as he wondered if he could ever serve his Lord again. We must wait until after the resurrection to discover what happened next in his life. In the meantime, let's face the truth about ourselves. Let's ask God to show us everything that the enemy wants to condemn us with, but which Jesus wants to turn around into a blessing!

SUMMARY

Peter vowed that he would never betray Jesus - even if everyone else left Him! But Scripture tells us that, despite all his protestations, when he was facing fear and danger, all his commitments to loyalty and faithfulness just melted away. He was left with his fears and fled with the rest of them. Then, when he tried to get close to where Jesus was being questioned by the High Priests, on three separate occasions he disowned Jesus, exactly as Jesus had prophesied. Peter was a broken man as he realised what he had done. When the cock crowed, he had to face the truth about himself.

PRAYER

Help me, Lord, to own the truth about myself and recognise if I've made similar mistakes to Peter when faced with circumstances out of my control. Show me, Lord, if I've betrayed You by telling lies, and doing things that are unworthy of my commitment to You. I want to confess these before You and ask for Your forgiveness. In Jesus' name, Amen.

JESUS BEFORE PILATE AND HEROD

Whilst Peter was going through his own personal crisis, following his triple betrayal of his Lord and Master, Jesus was being dragged from the house of the High Priest to the palace of the fifth Procurator of the Roman Province of Judaea, a man better known to history as Pontius Pilate.

The chief priests had established that they had grounds to accuse Jesus of blasphemy. According to their laws blasphemy was a religious crime punishable by death, and so the next stage of the procedure was to receive the support of the Roman authorities and get the death penalty endorsed. For this they needed Pontius Pilate's co-operation, so they decided to colour the evidence in the hope of making it more convincing. They put in some further accusations that might be of more interest to Rome in preparation for the time of cross examination.

MORE FALSE ACCUSATIONS

If Jesus was claiming to be the Son of God and this was a lie, then the accusation of blasphemy would have been right according to the Law.

The religious authorities didn't give any credence to the idea that Jesus actually was the Son of God and so was speaking the truth.

Blasphemy, however, wasn't a charge that interested Rome, so they told Pilate that they had *'"found this man subverting our nation"'* who *'"[opposed] payment of taxes to Caesar … and [claimed] to be Christ, a king"'* (Luke 23:2). Their hope was that, in saying Jesus was a king, Rome would decide they didn't want to have another authority in the land that could cause them problems. Pilate, however, although he may have been a weak man who eventually sanctioned the execution of Jesus, at least he was honest enough to disagree with the charges laid at Jesus' feet.

When the chief priests brought their accusations to Pilate, Jesus made no attempt to defend Himself – since what they said was untrue. This amazed Pilate (Matthew 27:14) so he asked Him if He was, as claimed, *'the king of the Jews'*. Jesus simply acknowledged the fact, saying *'"It is as you say"'* (Luke 23:3). He was proving no threat to either Pilate or Rome.

So Pilate *'announced to the chief priests and the crowd "I find no basis for a charge against this man"'* (Luke 23:4). But this did not satisfy the chief priests, who were looking for blood. So they told Pilate that Jesus *'"[stirred] up the people all over Judea by his teaching. He started in Galilee and [had] come all the way here'* (Luke 23:5). At this, Pilate saw a way of escape, for, as a Galilean, Jesus was under King Herod's jurisdiction. So because Herod happened to be in Jerusalem at that time, Pilate sent Jesus to him.

Herod had already heard a lot about Jesus and had been trying to find an opportunity to meet Him. He was keen to see a miracle but was to be disappointed. Although he asked Jesus lots of questions, he received no response to any of them. So *'Herod and his soldiers mocked him. Dressing him in an elegant robe, they sent him back to Pilate'* (Luke 23:11). Herod could find nothing to charge Jesus with either, so he sent Jesus back to Pilate's court. Herod hadn't solved Pilate's problem.

HE'S INNOCENT
Pilate then called back the Jewish authorities and told them:

'"You brought me this man as one who was inciting the people to rebellion. I have examined him in your presence and have found no basis for the

charges against him. Neither has Herod, for he sent him back to us; as you can see he has done nothing to deserve death. Therefore I will punish him and release him"' (Luke 23:14-16).

Time was passing and the chief priests were losing their battle to get Jesus crucified. Neither Pilate nor Herod would co-operate with them.

Pilate could see that an ugly scene was developing and if he didn't collaborate with the Jews, things could get even more difficult. So he *'then went back inside the palace, summoned Jesus and asked him, "Are you the king of the Jews?"'* (John 18:33). In His reply Jesus expressed a profound truth: *'"My kingdom is not of this world. If it were, my servants would fight to prevent my arrest by the Jews. But now my kingdom is from another place"'* (John 18:36).

When Pilate responded by saying *'"You are a king then"'*, Jesus answered, *'"You are right in saying I am a king. In fact, for this reason I was born, and for this I came into the world, to testify to the truth. Everyone on the side of truth listens to me"'* (John 18:37). *'"What is truth?"'* Pilate asked. But without waiting for an answer he went out again to the Jews and said, *'"I find no basis for a charge against him"'* (John 18:38).

Through this brief interchange between Jesus and Pilate, in which Jesus simply explained that His kingdom was not of this world, Pilate realised that this king was no threat to Rome. Rome was only interested in the kingdoms of this world. Jesus might have been mad, or He might have been speaking a truth which Pilate couldn't understand, but He definitely wasn't a threat to Rome!

It's easy for us to understand, with the benefit of two thousand years of Christian heritage, that the Kingdom of God is a spiritual kingdom, whose power and authority far exceeds anything that Rome could ever muster. But for Pilate this was all new. He was hearing and learning things under the most severe pressure. It was all totally beyond anything he could have possibly understood. He was on a dramatic learning curve of spiritual truth. But one thing was clear, whoever and whatever Jesus was fighting, Rome was not on His agenda. So Pilate didn't need to exercise Roman authority and have Him executed.

'"What is truth?"' Pilate had asked Jesus. Now he was once again confronted by his own thoughts on the inside, and an increasingly angry Jewish crowd on the outside. So in an attempt to satisfy their desire for

blood and at the same time save Jesus from the ultimate penalty, Pilate had him flogged.

Flogging under Roman law wasn't a gentle procedure. The lashes, with bits of metal embedded in the ends of the leather strands, literally ripped the skin and the flesh from the back of the prisoner. It wasn't unusual for prisoners to die from the consequences of flogging. Then:

'the soldiers twisted together a crown of thorns and put it on his head. They clothed him in a purple robe and went up to him again and again, saying, "Hail, King of the Jews." And they struck him in the face' (John 19:2-3).

'Once more Pilate came out and said to the Jews, "Look, I am bringing him out to you, to let you know that I find no basis for a charge against him"' (John 19:4).

Jesus was now standing there, in front of the crowd, wearing the purple robe and the crown of thorns, and Pilate said to them *'"Here is the man"'* (John 19:5), hoping that the pitiful sight of a man almost flogged to death by the Roman soldiers would appease their desire for blood.

But it had the opposite effect and *'as soon as the chief priests and their officials saw him, they shouted, "Crucify, Crucify"'* (John 19:6) and insisted that they had a law, according to which he must die *'"because he claimed to be the Son of God"'* (John 19:7).

When Pilate heard this, John tells us *'he was even more afraid'* (John 19:8) and went back into the palace to ask Jesus *'"Where do you come from?"'* (John 19:9). But once again Jesus didn't answer his question. Pilate was now frustrated at Jesus' apparent lack of co-operation. After all he was actually trying to help Him so he said *'"Don't you realise I have power either to free you or crucify you?"'* (John 19:10).

Jesus' response encapsulated a mountain of theological truth in a few words: *'"You would have no power over me if it were not given you from above. Therefore the one who handed me over to you is guilty of a greater sin"'* (John 19:11). Jesus was stating that it was through God's power and authority that the universe and everything in it was brought into being. Pilate would have no power or authority under Rome if it wasn't for God in the first place.

But from that position of power and authority, Pilate was being asked to judge a man whom he had no desire to condemn. Jesus went on to absolve Pilate of the greater part of the blame for what was happening to Him and implicated the High Priest when He said *'"the one who handed me over to you is guilty of a greater sin"'* (John 19:11).

FREE BARABBAS!

Pilate's efforts to free Jesus were getting nowhere. There was only one more thing he could do, which he was sure would get Jesus released, for *'it was the governor's custom at the Feast to release a prisoner chosen by the crowd'* (Matthew 27:15). Barabbas was a notorious and dangerous criminal who *'had been thrown into prison for an insurrection in the city, and for murder'* (Luke 23:19). There was no way, Pilate thought, the people would want Barabbas to be released, so he would give them the choice of Jesus or Barabbas.

Pilate calculated that the crowd would be obliged to choose Jesus. But he had seriously underestimated the hatred and the determination of the chief priests and the power and influence they had over the people. Pilate was shocked when the people began to shout for Barabbas to be freed and for Jesus to be crucified. His plan had failed.

HAVE NOTHING TO DO WITH THIS INNOCENT MAN

Suddenly all of Pilate's clever plans to get Jesus released had come to nothing. While he had correctly judged Jesus to be an innocent man, it was Pilate himself who was now on trial. As Governor, he had the authority to release Jesus and tell the chief priests to go away. But he probably feared an insurrection would be started by the Jewish authorities if they didn't get what they wanted. The last thing Pilate wanted was news of an insurrection, in the troubled province of Judea, to get back to Rome. Pilate was keeping an eye on his career path and didn't want any black marks against his reputation.

He was on the verge of making the choice that it was better for Jesus to die, even if He was innocent, when a message came from his wife. *'"Don't have anything to do with that innocent man, for I have suffered a great deal today in a dream because of him"'* (Matthew 27:19). Pilate was supernaturally warned through his wife's dream. God had given him a very good reason to be strong and resist the pressure of the Jewish authorities, but fear and expediency ruled the day and he ignored the dream.

There was an occasion in my own life when God clearly warned me not to have anything to do with a certain man, but I thought I knew best. For reasons of possible financial gain in my business, I ignored the voice of God and went ahead, despite the warning. It was the worst decision I had ever made. Had it not been for the grace of God, who dramatically intervened following my deep repentance and change of direction, I would certainly have lost my business, been made bankrupt and could, even, have lost my life. I learnt the hard way that it's a very dangerous thing to ignore the warnings of God.

Pilate was putting himself in a dangerous place with God when, because of the pressure he was under from the chief priests, he ignored the warning that came through his wife's dream. Despite her dream he went ahead with his plan to set free whichever prisoner the crowd asked for, even if it did mean releasing a notorious criminal and killing an innocent man.

By this time the crowd were shouting for Barabbas and if Pilate didn't agree to their request he would lose face. He then addressed the crowd, and asked:

> *"'What shall I do, then, with Jesus who is called Christ?" They all answered, "Crucify him." "Why, what crime has he committed?" Pilate asked. But they shouted all the louder, "Crucify him"'* (Matthew 27:22-23).

Pilate was now trapped by his own plan. He didn't want to have Jesus executed. But things were turning nasty and, unless he agreed to the crowd's demands, he could still have the rebellion on his hands that he dreaded. Pilate had crossed a line in his thinking. He'd gone beyond the point of no return and he would have to explain to his wife, and one day to God, why he hadn't intervened to save the life of an innocent man.

PILATE WASHES HIS HANDS

When Pilate decided that he had no alternative but to hand Jesus over to be crucified he was determined that the chief priests and the people should know that this was their choice and not his. Pilate took a bowl of water and washed his hands publicly in front of them all, saying, *"'I am innocent of this man's blood. It is your responsibility'"* (Matthew 27:24). The meaning of this simple act has become known across the world throughout history.

Pilate was trying to please his wife and absolve his conscience by declaring that the death of Jesus would not be his personal responsibility – even though the power of life or death was clearly in the hands of the Roman Governor. To 'wash your hands' of something has entered into the language of most nations as a phrase meaning that you aren't taking any responsibility for whatever happens.

The chilling response which came from the crowd, and which has become a curse on unredeemed Jewish people for all generations since, was *"'let his blood be on us and on our children'"* (Matthew 27:25). I believe this has had an enormous impact on the people of God down through history. It has acted like a curse which has blindfolded the spiritual eyes of the Jewish people, preventing them from seeing the truth about who Jesus is.

But today God is removing that blindfold from the eyes of many Jews who are discovering that Yeshua (Jesus) is their Messiah too. Next, we'll take a closer look at what was happening in this respect, and at what the apostle Paul had to say about it.

SUMMARY

Having decided that Jesus had committed blasphemy and deserved to die, the chief priests tried to convince Pilate of the need to endorse the death penalty by making further false accusation against Jesus. But Pilate couldn't find anything that Jesus was guilty of, and neither could King Herod. Pilate's wife told him not to have anything to do with that innocent man (Jesus) but, because of the pressure on him from the Jews, Pilate decided to release either Barabbas or Jesus. Pilate was shocked when they chose Barabbas. He therefore washed his hands of the matter and the Jews took upon themselves the consequences of what they were doing.

PRAYER

Thank You, Jesus, for Your amazing fortitude in enduring the false accusations and mockery of foolish men. I'm so grateful, Lord, that You pressed on to fulfil the calling on Your life so that I could be free of Satan's claim on mine. Help me, Lord, to always appreciate what You went through in order to set the captives free. In Jesus' name, Amen.

THE CENTRE POINT OF HISTORY

And so it was that Pilate gave in to the pressure of the chief priests to get Jesus executed. Fear controlled both his emotions and his decisions. He ignored the warning words of his wife and submitted the mighty power of Rome, the world's most powerful people, to the hatred and anger of Jewish leaders who, themselves, were frightened of the power and authority that Jesus had, and which they didn't.

Step by step the prophecies about Jesus were being fulfilled, in remarkable detail. And in the middle of all this Pilate did an extraordinary thing: he took a bowl of water and washed his hands publicly in front of them all, saying, *"'I am innocent of this man's blood. It is your responsibility'"* (Matthew 27:24).

LET HIS BLOOD BE ON US

The chief priests were so determined to get Jesus executed that by now they would stop at nothing to achieve their objective. When a corporate spirit consumes a crowd their behaviour reflects the raw emotion emanating from the carnal nature. They wanted Jesus dead and, if accepting responsibility for His shed blood would help the process along, so be it.

It was no surprise, therefore, that *all the people answered, "Let his blood be on us and on our children!"'* (Matthew 27:25). So, feeling relief from personal responsibility for the execution of Jesus, Pilate *'released Barabbas to them … [and] … handed him over to be crucified'* (Matthew 27:26).

At this point it was as if a large, round stone had been pushed over the brow of a hill and had started to roll. Gravity and momentum would make the stone unstoppable until it reached the bottom of the hill and could roll no further. As Pilate handed Jesus over to His captors, spiritual gravity took over. The events of the next few hours would just keep on rolling until Jesus had breathed His last, and His body had come to a halt at Calvary, the hill of eternal destiny.

We will walk together with Jesus and the disciples through the events of the next few hours of His life but, before we do so, we need to spend a short time looking again at the significance of those awesome words spoken by the chief priests, including the High Priest, and the crowds, when they took personal responsibility for the shed blood of Jesus and the death of the Son of God.

I mentioned specifically that the High Priest, Caiaphas, was implicated in everything that happened to Jesus, because he was the spiritual head of the nation. He was the one who had all the spiritual and legal authority over the people of Israel. To the Jews the High Priest was their spiritual covering.

The decisions and choices he made weren't carried out in the isolation of his private life. He was a public man and there were public consequences for what he did. And on this occasion his involvement in accepting responsibility for the blood of Jesus would affect every Jew from that moment on. Caiaphas and all the Jews there understood this principle – they even expressed it out loud when they said that Jesus' blood would not only be on them, but also on their children (Matthew 27:25).

We have seen this principle at work on many occasions. If, for example, a minister of a church falls into sin, those under his covering are vulnerable to falling into similar sins. Sin gives the enemy a right to operate in all their lives, causing untold spiritual harm. When a man falls into sexual sin, he's opening up the potential for his children and his children's children to be affected by a generational spirit. Those who are under our covering are affected by the things we do (Exodus 34:7).

The High Priest, the chief priests and the elders were blinded to the truth about Jesus by their own rebellious anger. They could no longer see reason, and not only did they bring cursing, through the work of the enemy, into their personal lives, but into everyone under their spiritual covering – in this case the whole Jewish people. Spiritual blindness was the inheritance they gave to the Jewish people for many generations.

PAUL EXPLAINS THE BLINDNESS OF THE JEWS

In his letter to the Romans, the apostle Paul explains what happened when the Jews, who were desperate for their Messiah to come, did not recognise Him and rejected the Son of God: *'God gave [Israel] a spirit of stupor, eyes so that they could not see and ears so that they could not hear'* (Romans 11:8, Isaiah 29:10); *'their eyes [became] darkened so they [could not] see'* (Romans 11:10, Psalm 69:23).

Then Paul explains that the Jews haven't fallen beyond recovery but that, for a season, because of their rejection of Jesus, the Gentiles would have the chance of salvation. Paul, however, prays that the Jews would eventually be provoked to jealousy and begin to want what this salvation too. Then, says Paul, *'what will their acceptance be but life from the dead?'* (Romans 11:15).

'Israel,' he says, *'has experienced a hardening in part until the full number of the Gentiles has come in'* (Romans 11:25). But then the day would come when the Jews would see for themselves the reality of who Yeshua (Jesus) really was and is, for *'God's gifts and his call are irrevocable'* (Romans 11:29). What God had planned for the Jews could never be taken from them.

The thrilling thing is that we're privileged to be living in the days when the Jews are beginning to rise from the dead! Not only has God preserved the Jewish people, against all odds, and gathered them back as the nation of Israel into their own land, but He's also gathering together a body of Messianic believers whose eyes are now fully open. They too are now receiving the mercy that God planned for them in the first place, through the witness of the Gentiles!

What an amazing and wonderful story. The Messiah of the Jews became the Saviour of the Gentiles and now Jews are once again recognising their

Messiah through the witness of the Gentiles, and the Body of Yeshua is growing in the land of Israel. Scripture is being fulfilled before our very eyes. These really are some of the most exciting days of history.

The blindfold is falling away from the Jews and one day, when all Jews recognise their Messiah, what a message will go out into this fallen world as God takes the Jew and Gentile and *'creates in himself one new man out of the two, thus making peace, and in this one body reconciles both of them to God through the cross'* (Ephesians 2:15-16). Watch the news headlines! God is on the move!

THE CENTRE POINT OF HISTORY

For nearly two thousand years time has been measured by the moment the cross was planted on Calvary's Hill, and a totally sinless man was taken there to die. Satan knew that if Jesus died in a sinless condition the ruling spirit of death would have no power over Him.

Today, the powers of universalism and political correctness are wanting to rewrite all our calendars to eliminate Jesus from our dating system, so we now live in CE, the Common Era, instead of AD (*Anno* Domini - meaning the Year of our Lord), and talk about BCE (meaning before the Common Era, not Before Christ). But no amount of political engineering of calendars can change the fact that all the saints of previous history had been waiting for this moment, when the promise of Genesis 3:15 would be fulfilled, and the One who was born of woman would crush the head of the serpent.

All those who had died in faith before Jesus came, were anticipating their release into the presence of God for eternity. But that could only happen when Jesus turned the key in the lock of the gates of death – gates that had swung shut on fallen man in the Garden of Eden, and which only began to be opened when Jesus said Yes to drinking the cup of God in the Garden of Gethsemane.

You may think that we are spending quite a long time meditating on all the events that surrounded the death and resurrection of Jesus but, unless we have come to the place of truly understanding all that was going on in both the spiritual and the physical realms at this turning point of history, we won't be fully equipped to run the race of life which stretches out before us from time into eternity.

THE CENTRE POINT OF HISTORY

Paul summed up the attitude that we should have so well when he said:

'Your attitude should be the same as that of Christ Jesus: Who, being in very nature God, did not consider equality with God something to be grasped, but made himself nothing, taking the very nature of a servant, being made in human likeness. And being found in appearance as a man, he humbled himself and became obedient to death – even death on a cross!' (Philippians 2:5-8).

In our own *Journey to Freedom* pilgrimage of understanding, this is the path we need to tread, the pathway of humility. It is only as we humble ourselves that God can lift us up (Psalm 147:6). I recently came across this profound quote from the writings of Dr Alexander Maclaren (1826-1910). What an encouragement they are to us as we prepare ourselves for walking with Jesus to Calvary's cross.

'The seed must die if a harvest is to spring from it. That is the law for all moral and spiritual transformations. No man can be fruit-bearing unless he sacrifices himself. We shall not "quicken" our fellows unless we "die" either literally or by the not less real martyrdom of rigid self-crucifixion. Self-renunciation guards the way to the "tree of life". The world's war cries today are "Get" and "Enjoy". But Christ's command is "Renounce!" But in renouncing we shall realise both of these other aims, which they who pursue them only, never attain.'[1]

There is so much in these words that needs to be thought through deeply. Especially the conclusion, that it's only those who renounce what comes from the carnality of the flesh who truly get what they can enjoy for ever – for both time and eternity. And this is radically different than the carnal things people want to get and enjoy!

I pray that, as you think on all that Jesus did for you, through His willingness to lay down His life, you will want to walk with Him on the path of humility. When God opens doors, we know He will bless us as we walk through them in obedience. And the character that God grows and develops in our lives, as we walk with Him, is priceless and eternal and will give us the courage to fulfil our destiny in Him, notwithstanding the barriers and hurdles that the enemy lays in front of us.

SUMMARY

When Pilate released Barabbas to the crowds, he washed his hands of responsibility for the death of Jesus. The chief priests and all the people took upon themselves this responsibility and brought upon themselves the consequences of the shed blood of Jesus. This blinded the eyes of understanding of the Jewish people. But today God is steadily removing the blindfolds and Jewish people are discovering what Paul prophesied in Romans 11 as Jews are 'raised from the dead' through coming to know their Messiah.

PRAYER

Thank You, Lord, that You never stopped loving Your people and that even today You're restoring to Jewish people an understanding of who their Messiah is. Help me, Lord, to walk in the ways of Jesus so much that all the people I meet will see Jesus in me and be drawn to Him. In Jesus' name. Amen.

[1] Public domain

STAGE 3

The Passion and Death of Jesus (2)

"Jesus' words of forgiveness to the Roman soldiers echo down the years of time as a constant challenge to those who think they have an excuse to be unforgiving."

Stage 3, Chapter 1

THE CRUCIFIXION OF JESUS

The Christian celebration of Easter embraces our remembrance of the death of Jesus, on what has always been known as Good Friday, and then the joyful celebration of the resurrection on Easter Sunday morning. That first Easter was, of course, at the time of the annual Passover celebration.

The early church wrestled with the huge issue of what major festivals Christian believers should celebrate. Eventually, the Christmas celebration was fixed for the 25 December and the date of Easter Sunday was fixed, after the Council of Nicaea in AD 325, as the first Sunday after the full moon following the Spring Equinox.

Sadly, today's Easter celebrations have taken the form of a national holiday in most western nations, which is now largely dissociated from the true significance of the weekend. What happened in Jerusalem on that first Easter has been lost in a sea of Easter eggs, chocolate, Easter bunnies and hundreds of other activities, which are now part of an annual calendar of events, all of which mask the true significance of this most important of dates in the Christian calendar.

PERSONAL NOTES

PERSONAL NOTES

Many children growing up in today's secular world have no idea whatsoever what the celebration of Easter is all about – other than an opportunity to gorge themselves on chocolate during the school holidays!

EASTER

In her cycle of twelve plays, *The Man Born to be King*[1], broadcast by the BBC during the Second World War, Dorothy L Sayers chronicles the whole life of Jesus, including all the events of the last week of His life. The complete series is a truly remarkable dramatic work by a woman who really knew her subject. The original plays were produced by one of the finest dramatic pioneers of the twentieth century, Val Gielgud.

When commenting on the impact the series was making, Dorothy Sayers said that 'It is curious that people, who are filled with horrified indignation whenever a cat kills a sparrow, can hear the story of the killing of God told Sunday after Sunday and not experience any shock at all!'[2] The crucifixion has been sanitised to such an extent that people no longer have any idea what it meant for the Son of God to suffer for the sin of mankind.

So as a counter to the trivialisation of the Easter story I'd like to begin this stage of *Journey to Freedom* by taking a closer look at just what crucifixion was really like. For Jesus knew exactly what lay ahead of Him when, in the Garden of Gethsemane, He said Yes to God and agreed to drink the cup of suffering which lay ahead of Him.

ROMAN CRUCIFIXION

Roman crucifixion was a cruel procedure. Death for the victim would come slowly, in excruciating pain and suffering. It was specifically designed to be a long, drawn-out process and was always carried out in a prominent public place. The sight of such pain and anguish was part of the Roman way of subduing the people of a province.

Once someone had witnessed the terrible suffering that crucifixion caused, they would want to avoid the possibility of ending up on a cross themselves. Crucifixion was a hugely effective means of controlling the masses, who would then be slow to commit any rebellious action that might result in them having to endure a similar fate.

There are many contemporary records of crucifixions from around the time of Jesus, all of which substantiate the Gospel records as being an accurate account of what actually happened to Him. Crucifixion was specifically designed to be the most humiliating of procedures and was used, especially, for people who had no rights whatsoever, such as slaves. Roman citizens were exempt from being crucified – it was considered a far too disgusting and degrading form of execution for them.

Jesus wasn't a Roman citizen, so crucifixion was the only form of death for Him. He was reduced to suffering the same fate as those at the bottom level of society. He could not have been more humbled than this.

It was common for crucifixion victims to suffer the terrible agony of being beaten before they were crucified. This was carried out with a scourge which had sharp bits of metal embedded in long strands of leather. When it was used on the prisoner's back it would remove most of the skin. Then, while suffering the extreme agony this brought, the victim would be made to carry the horizontal beam of his own cross from the place of flagellation to the place of crucifixion. It was placed on his back which was now raw and bleeding. Anything that increased the suffering of the victim was done so that the terrible sight would have an even greater effect on subduing the people who witnessed it.

The Romans would normally position a crucifixion site just outside the gates of most of the towns they governed, in places where the people couldn't avoid seeing what had happened to their fellow-citizens. Here the arms of the prisoner would be tied to the cross piece while he was lying on the ground, so that the nails could then be firmly put in place through the hands or between the bones of the wrist. Finally the prisoner would be lifted to a vertical position and the cross piece secured in place with the prisoner hanging by his arms. Finally the feet would be nailed to the post and the prisoner would be left to die in immoveable agony.

There were many different causes of actual death – ranging from loss of blood to asphyxiation. Sometimes, when the victim was taking longer to die than was convenient for the Roman soldiers, who had to remain on duty while the victims were still alive, they would break the legs of the prisoner. Then he could no longer support his body against the nails through the feet. Apart from the further agony of the broken legs, this caused the weight of the body to pull down on the chest, making

PERSONAL NOTES

breathing extremely difficult. Death through asphyxiation would come quickly after that.

Crucifixion was one of the most agonising and gruesome forms of death ever devised by human beings. This was the death that the Son of God voluntarily chose, because of His love for you and for me.

So, what does the cross of Christ actually mean to you and me? This is what James Boice said, 'The cross means this, Jesus taking our place to satisfy the demands of God's justice and turning aside God's wrath.'[3] And Billy Graham expressed it this way: 'In the cross of Christ I see three things: First a description of the depth of man's sin. Second the overwhelming love of God. And third the only way of salvation.'[4]

Martin Luther said, with passion in his heart, 'No man understands the Scriptures, unless he is acquainted with the cross.' Let's now do just that, get acquainted with the detail of what the Scriptures tell us about the cross and the crucifixion of Jesus Christ. *'For the message of the cross is foolishness to those who are perishing, but to us who are being saved it is the power of God'* (1 Corinthians 1:18).

THE SOLDIERS TAKE OVER

Jesus had already been flogged by the soldiers until His back was skinless and raw. This was one of Pilate's failed tactics to try and save Jesus from the ultimate punishment. So, when He was finally handed back to the soldiers for crucifixion, He had already suffered the terrible agonies of flagellation.

He then had to carry the heavy wooden cross-beam across His broken and bleeding back, but the burden was beyond Him. The soldiers had no intention of carrying the cross-beam for Him. So, to help them get the prisoner from Pilate's palace to Golgotha (which means 'The Place of the Skull') (Mark 15:22), where crucifixions were carried out, the soldiers grabbed a passer-by, Simon from Cyrene, to help them. Simon *'was on his way in from the country, and [they] put the cross on him and made him carry it behind Jesus'* (Luke 23:26).

By now a large number of people were following Jesus, *'including women who mourned and wailed for him'* (Luke 23:27). Almost certainly these included Mary and Martha from Bethany, Mary, the Mother of Jesus, Mary Magdalene and many others. It was at this moment that

Jesus turned to them and uttered words which are only rarely referred to in sermons about the Easter story, but which are of profound, prophetic significance:

> '"Daughters of Jerusalem do not weep for me; weep for yourselves and for your children. For the time will come when you will say, 'Blessed are the barren women, the wombs that never bore and the breasts that never nursed!' Then they will say to the mountains, 'Fall on us!' and to the hills, 'Cover us!' For if men do these things when the tree is green, what will happen when it is dry?"' (Luke 23:28-31).

Charles Spurgeon clearly explains the first part of Jesus' prophetic word (when He tells the women not to weep for Him, but for themselves and their children): 'You need not weep because Christ died, one tenth as much as because your sins rendered it necessary that he should die. You need not weep over the crucifixion, but weep over your transgression, for your sins nailed the Redeemer to the accursed tree. To weep over a dying Saviour is to lament the remedy, when it was wiser to bewail the disease. To weep over the dying Saviour is to wet the surgeon's knife with tears. It was better to bewail the spreading tumour, which the knife must cut away!'

Oh how true are those words of Spurgeon. Yes, of course we can weep over the terrible suffering that Jesus experienced on our behalf, and weep we must. **But if we do that and fail to weep over the sin that sent Him to the cross, we have not even begun to understand what the sacrifice of Jesus is all about.**

Jesus then talks about a time that is yet to come, when the fullness of sin would be worked out in this fallen world. This is a passage which parallels Jesus' warnings about the End Times in Matthew 24:16-25, when Satan and the powers of darkness will seek to do their worst, in the days before the return of Jesus the King. For these days will, indeed, be the most wonderful, but also the most terrible days for mankind, and especially for believers who are holding their ground against the onslaught of the enemy.

They will be wonderful days because in those times the Gospel of the Kingdom will be preached with great blessing and effectiveness across the world. The church will 'become a dwelling in which God lives by His Spirit' (Ephesians 2:22). But they will also be terrible days because Satan

PERSONAL NOTES

will be working to the limit of his powers to stop the word of blessing from achieving God's ultimate aim across the world.

For, as Jesus says, if men would do such terrible things to the Son of God *'when the tree is green'*, meaning the beginning days of this redeeming work of God on earth, what will happen when *'it is dry'* – when the enemy's work is fully developed in the mind and heart of men.

I find these words of Jesus, at this critical moment in His own pilgrimage to Calvary, so incredibly profound and meaningful. He could quite legitimately have spoken words of self-pity and personal grief. Instead He continued to focus on the reason for His suffering. He didn't allow Himself one moment of self-pity or personal comfort – He was truly drinking the cup of suffering that He'd agreed to drink when He knelt in the Garden of Gethsemane and agonised with His Father over what was to come.

Jesus was accompanied in crucifixion by two criminals who had been sentenced to die in the same way. When they reached the place of the Skull, the Roman soldiers laid Him down and nailed His hands to the cross-beam. Then, after raising the cross to an upright position, they nailed His feet to the vertical post. And so the Son of God was now *'**lifted up**'* to die.

THE BRONZE SERPENT

Hundreds of years earlier, on their way from Egypt to the Promised Land, the Israelites sinned by speaking against God and against their leader, Moses. As a result, God sent venomous snakes amongst the people to show them how sin removes His protection. Many of the people were being bitten and dying.

It's amazing how easily trouble in our lives brings us back to God! The people were desperate, and they soon acknowledged their sin, saying, *"We have sinned when we spoke against the LORD and against you. Pray that the LORD will take the snakes away from us"* (Numbers 21:7).

Moses prayed, and God gave them His answer. He didn't remove the snakes but provided a remedy for the sin. It was to be a constant reminder of who it was who had rescued them from Egypt. *'The LORD said to Moses, "Make a snake and put it on a pole; anyone who is bitten can look at it and live." So Moses made a bronze snake and put it on a pole. Then when anyone was bitten by a snake and looked at the bronze snake, he lived.'* (Numbers 21:8-9). And so the results of their sin became a means of driving the people back to God in repentance, and then trusting Him for their healing.

So, way back in those days in the wilderness, God had established a prophetic principle for His people. For those with eyes to see it would become a teaching lesson for all time to come, of how God intended to deal with the eternal consequences of sin – man would have to choose to look to Him and to no other. So, when Jesus was teaching about why He had come into the world He said:

> *"'Just as Moses lifted up the snake in the desert, so the Son of Man must be* **lifted up***, that everyone who believes in Him may have eternal life. For God so loved the world that he gave his one and only Son, that whoever believes in him shall not perish but have eternal life'"* (John 3:14-15).

Less than three years later, this prophecy that Jesus had made about Himself was fulfilled. When He was being nailed to that piece of wood at the Place of the Skull and **lifted up** on the cross-beam above the crowds He didn't become a bronze serpent but He became a living sacrifice for the sins of the whole world.

The sin of the Israelites was rebellion against God. In reality every single sin we commit is also an act of rebellion against God. The only remedy for sin is to look to the One who was **lifted up** for us, in our place, that we might live.

SO WHY DID HEZEKIAH DESTROY THE SNAKE?

The bronze snake that Moses had made had been preserved by the people as a symbolic reminder of what God had done for them in the past. But, as with so many things in our lives, the symbols of freedom for one generation can become an object of idolatry in the next!

When Hezekiah came to the throne, after the reign of one of the worst Kings in Judah's history, he wanted to walk in the ways of David, in respect of his relationship with God. Hezekiah had a godly mother and her influence had been critical in raising the young man. The previous king, Ahaz, had led the whole nation into occult idolatry, so Hezekiah set about cleansing the temple and cleansing the nation. *'He removed the high places, smashed the sacred stones and cut down the Asherah poles'* (2 Kings 18:4). These were the obviously evil artefacts of occult worship.

But he also did something else – he *'broke into pieces the bronze snake Moses had made, for up to that time the Israelites had been burning incense to it'* (2 Kings 18:4). What had been used to point the people to the God who healed them had, itself, become an object of worship that was leading the people into idolatry. The bronze serpent, which would probably have been considered to be one of the nation's greatest artefacts from their history, had become a stumbling block to relationship with God. So it had to go!

A LESSON FOR US TODAY

What a lesson this must be for us today – it is so easy for us to make an idol out of the things God uses to bring us blessing. People can even end up worshipping and idolising the cross on which Jesus died instead of having a real relationship with Jesus as their personal Saviour. The emblem can become a substitute for the real object of our worship, which is Jesus Himself.

Because our Ellel Centres have been so used by God to bring healing and blessing into the lives of thousands of people, it would be easy to fall into the trap of the Centres themselves becoming more important than our relationship with God, so that yesterday's blessing become tomorrow's idol!

Before we move on to look at some other important aspects of the day Jesus died, may I encourage you to spend a few minutes making sure that there's nothing in your life that's become an idol, an object of worship, that operates in your life more like 'a lucky charm', than a reminder of who God is and what His Son has done for you.

SUMMARY

Crucifixion was the most cruel of punishments. It was deliberately designed to make death as painful and as long drawn-out as possible, as a warning to others not to rebel against Rome. It was such an undignified way of dying, that criminals who were Roman citizens were exempt from having to endure it. There was no exemption for Jesus who suffered the worst possible death on behalf of sinful mankind. Jesus was lifted up in the same way as the bronze serpent had been lifted up in the desert wilderness, so that those who look to Him will live - they will be forgiven and because of what He suffered they can also know His healing.

PRAYER

Thank You, Lord, for everything You suffered on my behalf. I'm sorry for the sin in my heart, which made the cross necessary. I'm amazed that You loved me and all mankind so much that You went through all that suffering. Help me, Lord, never to make an idol of the things You use to bring me blessing, but to always remember that my relationship with You is more important than anything else in whole of the universe. In Jesus' name, Amen.

1   Sayers, Dorothy L (1943), The Man Born to Be King: A Play-Cycle on the Life of Our Lord and Saviour Jesus Christ, Written for Broadcasting, (Wm B Eerdmans, 1943)

2   Sayers, Dorothy L, quoted in: Thiede, Carsten, Rekindling the Word (Trinity Press International, 1995), p 116

3   Boice, James, The Centrality of the Cross (an address to the Philadelphia Conference on Reformed Theology, 1997)

4   Graham, Billy, Peace with God: The Secret of Happiness, Revised ed (Thomas Nelson, 2012)

Stage 3, Chapter 2

FATHER, FORGIVE

The Gospel writers each record different details about the crucifixion of Jesus. But all tell us that Jesus wasn't alone when He was lifted up on His cross. There were two other criminals crucified at the same time – *'one on each side and Jesus in the middle'* (John 19:18).

We are also told that *'Pilate had a notice prepared and fastened to the cross. It read JESUS OF NAZARETH, THE KING OF THE JEWS… and the sign was written in Aramaic, Latin and Greek'* (John 19:19-20). It seems that this was done deliberately by Pilate, to annoy the Jewish leaders. They certainly didn't like it and protested to Pilate, saying *'"Do not write 'The King of the Jews,' but that this man claimed to be king of the Jews"'* (John 19:21).

But the memory of his conversation with Jesus, and the warnings from his wife, must have been fresh in Pilate's mind. He had heard Jesus say that He was the King of a Kingdom that's not of this world, and so he retorted to the chief priests *'"What I have written, I have written"'* (John 19:22). Pilate had no intention of changing what he had written (in three different languages for everyone to read) on the sign that had been nailed to the cross.

FATHER, FORGIVE THEM

The soldiers who had nailed Him to the cross were not personally responsible for what was happening to Jesus. They were soldiers under authority, and they were simply carrying out the orders given to them by the centurion in charge of the execution squad. Jesus looked on them with compassion. Even in this, the direst moment of His short life, Jesus was concerned for everyone who was having to participate in the drama of the cross, especially the soldiers who had been obliged to drive the nails through His body as part of their job.

His prayer to His Father, which the soldiers will surely have heard Him speak, must have been one of the most astounding prayers ever made: '"*Father, forgive them, for they do not know what they are doing*"' (Luke 23:34). And how totally true was Jesus' statement. Those Roman soldiers knew they were crucifying a human being, but they had no idea what they were really doing! In particular, they had no idea that they were nailing a man to a piece of wood who had never sinned, and was not subject to the curse of death, which was the lot of every other fallen human being.

Jesus had remained without sin. As a sinless person He didn't deserve to die like every other human being, and He certainly wasn't guilty of the charges that had been levelled against Him by the Chief Priests. He was innocent on every count. But He was still dying. The unfairness was mind-boggling to the extreme.

In the beginning humankind turned its back on the God who made humanity, and broke relationship with Him. As a result, death entered into the human race. So it was our sin that caused the Father to put the only possible rescue plan into effect, one that could restore the broken relationship between God and humankind.

There is no one else who has ever walked the face of this earth, either before or since, who suffered such terrible injustice. No one else has ever had a greater excuse to blame others and cry out, "Not fair." But, not only did Jesus walk in personal forgiveness toward all of those who were the agents of His suffering, He also asked God to forgive them!

To ask God to forgive, in circumstances such as this, was an extraordinary demonstration of what Jesus meant when He said, '"*Bless those who curse you, pray for those who mistreat you*"' (Luke 6:28, *NASB*). Jesus was asking His Father to allow those who had persecuted Him to enter into the wonderful benefits that He had planned and purposed for them, benefits such as joy, release from bondage and, the greatest of all, a relationship with Himself.

All the angels of heaven must have bowed in silent wonder as they saw their beloved Jesus turn His back on resentment, bitterness, anger and revenge and ask the Father to forgive those who were causing His death. What a man! What a God!

THE NEED FOR A FORGIVING HEART

We have looked several times at different aspects of forgiveness in our *Journey to Freedom*. The subject just will not go away! And here it is again, right in the middle of the events that led to the death of Jesus on that first Good Friday. It's impossible to ask God to forgive those who have hurt us, without first being willing to forgive them from the heart ourselves. Otherwise the thoughts and desires of our own heart will be opposed to what we are asking God to do, and it is those thoughts, desires and intentions that God sees and judges (Hebrews 4:12-13). As we have already discovered, Jesus even said that if we don't forgive those who have hurt us, then our Father in heaven will not forgive us! (see Matt. 6:15).

People are often surprised to find that this is in the Bible. Surely God wants to forgive us, they say. Yes, He does, but He has also given us a choice; and He won't override the choices we make. **If we choose not to forgive those who have hurt us, we put ourselves under their control. If we are under their control, we cannot be free for God to heal us and set us free.** If Jesus had not chosen to forgive all those who had hurt Him, He would have been allowing them to control Him, and that would have changed His relationship with Father God, and given Satan the access he had been desperately wanting to undermine the work that Jesus was doing for mankind on the cross.

Jesus even told us to love our enemies! He knew that if we reacted in bitterness of heart against those who oppose us and who even do bad things to us, we would be in bondage to those people for as long as we live. He knew that if we ignore this vital principle, we will find that our reaction to what others have done to us could do us as much harm as the original offence. He wanted us to be free from all that. Only when we have truly forgiven others are we able to be free, and then pray Jesus' prayer, *'Father, forgive them'*, for ourselves from the heart.

THE POWER OF THE PRAYER

The prayer Jesus prayed from the cross, *'**Father, forgive them**'* is, quite simply, one of the most powerful prayers that you can ever pray:

- It transforms your relationship with God
- It denies Satan any further hold on your life
- It releases the power of the Holy Spirit into your life
- It restores your soul
- It opens the door to God's healing.
- It transforms your relationships with other people

But none of us can truly pray this extraordinary prayer until we have learned to forgive others for what they have done to us. And sometimes, we need to forgive ourselves before we can turn our hearts toward blessing others.

STEPHEN PRAYS THE JESUS PRAYER

Stephen, the first Christian martyr, learned this lesson of forgiveness well. He had such a forgiving attitude toward his accusers that when he was being stoned to death, watched by the man who would become the apostle Paul, he too was able to pray like Jesus. Using words very similar to those Jesus used from the cross, he prayed, *'"Lord, do not hold this sin against them"'* (Acts 7:60).

How important it is that we learn to live like this in the ordinary circumstances of life, and not just when facing the extremes of persecution that Stephen and countless others have faced through the centuries! Learning to pray like Jesus could be the most important thing you will ever do. It is God's master key, specially designed to unlock the most stubborn of problems in your life. (For further information, see my book *Forgiveness – God's Master Key*, Sovereign World Ltd 2009).

The prayer 'Father, forgive' is the spiritual dynamite that God uses to blow apart the prison doors – those doors that can keep us locked into the pain of the past. It is the most powerful prayer on earth.

THE SOLDIERS DIVIDE HIS CLOTHING

There were four soldiers who crucified Jesus. It was normal for a prisoner to suffer the indignity of being crucified naked and for his clothing to be divided between the soldiers. When they came to Jesus' clothing, they didn't want to tear His seamless garment into four pieces. Instead they decided to cast lots to determine who would get it (John 19:24). Perhaps they had been impacted by what Jesus had prayed to His Father for them?

For whatever reason, once again, one more of the many prophecies about the Messiah was amazingly fulfilled. David, inspired by the Holy Spirit, had written, *'They divided my garments among them and cast lots for my clothing'* (Psalm 22:18, John 19:24).

So the prophecies about Jesus were still being fulfilled, in the finest of detail, during those final hours of Jesus' life.

AND WHAT ABOUT THE OTHERS WHO DIED?

Yes, there were two criminals who also died that day. They were crucified alongside Jesus for things they had done and, according to the laws in force at the time, they were receiving the required punishment.

There was a significant difference, however, between the two criminals' attitudes towards Jesus. *'One of the criminals who hung there hurled insults at Him: "Aren't you the Christ? Save yourself and us!"'* (Luke 23:39). This question to Jesus must have been spoken with much sarcasm, for the other criminal rebuked him, saying *"'Don't you fear God, since you are under the same sentence? We are punished justly, for we are getting what our deeds deserve. But this man has done nothing wrong"'* (Luke 23:39-41).

Here the second criminal is making a clear statement of faith as to who Jesus is. *"'This man has done nothing wrong"'* is as simple and straightforward a statement as you will ever get about the sinless nature of the Son of God. And if He has done nothing wrong, then the title written by Pilate, and nailed to the cross of Jesus, must be true. He is a King – but not of this world. And if that's the truth then this man must be God Himself.

The second criminal knew and recognised that all men had sinned. But if Jesus had done nothing wrong, then He must be who Pilate had said He was. And so he spoke out loud, *"'Jesus, remember me when you come into your kingdom"'* (Luke 23:42). This was a statement of faith and

PERSONAL NOTES

trust in the Man who was being crucified alongside him. He was already believing that death would not conquer Jesus and that there was going to be life after death!

Jesus' reply to the crucified criminal has been such an amazing encouragement to sinners of every generation since, "'I tell you the truth, today you will be with me in paradise'" (Luke 23:43). The message people have received from these words of Jesus is very simple: 'If there was hope of resurrection life for a crucified criminal, then perhaps there's hope for me!'

The dying criminal looked to Jesus and discovered that, as he looked at the Lamb of God who was taking away the sin of the world (John 1:29), he received life in exchange for a look of faith at the Saviour. This wonderful truth was powerfully expressed in the words of one of the great Gospel hymns by Miss A M Hull (1825-1882):

There is life for a look at the Crucified One,
There is life at this moment for thee;
Then look, sinner, look unto Him and be saved,

Unto Him who was nailed to the tree.
Oh, why was He there as the Bearer of sin,
If on Jesus thy guilt was not laid?
Oh, why from His side flowed the sin-cleansing blood,

If His dying thy debt has not paid?
It is not thy tears of repentance or prayers,
But the blood, that redeemeth the soul;
On Him, then, who shed it, thou mayest at once

Thy weight of iniquities roll.
Then doubt not thy welcome, since God has declared
There remaineth no more to be done;
That once in the end of the world He appeared,

And completed the work He begun.
Then take with rejoicing from Jesus at once
The life everlasting He gives;

And know with assurance, thou never canst die
Since Jesus, thy Righteousness, lives.

SUMMARY

Even in His dying hours, Jesus was expressing love, compassion and concern for others. It was a remarkable moment when Jesus asked the Father to forgive those who were killing Him, because they didn't know what they were doing! But what an example Jesus set for us all in terms of how to forgive – even our enemies. Jesus was putting into practice the very instruction He had given to His disciples – to bless those who curse you! And at the last He was giving hope for eternity to one of the two criminals who died alongside Him – the one who believed that Jesus was indeed who the sign on the cross said He was!

PRAYER

Thank You, Lord, for showing me how, even in the depths of pain and suffering, it's possible to love and forgive those who are hurting me. Help me, Lord, not to be a believer who only knows the truth in my head. I want to put my faith into practice at all times and follow Jesus' amazing example. I don't want to give the enemy any ground in my life through holding others in bitterness and unforgiveness. I am trusting You afresh with all my decisions and the attitudes of my heart. Thank You, Lord, that there is always life for those who look in faith to the Lamb of God who was slain for sinful man. In Jesus' name, Amen.

PERSONAL NOTES

Stage 3, Chapter 3

THE LAST TEMPTATION OF CHRIST

Temptation comes in many forms. There are temptations to indulge in all sorts of soulish desires; temptations to harm others in order to protect or elevate oneself; temptations to steal other people's property; temptations to break any one of the Ten Commandments; temptations to laziness or self-indulgence; and then there was the temptation that Jesus faced when being crucified, *'"come down from the cross and save yourself"'* (Mark 15:30).

Jesus is the only person who has ever walked this planet for whom those words would be a real temptation as opposed to a sarcastic jibe. Those who passed by and *'hurled insults at him, shaking their heads'* (Mark 15:29) thought they were making sarcastic jibes to an impotent man. In reality they were speaking the words of Satan to an innocent man who, if He chose, could have done exactly what they were suggesting. But then, that's exactly what Satan wanted Jesus to do! Satan had, by now, realised, that if Jesus were to die willingly, as a result of His own free-will choice, then death would have no hold over Him.

SATAN'S PLANS AGAINST SINLESS JESUS

Since the moment that Jesus, the totally sinless Son of God, was born as Son of 'Man', Satan had been on the defensive. God had previously given man authority over planet earth but he had given away that authority to Satan. Adam had allowed the curse of sin to come into the human race and Satan was in charge. He had no fear that his authority would be taken from him … until Jesus came. For the only person who could regain authority over planet earth was another sinless human being.

Jesus was different. He was not an 'ordinary man'. Yes, He was wholly man, but He had been conceived in Mary by the Holy Spirit of God, not through normal sexual relationships between a man and a woman but through the direct intervention of God. So there was no generational sin in Jesus' life and Satan, therefore, had no authority over Him. And as the Word of God clearly said that Jesus had come to set the captives free (Isaiah 61:1), Satan had every reason to be concerned about His arrival on the planet. For setting the captives free could only ever mean setting people free from the domination and control of Satan!

So, for thirty-three years Satan had been doing everything he possibly could to bring Jesus under his spiritual control, either by taking His life or by tempting Him to sin. Either way, Satan would then have achieved His objective. If Satan had succeeded in having Jesus killed against the will, plans and purposes of God, then Satan would have proved and established his authority over the Godhead.

DEATH PLOTS

So, Satan's first plan to deal with the threat of Jesus' presence on earth, was to try and eliminate Jesus one way or another. First he tried to kill Him off as a baby when he prompted King Herod to kill all the baby boys in Bethlehem (Matthew 2:16). But Joseph was warned in a dream and the family made their escape to Egypt.

Then, when Jesus' ministry began, he managed to turn the crowds against Jesus in Nazareth, when He said that Isaiah's prophecy (Isaiah 61:1) was then being fulfilled. As a result the people were filled with anger, rose up against Jesus and tried to throw Him off a cliff to kill Him (Luke 4:29).

Later, Satan tried to drown Jesus, with all the disciples, when He was asleep in the boat. He chose that critical moment, when it looked as though Jesus was 'off duty and sleeping', to stir up a sudden and furious storm, which threatened to sink the boat (Luke 8:24). The disciples woke Jesus up, saying, *"Lord, save us! We're going to drown!"* (Matthew 8:25). But Jesus rebuked the disciples for being concerned, saying, *"You of little faith, why are you so afraid?"* (Matthew 8:26). Then He *'rebuked the winds and the waves, and it was completely calm'* (Matthew 8:26). As far as Jesus was concerned, He was completely in control of the situation, even when He was asleep. He had no fear that Satan could take His life!

TEMPTATIONS

The only other way that Satan could establish his supremacy over God was by enticing Jesus to use His own free will to make a sinful choice. In that way Jesus would come under Satan's control, just as mankind had come under his control when our first parents took of the fruit in the Garden of Eden. We've already looked at the specific temptations that Jesus faced when He was fasting in the wilderness (see *Journey to Freedom*, Book 4) . And I've no doubt that Satan was constantly looking for opportunities to tempt Jesus throughout His life and ministry.

In the Garden of Gethsemane Jesus voluntarily chose to drink the cup of suffering and fulfil His calling and destiny in obedience to the plans and purposes of the living God. From that moment on, the death of Jesus at the hands of the chief priests and the officers of Rome would be contrary to Satan's objectives. For, if Jesus was choosing to die willingly, fully participating with Father God in His amazing rescue plan for the human race, Satan would have to face an even bigger problem!

If Jesus were to die, without ever having sinned, neither death itself nor Satan could have any control over Him. Satan would have to face the reality that Jesus had overcome death, and on the other side of the crucifixion there was going to be a resurrection. That was something Satan dreaded more than anything else. It must be stopped!

SATAN'S FINAL CHANCE

As we've already seen and understood, crucifixion is a horrendously painful and cruel way to die. There's no-one who wouldn't want to escape from the Roman crucifixion process of being publicly nailed to a cross. The Romans knew what they were doing. The nails were driven home well. They wouldn't fall out. Were a prisoner to have ever managed to escape, the consequences would have fallen on the soldiers responsible for the crucifixion. The soldiers would have lost their own lives. There's no way they would take chances by not doing the job properly. There's no record in history of anyone escaping from the nails of their cross.

None of the Roman soldiers, or the criminals who were dying alongside Jesus, or any of the passers-by, would have understood that this prisoner dying on the cross was unlike any other. He could have escaped! Jesus had the power and the authority to instruct the angels of heaven to extract the nails and release Him. There were twelve legions of angels available, ready to respond to whatever Jesus wanted (Matthew 26:53).

So, when:

'the chief priests, the teachers of the law and the elders mocked him and said, "He saved others, but he can't save himself. Let him come down from the cross, and we will believe in him. He trusts in God. Let God rescue him now if he wants him, for he said, "I am the Son of God"' (Matthew 27:41-43),

their challenge to Jesus was far more real than any of them can ever have imagined. And as far as Satan was concerned, this was his last chance to try and trap Jesus into falling into temptation.

The temptation to rise to the challenge of the chief priests and show them who He was must have been very great. Jesus was experiencing sheer human agony. Surely we would all do anything possible to escape from such agonising pain. Jesus was totally human – make no mistake, He felt the pain. He wasn't insulated from all the suffering of the cross.

What a massive temptation. Here was a wonderful opportunity to prove once and for all that every word He'd said was true. At the same time He could escape from the agony of the cross. But, if Jesus had given in to the temptation, summoned the angels and come down from the cross, He would have been obeying Satan. It was Satan's subtle inspiration behind the words of temptation and challenge that were being hurled at Jesus from all sides.

This temptation was similar to the tests He'd already been put through in the wilderness – to use His power to serve Himself. Jesus had come to earth in obedience to God and to serve mankind. If He had chosen to use His power to serve Himself, and exempt Himself from the sufferings of man, He would have been using His free will to enter into rebellion against His Father. At that point Satan would have won, Jesus would have come under Satan's authority and the glorious rescue plan from heaven would have failed. And all of mankind, without exception, would have been condemned to eternal separation from God. Jesus could have saved Himself by coming down off the cross, but in saving Himself the hope of man would have died.

Man's only hope of escaping eternal death was in God's plan for Jesus to die and then, because He is without sin, to be raised again from the dead and become our Living Hope. How I praise God that Jesus faced the prospect of death and rejected the last temptation Satan threw at Him.

I love the words *'It wasn't the nails that held Him to the cross – it was His love for you and for me.'* It was for our sake that the angels remained unemployed on that most awesome day of history. The last temptation of Christ had failed to achieve its goal.

DESTROY AND REBUILD THE TEMPLE!

One of those passing by the cross, reminded Jesus that He'd said He was going to *'destroy the temple and build it in three days'* (Mark 15:29). They were making fun of the helpless victim and laughing at the stupidity of the idea that Jesus had proposed. But in their mockery, they were proclaiming the very truth of what Jesus had meant when He said He would rebuild the temple!

Jesus was always filled to overflowing with the presence of God's Holy Spirit and the apostle Paul wrote that our *'body is a temple of the Holy Spirit'* (1 Corinthians 6:19). The body of Jesus was about to be destroyed, but in three days it was going to be resurrected (the temple was going to be rebuilt). When the enemy mocks, God smiles – God had His focus on what was going to happen three days later – and very soon that's where our focus in *Journey to Freedom* will be also.

A FINAL WORD

The essence of the last temptation of Christ was Satan's final attempt to stop Jesus fulfilling His destiny. In reality, that is the tactic that's at the heart of all Satan's work. He hates it when we become what God wants us to be and when we do what He's called us to do.

I'm personally praying for each one of you, as you work your way through *Journey to Freedom*. I'm especially praying that, when the enemy devises temptations to distract you from the way God has laid out for you, you'll recognise the temptations for what they are and you'll have the courage to resist them, at all costs. Never forget that there's a crown of life awaiting you in eternity!

SUMMARY

The final temptation of Jesus was to come down off the cross. Through performing this amazing miracle He would have proved to all His tormentors that He was who He said He was, and He would have escaped the agony of crucifixion. But His calling and destiny were to endure the cross. It was necessary because of God's love for mankind and, if Jesus had not pressed on and overcome death, mankind would never have escaped from Satan's control. His love kept Him on the cross and there He died to set the captives free – including you and me!

PRAYER

Thank You so much, Lord, that You resisted the final temptation Satan threw at You and that You chose to endure the cross because of Your love for mankind. We don't deserve such love but we're so grateful. Help me, Lord, when I am tempted to walk away from my destiny and calling, to remember what You did for me. In Jesus' name, Amen.

Stage 3, Chapter 4

THE DEATH OF JESUS

We now turn to the final sufferings of Jesus at the very end of His earthly mission. But before we do so, let me ask you a question: **Do you want to know Christ and the power of His resurrection?**

I am sure that every one of you who has travelled this far through our *Journey to Freedom* journey would answer a resounding Yes to this question! Then let's read the full Scripture from Philippians 3:10 when Paul said:

*'I want to know Christ and the power of his resurrection **and the fellowship of sharing in his sufferings, becoming like him in his death,** and so, somehow, to attain to the resurrection from the dead'.*

Here is my own, rather amplified, version of this wonderful Scripture:

'I want to know and experience the anointing of God that was on Jesus, God's Son. And I want to live my life every day in the same dynamic power that God used to raise Jesus from the dead. In order to experience

this incredible blessing in my life, I choose to fellowship with Jesus in the sufferings He went through on my behalf. I realise that without death there can be no resurrection, and I want to die to everything in my life that would be an obstacle to realising my destiny and prevent His resurrection life transforming me from the inside out. I choose to fellowship with Him in whatever sufferings come my way as a result of walking forward in obedience to Him, and one day, through God's great love and mercy, I look forward to celebrating with Him in my own resurrection from the dead to eternal life in glory.'

Now we must walk with Jesus through everything that happened as His earthly life was drawing to a close, in those final steps of suffering that led to His death, before He was gloriously resurrected.

HERE IS YOUR MOTHER

When people are dying they like to make provision for those who are to be left behind. And those who are closest to the person dying are often gathered around the bedside. In Jesus' case there was no bedside, only the foot of a cross. And there was no written will, for Jesus had no earthly possessions. But what He left behind was far more valuable than anything else the world had ever seen or known – a knowledge of the truth about God and the way to Him, a gift of salvation for those who would choose to believe and the promise that He was going to prepare a place for all those who knew and loved Him (John 14:1-6).

As the moment of Jesus' death drew closer, those who specially loved Him were naturally as close to Him as they could get.

'When Jesus saw his mother there, and the disciple whom he loved standing nearby, he said to his mother, "Dear woman, here is your son" and to the disciple, "Here is your mother." From that time on, this disciple took her into his home' (John 19:26-27).

Even while enduring the agonies of His own death Jesus was concerned for the woman who had been so highly favoured by Father God, the one chosen to carry and bear His Son. Jesus was making provision for her future care. It's generally assumed that the disciple Jesus was asking to care for His mother was John, the writer of the Gospel which records this conversation.

THE LAST PROPHECY TO BE FULFILLED

Everything was now in place. His mother was cared for and there was nothing left for Jesus to do but die. However, there was still one unfulfilled prophecy. Even in the agonies of His final moments, the integrity of the Word of God was at the forefront of His thinking.

Hundreds of years previously King David poured out his heart to God. He brought everything before the Lord but, in so doing, became close to the heart of God. And in that place, God filled his spirit with prophecies. So when David wrote what we call Psalm 69 it was a glorious expression of his own circumstances and prayers, linked with things he knew were from God even though they were beyond his capacity to understand.

In the Psalm David talks about himself and his own situation, whilst speaking prophetically about Jesus (the Son of David) and what would happen to him. His words are a prophetic description of what Jesus was to endure in order to bring salvation as a gift to mankind:

'I am scorned, disgraced and shamed ... scorn has broken my heart and left me helpless ... they put gall in my food and gave me vinegar for my thirst' (from Psalm 69:18-21).

Before Jesus was crucified He had been offered *'wine to drink, mixed with gall; but after tasting it he refused to drink it'* (Matthew 27:34). It was laced with gall (or myrrh – Mark 15:23), a bitter substance that was a drug. It was usually offered to those being crucified to reduce their searing pain at the moment of being impaled on the cross, to make it easier for the soldiers to put the nails through the body and do their job. A modern day equivalent would be the anaesthetic that is given by a dentist before drilling a person's teeth. Without the anaesthetic the pain levels are so high that it is extremely difficult for the dentist to do his job.

But for Jesus to have taken the drug would have been a sin, insulating Him from the suffering that was the very core of His calling under God.

So having tasted it, He rejected it. However, having been nailed to the cross Jesus was still thirsty and so, in fulfilment of the Scripture, He cried out

"'I am thirsty" – a jar of wine vinegar was there, so they soaked a sponge in it, put the sponge on a stalk of the hyssop plant, and lifted it to Jesus' lips. When he had received the drink, Jesus said, "It is finished"' (John 19:28-30).

The final prophecy had been fulfilled; there was nothing left for Jesus to do. All the items on the agenda of God had been completed in preparation for the moment that changed the history of the world, and Jesus cried out those extraordinary words *"It is finished."*

DARKNESS OVER THE LAND

The work Jesus came to do was finished. He now hung between life and death. *'From the sixth hour until the ninth hour darkness came over all the land'* (Matthew 27:45). Luke adds that *'the sun stopped shining'* (Luke 23:45). John Wesley comments on the 'heathen philosopher' who, seeing it, knew that 'it could not be a natural eclipse, because it was at the time of the full moon, and continued three hours together.' This heathen man cried out, '"Either the God of nature suffers, or the frame of the world is dissolved."'[1]

The God of nature, the Creator of the universe and the Father of our Lord Jesus, was indeed suffering. By this darkness God testified his abhorrence of the wickedness of man that was then being laid upon the shoulders of His Son. Matthew Henry, one of the greatest ever commentators on Scripture, said, 'During the three hours which the darkness continued, Jesus was in agony, wrestling with the powers of darkness, and suffering his Father's displeasure against the sin of man, for which he was now making his soul an offering. Never were there three such hours since the day God created man upon the earth, never such a dark and awful scene; it was the turning point of that great affair, man's redemption and salvation.'[2]

MY GOD, MY GOD

At the end of these three hours, during which Jesus took all the consequences of the Fall of man upon Himself, He cried out in a loud voice, using the words of Psalm 22:1, *"'Eloi, Eloi, lama sabachthani?" Which means, "My God, my God, why have you forsaken me?"'* (Matthew 27:46). Jesus was now separated from His Father. He was now experiencing what would have been the eternal condition of mankind – separation from God and being without hope, in the control of Satan, for eternity.

As we have already seen, Jesus could have saved Himself from death, even after He had been nailed to the cross. But once He had died the situation would change. For Jesus to choose to die as a man was an extraordinary demonstration of faith and trust in His Father. He was trusting that God would honour His Word and raise Him to life once again. **For when Jesus allowed the burden of man's sinfulness to be placed upon His shoulders, He was putting Himself in a place from which He could not rescue Himself. I believe that at that point Jesus was helpless to save Himself. He was trusting totally in the God who had abandoned Him, to rescue Him.**

Abraham was willing to take his son, Isaac, and place him on the altar of sacrifice, trusting that God would provide an alternative sacrifice. Just at the critical moment the *'angel of the LORD called out to him from heaven'* (Genesis 22:11) and Abraham's faith in God was rewarded as *'there in a thicket he saw a ram caught by its horns'* (Genesis 22:13). This time, no alternative sacrifice had miraculously appeared on Calvary's hill, and Jesus was trusting that after a death when He was, as it were, buried by all the sins of mankind, Father God would stretch down His hand and lift the One who was without sin, out from the hell of sinfulness into the heaven of resurrection life.

'Jesus called out with a loud voice, "Father, into your hands I commit my spirit". When he had said this he breathed his last' (Luke 23:46).

In commenting on this Matthew Henry said, 'Christ, just before he expired, spoke in his full strength, to show that his life was not forced from him, but was freely delivered into his Father's hands. He had strength to bid defiance to the powers of death, and to show that by the eternal Spirit he offered himself, being the Priest as well as the Sacrifice, he cried with a loud voice. Then he yielded up the spirit. The Son of God upon the cross, did die by the violence of the pain he was put to. His soul was separated from his body, and so his body was left really and truly dead. It was certain that Christ did die, for it was needful that he should die. He had undertaken to make himself an offering for sin, and he did it when he willingly gave up his life.'[3]

THE WORLD IS SHAKEN AND THE CURTAIN TORN

At that very moment, when Jesus gave up His life to death, the whole world was shaken, even to the extent that rocks split, tombs broke open and:

> *'the bodies of many holy people who had died were raised to life. They came out of the tombs, and after Jesus' resurrection they went into the holy city and appeared to many people'* (Matthew 27:52-53).

The resurrection of these saints was a totally extraordinary and miraculous event, but it was nothing in terms of its significance to what happened to the curtain inside the temple in Jerusalem. The curtain separated the temple courts from the most holy place, the place where only the High Priest was allowed to go, once a year, into the presence of God, to make atonement for his own sins and the sins of the people. The curtain he went through was about sixty feet high (20 metres), four inches (10 centimetres) thick and was fashioned from blue, purple and scarlet material and fine twisted linen (Exodus 26:1).

At the very moment when Jesus gave up His spirit, and physically died, *'the curtain of the temple was torn in two from top to bottom'* (Matthew 27:51). It was torn by God from above, the place where God dwells, to the bottom, the place where man resides. It dramatically symbolized that Jesus' sacrifice and the shedding of His blood was a sufficient atonement for sin, and that the way to God was now open to all people (whether Jew or Gentile) for evermore.

Other sacrifices for sin would no longer be needed, because the one, perfect, totally sufficient sacrifice had already been made. God had done it! The temple symbolised the season of the Old Covenant. A New Covenant was now replacing the Old, through which God said:

'I will put my laws in their minds and write them on their hearts. I will be their God and they will be my people … I will forgive their wickedness and remember their sins no more' (Hebrews 8:10, 12).

Through what happened at the cross we can now enter into the holy presence of Almighty God through Jesus. He is our great High Priest. No earthly priest is necessary. The veil separating God and man has gone forever, through His finished work on the cross. Believers may:

'enter the Most Holy Place by the blood of Jesus, by a new and living way opened for us through the curtain, that is, his body, and since we have a great priest over the house of God, let us draw near to God with a sincere heart in full assurance of faith having our hearts sprinkled to cleanse us from an evil conscience and having our bodies washed with pure water' (Hebrews 10:19-22).

The veil in the temple was a constant reminder that sin separates man from God. Through His death Jesus removed the barrier between God and man, and now those who believe in Him may approach Him with confidence and boldness (Hebrews 4:14-16), knowing that He has become the way of salvation for each one of us.

SURELY …

Jesus died. *'And when the centurion, who stood there in front of Jesus, heard his cry and saw how he died, he said, "Surely this man was the Son of God!"'* (Mark 15:39). Luke tells us that the centurion *'praised God'* (Luke 23:47).

This moment is the centre of everything that matters in this world and the next. The Lamb of God, the only one who could take away the sin of the world, had completed His assignment, and now hung from the cross, dead. As we look to Him, who took upon Himself your sin and mine, let's rejoice and give thanks.

In 1848, Cecil Alexander put all of this into the words of the well-loved hymn:

*There is a green hill far away,
outside a city wall,*

where our dear Lord was crucified
who died to save us all.

We may not know, we cannot tell,
what pains he had to bear,
but we believe it was for us
he hung and suffered there.

He died that we might be forgiven,
he died to make us good,
that we might go at last to heaven,
saved by his precious blood.

There was no other good enough
to pay the price of sin,
he only could unlock the gate
of heaven and let us in.

O dearly, dearly has he loved!
And we must love him too,
and trust in his redeeming blood,
and try his works to do.

SUMMARY

Everything had been completed. The chief priests had had their way and Jesus was nailed to the cross and preparing to die. But what the chief priests had planned for harm, God turned to good, being the very plan that He had laid down for the salvation of all men! Jesus made provision for His mother, the last prophecies were fulfilled, and the sin of the world was laid on the shoulders of the Son of God. As He hung there, Jesus experienced total separation from His Father. Then at the moment of His death, the curtain of the temple was torn from top to bottom signifying that a new way had been opened up for all men to come to God through His Son. And even the Roman centurion recognised who Jesus really was!

PRAYER

I stand amazed dear Lord at what You did for me. Thank You for willingly taking upon Yourself the burden of my sinfulness. Help me, Lord, as I choose to follow You, never to shrink from the way of the cross. I'm so grateful that there's now a way open for me to the Father – for this earthly existence and all of eternity beyond. In Jesus' name, Amen.

1 Wesley, John, Explanatory Notes on the New Testament (First published 1755; available to view on-line at: https://www.biblestudytools.com/commentaries/wesleys-explanatory-notes/matthew/matthew-27.html) Public domain

2 Henry, Matthew, Commentary on the Whole Bible, Complete and Unabridged (Hendrickson Publishers, 2008), originally published 1706

3 ibid

Stage 3, Chapter 5

THE BURIAL OF JESUS

As we have seen, a huge number of prophecies were fulfilled during the latter days of Jesus' life. Some people discount their significance saying that Jesus knew what they said and so only did what was necessary to fulfil them so they could be proved accurate. However, this argument holds little weight when you consider the very detailed way in which the prophecies continued to be fulfilled after Jesus died - when He was no longer there to influence events.

The chief priests didn't want the bodies left on the crosses during the Sabbath. So, to ensure that the victims died quickly they went to Pilate and asked that the three who had been crucified should have their legs broken so the bodies could be taken down (John 19:31).

As we have already seen, once the legs of a prisoner had been broken, the weight of the body could not be sustained against the nails holding the feet to the cross. The body would instantly slump downwards, making it impossible to breathe. Death through asphyxiation would come quickly.

Pilate didn't want any further problems with the Jews. Since Jesus was going to die anyway, he may even have thought it was kinder to break the legs to shorten the time of suffering. Whatever the reason, He gave the instruction, and a message was sent to the soldiers attending the crucifixion to hasten the operation by breaking the legs of the victims. Contemporary sources confirm that an iron bar for this purpose was part of the standard crucifixion equipment.

MORE PROPHECIES FULFILLED

So, the soldiers broke the legs of the two criminals who had been crucified on either side of Jesus, but:

> *'when they came to Jesus and found that he was already dead, they did not break his legs. Instead, one of the soldiers pierced Jesus' side with a spear, bringing a sudden flow of blood and water'* (John 19:33-34).

Many commentators and some medical authorities say that this is evidence that Jesus had died, not from the effects of the crucifixion, but from a broken heart. His heart of love could no longer withstand the weight of pain caused by carrying the sin of mankind.

That is surmise – but the flow of both blood and a clear fluid, probably from the area of the lungs, is abundant evidence that Jesus was indeed dead. In fact, it may have been a standard procedure of the Roman soldiers to pierce the side with a spear and look for evidence of the two liquids coming from the body. This would ensure the victim was really dead before the body was lifted down from the cross.

The Roman soldiers were not experts in either Jewish law or the interpretation of scriptural prophecy. They were just doing their job! But they were being watched by a group of grief-stricken family, friends and disciples and, in the rather quaint way in which John includes himself in his own account, he says:

> *'The man who saw it'* (meaning himself) *'has given testimony, and his testimony is true. He knows that he tells the truth, and he testifies so that you also may believe.'* He then tells us that *'these things happened so that the scripture would be fulfilled "Not one of his bones will be broken" and, as another scripture says, "They will look on the one whom they have pierced"'* (John 19:35-37).

We don't know whether John was aware of these Scriptures before Jesus died, or whether he researched them himself at a later date. It's most likely that he heard it from the disciples who walked to Emmaus after the resurrection and were joined by the risen Lord Jesus on the way. For on that walk, Jesus began with *'Moses and all the Prophets, and explained to them what was said in all the Scriptures concerning himself'* (Luke 24:27).

However it was that John had learned these truths, he now knew that when David had written, *'he protects all his bones, not one of them will be broken'* (Psalm 34:20) he was prophesying about what would happen to the Messiah when He died. And similarly, when Zechariah wrote *'they will look on me, the one they have pierced'* (Zechariah 12:10) he was adding more prophetic detail to the wealth of understanding about the Messiah that is scattered throughout the Old Testament Scriptures.

THE SECRET DISCIPLES

Joseph of Arimathea and Nicodemus were both men of influence and significance, and neither wanted the body of Jesus to be taken down and disposed of as a criminal by the Romans. They were both members of the Jewish ruling Council (the Sanhedrin)- and secret disciples of Jesus - 'secret' because they *'feared the Jews'* (John 19:38). Nicodemus was *'the man who earlier had visited Jesus at night'* (John 3:2) and Joseph is described as *'a good and upright man, who had not consented to [the Jewish ruling Council's] decision and action'* (Luke 23:50-51).

Since Pilate was unaware of Joseph's allegiance to Jesus (known disciples would have had no influence with him), he would have seen his request for Jesus' body as coming from *'a prominent member of the Council'* (Mark 15:43) who wished to bury Jesus properly and with dignity. Having checked with the centurion that Jesus had already died, Pilate then allowed Joseph to take the body (Mark 15:45).

This secret disciple of Jesus went with Nicodemus (John 19:39) and, having:

'bought some linen cloth, took down the body, wrapped it in the linen, and placed it in a tomb cut out of the rock. Then he rolled a stone against the entrance of the tomb. Mary Magdalene and Mary the mother of Jesus saw where he was laid' (Mark 15:46-47).

John tells us that Nicodemus brought with him *'a mixture of myrrh and aloes, about seventy-five pounds. Taking Jesus' body, the two of them wrapped it, with the spices, in strips of linen. This was in accordance with Jewish customs'* (John 19:39-40). The man to whom Jesus had told the astonishing truth of why He had come to earth (John 3:16), was now being used by God to bring fulfilment to this truth!

THE GARDEN TOMB

There is a place in Jerusalem which, even today, has the shape of a skull naturally hewn out of the rock face. It is a clear image identifying what is most credibly the place where Jesus was crucified. John says that Jesus, *'carrying his own cross, went out to the place of the Skull (which in Aramaic is called Golgotha)'* (John 19:17).

John tells us that the tomb in which Jesus was buried was *'at the place where Jesus was crucified'*. Here, *'there was a garden, and in the garden a new tomb, in which no-one had ever been laid'* (John 19:41). Matthew tells us that it was Joseph's *'own new tomb that he had cut out of the rock'* (Matthew 27:60).

The Sabbath began at dusk and there was no time to carry the body of Jesus to a tomb further afield, so Joseph used the new tomb that, no doubt, he had prepared for himself. So:

'because it was the Jewish day of Preparation and since the tomb was nearby, they laid Jesus there' (John 19:42). Then *'he rolled a stone against the entrance of the tomb'* (Mark 15:46).

And so it was that, at the end of Jesus' life, provision was made for His burial by two Jewish members of the Council who had believed in Him and were secret disciples. Today the Garden Tomb is a place of pilgrimage for believers. No-one knows for certain that this is the place where Jesus was laid, but having been there, all I can say is that it is a place where it's easy to sense the presence of God. But does it matter whether or not this was the exact place – not really! What really does matter is that Jesus is no longer there! No-one is ever going to find the bones of Jesus in some forgotten tomb.

THE FINAL ACT

The Jewish authorities had one more request to make of Pilate. On the next day they came to Pilate and said:

'Sir, we remember that while he was alive the deceiver said, "After three days I will rise again." So give the order for the tomb to be made secure until the third day. Otherwise his disciples may come and steal the body and tell the people he has been raised from the dead. This last deception will be worse than the first' (Matthew 27:63-64).

So Pilate released to them a guard of soldiers and told them to *'"make the tomb as secure as you know how. So they went and made the tomb secure by putting a seal on the stone and posting the guard"'* (Matthew 27:65-66).

I can imagine the Jewish authorities thinking they could now get on with life once again, knowing they had once and for all dealt with every eventuality associated with this man they believed to be a deceiver. Of course, if Jesus had been a deceiver, a Roman guard would have been sufficient to intimidate and repel any attempt by men to remove his body. But what if He wasn't? Such a possibility doesn't appear to have entered into their thinking!

The soldiers stood guard over a tomb, not realising they were leading up to the moment that would divide history and change the world forever! The next event in the story brought new life to a dark world. It's given you and me everlasting life and eternal hope.

SUMMARY

Even after Jesus had died, detailed prophecies were being fulfilled. David's words about His bones not being broken, and Zechariah's prophecy about Him being pierced, were precisely fulfilled by Roman soldiers who knew nothing of the Scriptures. After Jesus had died Joseph of Arimathea asked permission from Pilate to take His body down and bury it. And finally the Jewish authorities asked for a seal and a guard on the tomb to stop the disciples stealing the body and saying Jesus had been raised from the dead.

PERSONAL NOTES

PRAYER

Thank You, Lord, for the amazing ways in which the prophetic words of the Old Testament were fulfilled so precisely in the New. Thank You for teaching us that Your word is true and can be trusted. Thank You, Lord, for the secret disciples who made provision for Jesus at the end. Help me, Lord, to read Your word with an open heart, always listening to Your voice through what it says, and to be always thinking of what I can do to bless and serve You in every circumstance of life. I don't want to miss any opportunity of being of service to You. In Jesus' name, Amen.

STAGE 4

Resurrection Life!

"Christianity would be nonsense were it not for the resurrection. It is still nonsense to those who choose not to believe!"

THE RESURRECTION!

We concluded the last stage of our journey with Jesus crucified, dead and buried. His life had been brought to a sudden end at the hands of cruel men. His prophesies to His own disciples on the way up to Jerusalem had occurred:

> *'From that time on Jesus began to explain to his disciples that he must go to Jerusalem and suffer many things at the hands of the elders, chief priests and teachers of the law, and that he must be killed and on the third day raised to life'* (Matthew 16:21).

When Peter refused to believe what Jesus was saying and said, *'"Never, Lord, this shall never happen to you"'*, Jesus had rebuked him, saying *'"Get behind me Satan. You are a stumbling block to me; you do not have in mind the things of God, but the things of men"'* (Matthew 16:22-23). As far as Jesus was concerned, what Peter had said was so opposed to the plans and purposes of God that He had no alternative but to tell him that his words were from the devil himself. Satan never ceased to use every possible

PERSONAL NOTES

opportunity to try and divert Jesus from fulfilling His destiny. And what he tried to do for Jesus he will try and do for us.

Even though Jesus had carefully warned the disciples, they hadn't really understood or believed what He was saying. And this was still the case after He had gone up to Jerusalem and been killed! What Jesus had prophesied had actually happened.

After His death, if the disciples had really understood and believed they wouldn't have been hiding in Jerusalem after Jesus' burial. Instead they would have been watching at the tomb, waiting for the moment when Jesus rose again from the dead, as He had said He would! But they weren't anywhere to be seen! They certainly weren't expecting the resurrection to happen. Perhaps, in a way, they were less believing than the chief priests. At least the chief priests were afraid that it *might* happen!

Different groups of people had witnessed the death of Jesus:

1. **A Triumphant Group of Pharisees**

   They thought they had finally disposed of the one they called the 'deceiver', but who was more powerful and popular than they were. I can imagine them having something of a back-slapping celebration at how they had manipulated Pilate into agreeing to the crucifixion, and then to placing a Roman guard at the tomb to stop the disciples of Jesus from stealing His body.

2. **The Onlookers at the Cross**

   They had mocked Jesus when He was dying, probably including many of the people who had shouted for Barabbas to be released instead of Jesus.

3. **The Two Criminals Who Were Crucified Alongside Jesus**

   One of whom believed in Him and one didn't.

4. **The Roman Soldiers**

   They were the people who had actually crucified Jesus. They were just doing their job, but their close observation of Jesus in His dying hours, the three hours of darkness over the land and their experience of an earthquake at the precise moment He died, had led one of them at least to believe that Jesus *'was the Son of God'* (Matthew 27:54).

5. The Women

These included Jesus' own mother and Mary Magdalene, who had remained close to Him throughout His ordeal, and who had been His nearest supporters throughout the three years of His ministry.

6. Jesus' Disciples

At this particular moment they were some of the most frightened and confused people on the planet. It's hard to believe that they were the same people who had been chosen by Jesus to take the message of the Kingdom across the world. When He died, they were devastated by the apparent failure of their mission – they had given their all to follow Him and had been expecting so much. It appears that everything Jesus had said about what would happen after the crucifixion had evaporated from their thinking: *'they still did not understand from Scripture that Jesus had to rise from the dead'* (John 20:9).

None of these groups of people were ready for what happened next. Jesus had died, but death could not hold Him!

In the time between His death and resurrection morning, Peter tells us that Jesus:

'was made alive by the Spirit, ...[and] ... he went and preached to the spirits in prison who disobeyed long ago when God waited patiently in the days of Noah while the ark was being built' (1 Peter 3:18-20).

This is the only description in the Word of God that we are given about what happened, and it is beyond our full understanding. The ancient creeds of the church (which contain the statements of foundational Christian belief) tell us that Jesus *'descended into hell'*. We cannot, however, know exactly know where it was that Jesus was preaching to those *'spirits in prison'* in the hours following His death.

But what we do know is that the place of darkness with the departed sinners was no place for Jesus to stay, He was destined for glory! One day we will know and fully understand all these things. But at the moment, it's very much as Paul described it in 1 Corinthians 13:12 – we can only see a poor reflection of the truth, looking, as it were, through darkened glass.

RESURRECTION MORNING

The only way to keep a cork beneath the surface of water is to hold it there with your hand. And because Jesus was without sin, the only way that Jesus could be held beneath the 'waters of death' was if the Father's hand held Him there. But when you move your hand away from a cork, the water can no longer stop it from rising to the surface. To me this is a picture of what happened when Jesus had completed His work of overcoming sin and death. Father God removed His hand and the whole universe was shaken as Jesus, the Son of God, was raised from the dead – the 'waters of death' could not hold Him.

No words would ever be sufficient to describe the moment when the Lamb of God, returned to earth as the Lion of Judah, having conquered death and overcome every power of darkness. Out of the darkness, the Light of the World burst into time once more, and the only people on earth to witness that extraordinary resurrection moment were the Roman soldiers whom Pilate had placed as a guard!

The spirit of Jesus returned to His body and what was a body of flesh when Jesus died was instantly transformed into a spiritual body. No doubt every single eye in the spiritual realms was focussed on the tomb of Jesus as they anticipated what was happening. The powers of darkness would be looking on in sheer terror because, if Jesus was raised from the dead, then Satan and hell itself would tremble with fear.

But the angelic realms and all the hosts of heaven would have been watching with the sheer thrill and excitement of knowing that the Prince of Heaven had fulfilled His mission and would soon be returning to heaven's glory. Heaven must have been filled with great thanksgiving and celebration as the hosts of heaven worshipped the Father and looked forward to the Lamb being back on His throne.

That transforming moment when the energy of God filled the physical body of Jesus with the life of the Spirit was accompanied by the physical sign of a violent earthquake as:

'an angel of the Lord came down from heaven and, going to the tomb, rolled back the stone and sat on it. His appearance was like lightning and his clothes were white as snow.' (Matthew 28:2-3).

The Roman guards had seen nothing like it before. They were literally petrified by the experience. *'They shook and became like dead men'* (Matthew 28:4) as awesome shock and paralysing fear swept through their bodies. This was the moment when a door of hope was opened for repentant sinners! Prior to this every sin of mankind had further alienated a holy God from His increasingly sinful people. But when Jesus became the first-fruit of the resurrection, as He was raised from the dead, a way back to God from the dark paths of sin was established. This way has since been trodden by pilgrims of every generation as they have made their way, via the foot of the cross, to the very gates of heaven.

At that moment a living hope burst into the world. The earthquake that accompanied Jesus' resurrection was a parable of the spiritual earthquake that takes place every time a person is born again of the Spirit of God. Resurrection power is made manifest when the light of Christ first shines in the heart of a redeemed person. A spiritual earthquake marks the moment whenever one of earth's sinners is born again and becomes a saint of God. The enemy has to take notice of that fact. The spiritual transformation that occurs at conversion is, in itself, a prophetic picture of the physical transformation that will one day take place, when the Lord Jesus comes again to take His own to Himself.

Jesus was the first-fruit, and the first-fruit always anticipates the harvest that's to come. As God sees Jesus, the first-fruit of resurrection power, alive again, He knows for certain that He can anticipate a glorious harvest. It's a harvest of the souls of men and women at the close of time and they will populate heaven with the saints of God.

THE TWO MARYS AT DAWN

After the Sabbath was over, on the first day of the week, when the very first streaks of light were beginning to light up the sky of a new day, Mary Magdalene and Mary the mother of James made their way *'to look at the tomb'* (Matthew 28:1). They had a specific objective and it wasn't to see if Jesus was still there! They really loved Jesus and wanted to do everything they possibly could for the One who had meant so much to them, even though He was now no longer with them. Because of the hot climate they needed to prepare the body at the earliest possible moment.

They were prevented by the Jewish law from going to the tomb on the Sabbath, and so they waited until the earliest possible moment to go with the traditional spices they had prepared to anoint the body of Jesus. These spices were for the dead – not the living. The women did of course have another problem to resolve. The stone covering the entrance to the tomb was huge, and neither of them would be able to move it. So, *'on their way to the tomb, they asked each other, "Who will roll the stone away from the entrance of the tomb?"'* (Mark 16:3). Perhaps they were thinking Joseph had a gardener who might be able to help?

Because it had been done on the morning of the Sabbath they were probably unaware that Pilate had placed a guard on the tomb and that it had been sealed at the request of the chief priests. There was no way that the Roman guards would have let them get anywhere near the tomb on the third day. Their specific instructions had been to prevent any of Jesus' disciples entering the tomb, to stop them stealing the body – especially on the day when Jesus had said He would rise from the dead!

No-one could possibly have got to the tomb earlier than these women, so they would have been tremendously surprised, probably shocked, when *'they saw that the stone, which was very large, had been rolled away'* (Mark 16:4). Who could possibly have done that so early on the first day of the week?

The guards, who should have been there, were nowhere to be seen. They had fled in sheer terror at what had happened. After all, **they had been at the centre of an earthquake that had shaken the gates of hell and opened the gates of heaven!** By the time the women arrived the soldiers were on their way into the city to report *'to the chief priests everything that had happened'* (Matthew 28:11).

MORE DECEPTION!

The Jewish authorities now had an even bigger problem. The 'deceiver' had 'deceived' them! The guards were terrified, the body had gone and the chief priests were desperate! So they:

'met with the elders and devised a plan. They gave the soldiers a large sum of money, telling them, "You are to say, 'his disciples came during the night and stole him away while we were asleep.' If this report gets to the governor, we will satisfy him and keep you out of trouble." So the soldiers took the money and did as they were instructed.' (Matthew 28:12-15).

Before the resurrection the chief priests had the guard mounted to prevent the disciples from coming to steal the body of Jesus. Now, they were paying these very guards to tell people that's exactly what the disciples had done! Oh, what a mess people get into once they start to resist and distort the truth. One lie follows another as people desperately try to cover up the reality. The reality was that what the chief priests feared, had in fact happened, **JESUS WAS RISEN FROM THE DEAD** – and they could do absolutely nothing about it!

HE HAS RISEN!

Meanwhile the two Marys approached the tomb and the angel, who was sitting on the stone, spoke to them saying:

> '**"Do not be afraid, for I know you are looking for Jesus, who was crucified. He is not here; he has risen, just as he said."**' (Matthew 28:5-6) (emphasis added).

What joy this news has been for believers throughout Christian history. The words of the angel, '"*just as he said*"', give us such confidence **in everything** Jesus said. For, if what Jesus said about being raised from the dead came true, we can depend on absolutely everything else that He said. He and His Word are totally trustworthy.

Jesus' teaching, His prophecies, His forgiveness, His redemption, His call on our lives, the purpose and destiny He gives us, His promises of resurrection life and eternity with Him in heaven – everything that comes from Him, without exception, is true. This is fantastic news – but it's also very challenging news for all who would want to follow Him. The joyful news of the resurrection is God's seal on the truth of who Jesus was and is, but also of everything He said and did.

This truth is at the heart of my personal passion for *Journey to Freedom*.

I daily long that, as you absorb each unit of teaching, the eternal, unchanging and unchangeable truth about God, His Son, His Spirit and His Word will fill you to overflowing, and you will know the reality of His love, presence and power in every step of life's journey, until that glorious moment when you become part of the resurrection harvest at the end of time!

SUMMARY

The chief priests mounted a guard of Roman soldiers, but nothing in the whole universe could have prevented what God had planned for resurrection morning! The soldiers fled in fear, the angel rolled the stone away and then told the two Marys that glorious news, '"He is not here. He has risen, just as he said"' (Matthew 28:6). The chief priests had to devise further lies to cover up what had really happened, but the grave was empty, Jesus was alive and all believers can rejoice that the gates of heaven were opened for all eternity.

PRAYER

I am utterly amazed, Lord, at Your plan of salvation - the plan You worked out before time began for rescuing a people that would rebel against Your love. I am so, so grateful that the bones of Jesus will never be found. He has risen from the dead, and I can trust Him totally with everything I am, every day of my life. Oh, what joy there is to look forward to, when the first-fruit of the resurrection is followed by the harvest! Thank You, thank You, Lord. In Jesus' name, Amen.

Stage 4, Chapter 2

THE EMPTY TOMB AND JESUS APPEARS TO MARY

'"He is not here. He has risen, just as He said"'. **These words from the angel, to the women who came to the tomb with their spices, are the resounding echo that has gone down two millennia of time, declaring into the earthly and heavenly realms that God has visited this planet to redeem His children out of the hands of the enemy.**

There was a question the angel asked the women, which is still of enormous significance today, especially to everyone who's looking for spiritual answers to life in false religions. *'"**Why do you look for the living among the dead?**"'* (Luke 24:5) (emphasis added). A grave is a place for the dead, but Jesus wasn't in the grave and He can no longer be found in such a place! The founders of all the other world religions and philosophies, such as Confucius, Buddha, Mohammed, and Lenin are all safely ensconced in their graves. Jesus' tomb is empty! He is risen.

I well remember, as a teenager, rising at 3.00 am on Easter Sunday morning and travelling to the top of the largest hill in the vicinity that faced towards the east. There we sat in the dark singing choruses and Easter hymns until that critical moment when, after watching the advance of dawn across the landscape, the first hint of the shape of the sun appeared above the distant horizon. As one voice the hundred or so teenagers who were gathered there shouted out at the very top of their voices **"He is Risen"**. We were telling the world the good news. I doubt if anyone in their beds in the valley below could hear our voices. But it was a very evocative moment in my own Christian experience and has always remained in my memory.

THE EMPTY TOMB

Memorable though that teenage experience was, I would love to have been there two thousand years ago to see what happened on that first Easter morning! And I would love to know what the women were thinking as they talked directly to God's angel, when he gave them the message they all desperately needed and wanted to hear, but were not yet able to receive and believe.

> '*"Come"*' said the angel, '*"and see the place where he lay. Then go quickly and tell the disciples: He has risen from the dead and is going ahead of you into Galilee. There you will see him"*' (Matthew 28:7).

Whilst we may never know what the women were thinking, we do know exactly how they were feeling for, says Mark:

> '*trembling and bewildered, the women went out and fled from the tomb. They said nothing to anyone, because they were afraid*' (Mark 16:8)

It's interesting to note that Mark added an extra bit of information to his account of what happened on resurrection morning. The angel hadn't just said '*"go and tell the disciples"*', he'd said, '*"go, tell his disciples and Peter"*' (Mark 16:7). There are at least three reasons why the Holy Spirit prompted the angel to make special reference to Peter:

- It was Peter who had rebuked Jesus for saying these things would never happen to Him. Now, not only had Jesus died, but the final piece of the prophecy had been fulfilled – Jesus was alive again.

- It was Peter who had betrayed Jesus three times during Jesus' trial, and it was going to be necessary for Peter to be restored in his relationship with Him. Jesus needed Peter to know that He was still loved and very much wanted, despite his failure.

- Peter was going to be the one who would lead the emerging church, and his witness to all that was happening was going to be vital as the foundations of the church were going to be laid.

APPARENT CONFUSION!

When you read the different Gospel accounts of the resurrection, you may not find it easy to compare one Gospel with another and fit everything into your thinking and understanding! I recently watched a fascinating documentary television programme originated by the Greater Manchester Police. It was compiled out of research they were doing on how to interpret the apparently confusing witness reports from different people who were present at the same traumatic event.

Without telling any of the people what they were going to do, the police staged a dispute between two people coming into a crowded pub which led to a brawl, a fight and an apparent murder before their very eyes.

They then interviewed everyone present (the eye-witnesses of the event) and discovered that different people, despite sitting next to each other and watching the same incident happening, reported it in a completely different way. Some incidents were remembered clearly by some people, but not even noticed by others. Everyone knew what had happened but remembered it in very different ways. It was a fascinating insight into how the witness reports of traumatised people can all be true eye-witness accounts of the same event but can still have apparent discrepancies between them.

And so, let's go back to the accounts of the resurrection. The women and the disciples had been terribly traumatised by the events that surrounded the crucifixion. Then, on top of this, they went through a series of further shocking experiences. They got to the tomb and found the stone rolled away; a brilliantly radiant angel of the Lord talked to them as if he was a human being; they saw the empty tomb and the folded grave clothes; and Mary Magdalene had a sudden living encounter with Jesus. The last time she'd seen Him He was being carried as a dead body into the tomb! These were all seriously life-impacting and sudden experiences.

So, it's not surprising when you read the reports in the four different Gospels of what happened on resurrection morning, that there's an air of apparent confusion between the different accounts. However, at the same time there is an absolute certainty that everything being said is the whole truth and nothing but the truth – just as it was on the television programme.

Everyone was telling the truth, but they remembered different things and had different perspectives. For example, Mark recorded the fact that the angel had particularly added '"*and tell Peter*"' to his message to the women. Matthew hadn't included it at all in his equally truthful story Because all the accounts are different in some of the details it adds an even greater credibility to the authority of Scripture. If the disciples had made up their stories to try and deceive people in any way, they would have gone to great lengths to make those stories the same, in every detail.

NEWS SPREADS!

So, after their encounter with the angel, the women went and did exactly as the angel had told them and reported to the disciples what they had seen. They were '*afraid, yet filled with joy*' (Matthew 28:8), but they now had a further problem – the disciples didn't believe them! '*When they came back from the tomb, they told all these things to the Eleven, and to all the others… but they did not believe the women because their words seemed to them like nonsense*' (Luke 24:9-11).

Mary Magdalene had also been to the tomb at first light and it appears that she hadn't seen the angel at that time. She tried to put a more rational interpretation on events, saying, '*They have taken the Lord out of the tomb, and we don't know where they have put him*' (John 20:2).

Confusion reigned in their hearts! They desperately wanted Jesus to be alive, but their rational minds couldn't handle the facts. In their minds they were still seeing the dead body of Jesus being lifted into the tomb – yet their ears were hearing things that didn't make sense.

Then there was a report that some of the women had actually seen Jesus when they were rushing back to Jerusalem from the empty tomb.

Could their report possibly be true? They said that Jesus had suddenly met them and said, *"Greetings"*, and they had fallen at His feet and worshipped Him. Jesus had also said, *"Do not be afraid. Go and tell my brothers to go to Galilee; there they will see me"'* (Matthew 28:10)?

In the midst of so much confusion there was only one thing to do – to go and look for yourself,

'So Peter and the other disciple started for the tomb. Both were running, but the other disciple' (probably John talking about himself) *'outran Peter and reached the tomb first. He bent over and looked in at the strips of linen lying there but did not go in. Then Peter, who was behind him, arrived and went into the tomb. He saw the strips of linen lying there, as well as the burial cloth that had been around Jesus' head. The cloth was folded up by itself, separate from the linen. Finally the other disciple, who had reached the tomb first, also went inside. He saw and believed'* (John 20:3-8).

MARY MAGDALENE'S ENCOUNTER WITH THE RISEN JESUS

Having rushed to Jerusalem to tell the disciples what had happened, Mary must have turned back and followed Peter and John. After the two disciples had seen the empty tomb and returned to Jerusalem, Mary stayed there by herself weeping, trying to cope with her confusion and grief. Jesus had died and now His body had gone. Jesus had been everything to her.

Men had used and abused Mary throughout her life. Demons had played havoc with her whole being, but Jesus had not only loved her with the purest, non-sexual, love you could ever imagine, but He had delivered her from all her demons, healed her from her past and set her free to be the woman God had created her to be. When someone has been rescued by Jesus in this way, their love and loyalty to Him knows no bounds. I know, having seen on many occasions, the joy that Jesus' healing brings.

The tears were beginning to flow freely down Mary's face and she *'stood outside the tomb crying'* (John 20:11). As she wept, she plucked up the courage to bend over and look into the tomb again for herself:

'and saw two angels in white, seated where Jesus' body had been, one at the head and the other at the foot. They asked her, "Woman, why are you crying?" "They have taken my Lord away," she said, "and I don't know where they have put him"' (John 20:12-13).

Then Mary turned round, perhaps disturbed by a noise behind her, or just the sudden awareness that someone else was present. A man was standing there who asked her the same question as the angels: *'"Woman, why are you crying?"'* Then He asked, *'"Who is it you are looking for?"'* (John 20:15).

At this point Jesus was hiding His identity from her, and Mary, thinking He was the gardener, asked Him if He knew where Jesus had been put. Jesus couldn't stand the suspense of keeping her in ignorance any longer and looking at her, He simply said her name, in the voice that she knew so well, *'"Mary"'* (John 20:16).

That was it. Jesus speaking her name was sufficient. All her doubts were instantly swept away. The pain of grief was healed as the present reality overwhelmed her spirit, and from the depths of her heart she responded in the way she had always spoken to Him, *'"Rabboni"'* (John 20:16), which is Aramaic for 'teacher'.

Jesus responded by saying:

'"Do not hold on to me, for I have not yet returned to the Father. Go instead to my brothers and tell them, I am returning to my Father and your Father, to my God and your God"' (John 20:17).

When Mary returned to where the disciples were, it was a different Mary who burst through the door, not the one who had chased after Peter and John as they ran to the tomb earlier in the day. Her life had been turned upside down once more. She was totally transformed by her personal encounter with the risen Lord Jesus. It's easy to imagine the words tumbling out of her mouth *'"I have seen the Lord!"'* (John 20:18).

"I HAVE SEEN THE LORD"

I've often thought about two of the most remarkable exchanges that took place with Jesus either side of His death. The first one, just before He died, was with the criminal to whom Jesus had said, *"'Today you will be with me in paradise'"* (Luke 23:43). The second was just after He had risen from the dead and was with Mary Magdalene outside the tomb.

I've imagined Jesus arriving in paradise, accompanied by this unknown criminal, seeing him given a triumphant welcome as the first person to be saved from eternal death, following the death of the Saviour! And then, after the resurrection, we see that the first person to whom Jesus revealed Himself was a formerly demonised woman who had been redeemed! What an amazing picture of the depth of love that God has for fallen mankind!

I just love the reality of these two incidents, which together make an incredible declaration into a fallen world that there is no-one beyond redemption, or beyond the capacity to be healed and delivered by the Saviour.

When Jesus spoke Mary's name, she instantly recognised who He was. I'd like to encourage you to spend some time 'by the empty tomb' thinking about the death and resurrection of Jesus. Don't be ashamed to join Mary Magdalene in her tears and rejoice that the Saviour knows your name also. Then look to Him and experience His love. As you 'sit at the feet of Jesus', may your experience echo that of Mary Magdalene as you say in your heart, "I've seen the Lord!"'

SUMMARY

When the women went to the tomb on the first day of the week, they were shocked to find the stone had been rolled away and an angel telling them what to do. They ran back to the disciples, who couldn't believe what they were saying about Jesus having been raised from the dead. So Peter and John went to see for themselves. Then Mary Magdalene had her own remarkable encounter with the risen Jesus, when He spoke her name, "Mary" and she responded, "Rabboni". Her life was changed again at that moment and she ran back to the disciples again to say, "I have seen the Lord!"

PRAYER

Thank You, Lord, for showing me again how much You love those who've been hurt and broken by the experiences of life. Thank You, for revealing Yourself to Mary Magdalene and showing her Your love. Thank You for the way it speaks to me of how You love and accept all those, including me, who come to You in repentance and receive the gift of eternal life. I'm amazed at how much You love me. In Jesus' name, Amen.

THE WALK TO EMMAUS

It's hard for those who know the Bible not to think how stupid those first disciples were! Jesus had told them, probably on many occasions, that He was going up to Jerusalem and that He was going to die and then He would be raised from the dead. So why couldn't they just believe the reports that the women had brought to them and rejoice in the fulfilment of what Jesus said would happen?

It all seems so obvious! But what may seem obvious to us wasn't at all obvious to those first disciples. Jesus was asking them to believe something right outside their experience, and not only their experience but the collective experience of the whole human race. People don't normally have three days in their grave and then get up fully restored to life! Even though Jesus had told them in advance, the idea of being raised from the dead was so foreign to their understanding that it was easier to dismiss the possibility from their thinking than believe in faith for the impossible.

Peter struggled with believing the obvious. Even after seeing the empty tomb and the folded grave clothes *'he went away, wondering to himself what had happened'* (Luke 24:12). The disciples didn't automatically conclude that Jesus must have been raised from the dead!

The women had reported that an angel told them Jesus would meet with the disciples in Galilee. But this didn't mean that Jesus wouldn't appear to them before that, as the body of believers slowly came into a knowledge of the truth. As you read the different Gospels you can almost sense Jesus watching and listening to what they were saying and doing, and then planning how best to reveal Himself to them. It was important that He should have the opportunity to show them how Scripture's prophecies had been fulfilled.

THE WALK TO EMMAUS

On the very day that Jesus had been raised from the dead, two of His followers (not members of the Eleven) were walking out of Jerusalem to the village of Emmaus, about seven miles away. As they walked along the road *'they were talking with each other about everything that had happened'* (Luke 24:14).

There are many times when I've taken a walk with a friend, and in my younger days some of those were very long walks. As you walk, it's so easy to get engrossed in an interesting conversation – so much so that the miles can go by and you forget how far it is that you have travelled. Occasionally you meet others who are walking in the same direction and for periods of time they join you in the walk and can even share in the conversation.

When something big has happened, there's always a lot to talk about. The very process of talking things through helps people come to terms with reality. And these two friends needed to talk about a lot of things which didn't make much sense to them at that moment. They were hurting, confused and struggling with how they could ever get their lives back together after losing their Master to the chief priests of Israel and the Roman soldiers with their cruel nails.

They'd lived through the day of Jesus' trial. They'd seen the terrible event on Calvary's hill when Jesus was crucified. All their hopes and dreams were smashed as the Roman soldiers did their job. And now they couldn't even go and gain some comfort at the tomb, because His body had disappeared. They were trying to make sense of it all when they were joined along the road by a fellow traveller, who heard them talking and asked, '*"What are you discussing as you walk along?"'* (Luke 24:17). The fellow traveller was of course, Jesus, *'but they were kept from recognising him'* (Luke 24:16).

Obviously shocked by the ignorance of their new friend, they stopped for a moment, *'their faces downcast'* and one of them, Cleopas, asked Him, '*"Are you only a visitor to Jerusalem and do not know the things that have happened there in these days?"'* (Luke 24:18-19).

By His response (*"What things?"),* Jesus was clearly inviting them to tell Him everything that had happened, in their own words. So they recounted how Jesus of Nazareth was a powerful prophet *'in word and deed before God and all the* people' (Luke 24:19), and how the chief priests and Jewish authorities *'had handed him over to be sentenced to death, and they crucified him'* (Luke 24:20).

They then talked about all the hopes they'd placed in this man, Jesus, and of how they thought He was the one who would *'redeem Israel'* (Luke 24:21). At that time it was generally thought this meant to free the people from the control of Rome and restore the nation. Their hopes had been smashed at the crucifixion and now, three days later, some of the women had come back from the tomb with reports that His body had disappeared and that they'd even *'seen a vision of angels, who said he was alive'* (Luke 24:23).

This last statement helps us to understand why the disciples hadn't immediately believed the fact that Jesus had been raised from the dead when the women came back with their report. They thought the women had seen a vision rather than having had an actual conversation with an angel. They may even have thought that all the stress and trauma of the past few days had been too much for them and that they were 'seeing things'. This can happen with emotionally stressed people, but there's a huge difference between seeing a vision of an angel and actually seeing and talking with one. They'd put the women's experience down to a vision – not hard reality.

But then, the travellers said, '*"some of our companions went to the tomb and found it just as the women had said, but him they did not see"'* (Luke 24:24). Throughout this conversation I think Jesus must have been desperate to interject and reveal to them who He was, but He allowed them to express the depth of their frustration and pain before He responded.

THE GREATEST BIBLE STUDY EVER!

But when He did respond, He led them through what must have been the greatest Bible Study ever – a one-to-one exposition of all the prophetic words there are in the Old Testament Scriptures telling about Himself. That journey must have been the most enthralling journey ever taken, as Jesus took them by the hand and travelled with them through the history of Israel, bringing them right up to date.

But first He berated them kindly for their ignorance and unbelief, saying, *'"How foolish you are, and slow of heart to believe all that the prophets have spoken"'* (Luke 24:25). And then Jesus did something a Rabbi would often do when teaching in the Synagogue – ask the people a question to provoke their thinking before giving them his understanding of the correct answer. So Jesus asked them *'"Did not the Christ have to suffer these things and then enter his glory?"'* (Luke 24:26). And then, *'beginning with Moses and all the prophets, he explained to them what was said in all the Scriptures about himself'* (Luke 24:27). This man who had joined them for the journey certainly knew what was in the Scriptures, but for the time being His identity remained a mystery.

Can you imagine what it must have been like for these two as Jesus began giving them the answer to His own question? Firstly He took them through the five books of Moses. He must have shared with them about the sacrifice that Abraham was willing to make when he put his son, Isaac, on the altar. God intervened to save Isaac by providing a ram that was caught in a nearby thicket. What an incredible experience it must have been to hear Jesus explain how God had now intervened in history. The **Lamb of God** had now been provided as a sacrifice to save mankind from eternal death, not just to save one man, but to save all who would believe.

Then Jesus must have explained to them how the shed blood of the Passover lamb protected God's people from the angel of death, and how the Messiah had now become the **Passover Lamb.** The covering of His shed blood was now the protection of God's people for all eternity.

I would dearly love to have heard Jesus taking them through all the prophetic references to His coming. I'd especially love to have heard Him explain how Isaiah the prophet had described, in advance, the death of the coming Messiah and what His sacrifice would achieve for mankind (Isaiah 53). And, of course, there was so much more as *'he explained to them what was said in all the Scriptures concerning himself'* (Luke 24:27).

ON REACHING EMMAUS

When they got to their destination:

'Jesus acted as if he were going farther. But they urged him strongly, "Stay with us, for it is nearly evening, the day is almost over." So He went in to stay with them' (Luke 24:28-29).

The stranger who'd joined them for the journey and taught them so much from the Scriptures went into their home and joined them for a meal.

And, as they sat down together for a meal, the stranger *'took bread, gave thanks, broke it and began to give it to them'* (Luke 24:30). It was in this familiar act that they instantly recognised who He was. Jesus must have broken bread with the disciples on many occasions in His own unique way. But at that critical moment, when they were probably absolutely bursting with a hundred questions, *'he disappeared from their sight'* (Luke 24:31)!

It's no wonder that these two disciples described to each other their extraordinary experience by saying, *'"Were not our hearts burning within us while he talked with us on the road and opened the Scriptures to us?"'* (Luke 24:32). The effect of this experience was electrifying. Even though the day was over and it was now dark, and travelling at night was not particularly safe, they didn't want to wait till the next day to share the exciting news. *'They returned at once to Jerusalem'* (Luke 24:33). My guess is that they ran most of the way because they were so keen to share everything with the Eleven and all the other disciples.

IT'S TRUE!

It must have been a very dramatic moment when these two disciples from Emmaus, Cleopas and his companion, burst into the room and *'told what had happened on the way, and how Jesus was recognised by them when he broke the bread'* (Luke 24:35).

The thrill and the excitement in the room must have been electric!. Now they didn't only have a report from the women whose account they had formerly put down to having seen a vision, but they were hearing from two people who had spent several hours with the Lord. They were getting a line-by-line account of everything Jesus had said. These first-hand witness reports changed everything.

TRUTH TOUCHES THE HEART

When Cleopas or his companion said, *"'were not our hearts burning within us'"*, they were describing exactly how the truth about Jesus witnesses the presence of God to our spirits. Not only were their minds and understanding acknowledging the truth of what Jesus said, their spirits were being made alive. When you set fire to something, it burns and you feel the heat. When the presence of God sets fire to our spirit, then we feel the heat!

We must all have times in our lives when our hearts burn within us, when the presence of God is so real that we feel we can reach out and touch the Lord. It's moments like these that provide the marker posts of our Christian pilgrimage. They're the moments we can look back on and take great encouragement from, particularly at times of testing or temptation.

When we're going through such times the enemy may urge us to give up the struggle or give in to the comfort of falling into sin. It's then that we need to remind ourselves of all that God has done in our lives in the past, and keep moving forward in faith and with thanksgiving, knowing that He is with us, whether we particularly sense His presence or not. Be assured, He is with you and knows and understands.

Jesus probably wasn't ever present again with Cleopas and his companion in quite the same way. But the unforgettable inspiration of that time would live with them throughout life's journey. There have been certain times in the history of Ellel Ministries when I've felt that the presence of God was so real it was almost tangible. My heart burned within me and I knew without a shadow of doubt that God was with us. I have always drawn great strength and encouragement from the memory of those times.

Sometimes I get asked how people can have such experiences. I wish I could give you a formula but, if there was one, people would be tempted to use it as an exciting experiment, without having any real desire to walk in the steps of the Lord. My best response to such questions is simply to walk in obedience to everything that God asks you to do and to trust

Him for the outcome. Jesus was obedient to the cross and experienced resurrection. The fellowship of His sufferings always leads to the reality of resurrection life.

I pray that you will have your own experiences of sensing your heart burning within you in the presence of the Lord – you will never be the same again! It may even be that, as you read *Journey to Freedom*, there will be moments when you know God is very close and speaking directly into your spirit. When that happens give Him time and space and listen for His voice. You will not be disappointed.

SUMMARY

All of Jesus' disciples were despondent. Their hopes and dreams had collapsed. Two of them walked out of the city to Emmaus, talking between themselves on the way. Quite suddenly they were joined by another traveller who joined in their conversation and told them everything about the Messiah from the Old Testament Scriptures. The stranger was the risen Lord Jesus and they were treated to the most exciting personal Bible Study there'd ever been. It was only when He broke bread at their home in Emmaus that they recognised Jesus. They immediately ran back to Jerusalem saying "Our hearts burned within us" and told the Eleven, "It's true - He's alive!"

PRAYER

Thank You, Lord, that You have promised to be with us through life and that You revealed Yourself to these two disciples. Help me to recognise Your presence and to listen to Your voice so that I may grow in my understanding of the Scriptures and know how to read and use them as the lifetime manual of Christian living. I want my heart to feel the burning of Your presence. In Jesus' name, Amen.

JESUS APPEARS TO THE DISCIPLES AND THOMAS

It was still the evening of the first day of the week when Cleopas and his companion burst into the room where the disciples were gathered. They had run, or walked, as fast as they possibly could all the way back from Emmaus and were now pouring out their amazing story.

The doors were *'locked for fear of the Jews'* (John 20:19) but there must, nevertheless, have been quite a noise in the room as they all shared in discussing the astounding news that what the women had reported that morning was true! Now that the Lord had appeared to the two on the road to Emmaus, Jesus' own disciples must have been wondering when they too would have the privilege of seeing the risen Lord!

STARTLED SHOCK AND OVERWHELMING JOY

As they were talking, suddenly *'Jesus himself stood among them and said to them, "Peace be with you"'* (Luke 24:36). Despite hearing the voice of Jesus *'they were startled and frightened, thinking they saw a ghost'* (Luke 24:37).

PERSONAL NOTES

But their shock soon changed and they *were overjoyed when they saw the Lord'* (John 20:20).

Their moment had come; Jesus had not forgotten them. Despite locked doors, Jesus appeared in His resurrected body inside the room. Walls and doors were not an obstacle to Him. His presence brought the peace of God into the room and, once they had got over the shock, that peace would have descended on them and brought comfort to their hearts.

It had clearly been a disappointment to Jesus that the disciples hadn't believed the reports of the women and had not been expecting Him to rise again from the dead. Mark goes as far as to say that Jesus *'rebuked them for their lack of faith and their stubborn refusal to believe those who had seen him after he had risen'* (Mark 16:14).

It's easy for us to seem surprised at their lack of faith. We're part of an unbroken succession of believers who have known the facts of the resurrection for close on two thousand years. But I wonder how we would have responded if we'd have been in their shoes? My guess is that, despite the things that Jesus had said would happen, a man being raised from the dead, immediately after being horrendously beaten and then crucified by the Romans, would have stretched the capacity to believe for most of us.

Jesus asked them, *'"Why are you troubled, and why do doubts arise in your minds?"'* (Luke 24:38). But then He did the one thing that would have convinced you and me – it certainly convinced the disciples – He said:

> *'"Look at my hands and my feet. It is I myself! Touch me and see; a ghost does not have flesh and bones, as you see I have." When he had said this, he showed them his hands and his feet'* (Luke 24:39-40).

Slowly it was dawning on the disciples that this really was Jesus. No doubt they were trying to come to terms with a body having flesh and bones that had just walked through the wall of the room they were in. It does take a measure of radical faith to be really comfortable with such extraordinary facts. And while the disciples were certainly filled with *'joy and amazement'* (Luke 24:41), they were still struggling to actually believe what their eyes and their senses were telling them! (Luke 24:41).

In English we have a saying, 'it's too good to be true', which we use to describe the feelings and emotions a person might have when something sensationally good happens, but which they hardly dare believe is true to them. I'm sure that's the sort of emotional roller-coaster those disciples were going through.

How else could Jesus prove to them that it was Him and He was real? Then He had an idea and asked, *'"Do you have anything to eat?"'* (Luke 24:41). I'm sure this wasn't because Jesus was hungry, but because He simply wanted to demonstrate His present reality to them. So, *'they gave him a piece of broiled fish, and he took it and ate it in their presence'* (Luke 24:42-43).

Having established the reality of His presence with the disciples, Jesus then began to teach them once more what the Scriptures said about Him. He said:

> *'"This is what I told you while I was still with you: everything must be fulfilled that is written about me in the law of Moses, the Prophets and the Psalms"'* (Luke 24:44).

And just as He'd done for the two on the road to Emmaus, He showed them all that the Scriptures said.

THE MISSING DISCIPLE!

What an experience that must have been for the disciples – the risen Lord Jesus personally sharing with them from the Scriptures. There was only one problem. Thomas wasn't there. We have no idea where he was, all we know is that he *'was not with the disciples when Jesus came'* (John 20:24). The other disciples quickly told Thomas *'"We have seen the Lord!"'* (John 20:25) and, no doubt, told him everything else that had happened as well.

But then they hit the same problem with Thomas that had been their own problem just a few hours earlier. It was beyond Thomas' capacity to believe that what they were saying was true. In words that have made the name Thomas famous down the centuries, he said:

> *'"Unless I see the nail marks in his hands and put my finger where the nails were, and put my hand into his side, I will not believe it"'* (John 21:25).

Thomas' desire for proof has given him, rather unfairly, the name 'Doubting Thomas', but in reality he was no more or less doubting than all the other disciples had been, prior to having had their own personal encounter with the risen Lord Jesus themselves. All the disciples had doubted – not just Thomas! Thomas was just being honest with his own feelings and emotions, and perhaps 'Honest Thomas' would have been a fairer name for him. But nothing will change the perception that people have. For the rest of time he will be 'Doubting Thomas' in most people's minds.

Don't you just love Jesus? He knew Thomas wasn't there and He also knew how important it would be in the future for all the disciples, who were destined to become the apostles of the early church, to have had a direct personal encounter with Him.

A week had passed and despite the instruction they had been given through the angel to go on up to Galilee, they were still in Jerusalem. And, once again, they had locked themselves in the room where they met. This time Thomas was with them and once again *Jesus came and stood among them and said, "Peace be with you!"* (John 20:26). It's obvious from the text that Jesus had been waiting for the moment when Thomas would be there with them all, for He turned to Thomas and said, *"'Put your finger here; see my hands. Reach out your hand and put it into my side. Stop doubting and believe'"* (John 20:27).

I'm sure that Thomas must have been acutely embarrassed at his failure to trust the words Jesus had spoken before He was crucified, and also at his lack of faith and trust in what others had said had happened. For Thomas this was a supreme moment of personal revelation and teaching, drawing out of him that spontaneous, inspired expression of faith when he said to Jesus, *"'My Lord and my God'"* (John 20:28).

Jesus must have been thinking about those who'd believed the reports of the women, others who'd heard the good news of the resurrection, and the countless millions down the centuries to follow who would come to the same conclusion as Thomas (but without the benefit of a personal physical encounter with Him as the risen Lord). He said to Thomas, *"'Because you have seen me, you have believed; blessed are those who have not seen and yet have believed'"* (John 20:29).

Jesus always responds when we exercise our faith and trust in Him. Jesus manifested His presence in the place where the disciples were meeting and when people are born again of the Spirit of God, through believing in Jesus as their personal Saviour, He manifests His presence in their hearts. A journey of personal transformation begins. New life comes with the presence of the risen Saviour.

SO WHY WEREN'T THE WOUNDS OF JESUS HEALED?

People sometimes ask why it is that the wounds of Jesus weren't healed by God at the same time as He raised Jesus from the dead. For it would seem surprising that the ultimate healing – being raised from the dead – didn't also include the restoration of all the injuries Jesus incurred during His beating and crucifixion.

Clearly the wounds were important for Thomas, and probably the other disciples also. These unique scars proved who Jesus was, but this isn't the only reason why the wounds were still there.

In ancient times when two people groups reached an agreement over, say, access across a piece of land, or the supply of water from a river, then a special covenantal agreement was entered into between the representatives of the two parties to the agreement. The agreement was marked with the shedding of blood of a sacrificial animal, which was then eaten in a celebration, marking the establishment of the covenant. But it was also marked by the shedding of the human blood of the representatives who had negotiated the agreement between the two peoples.

The arm of each of the representatives would be cut with a knife and salt would be put into the wound to ensure that there would always be a noticeable scar when the wound healed. This was important. For it sometimes happened that when one party was exercising the rights they had acquired through the covenant, someone from the other party might challenge them over what they were doing.

There could then be an argument, even a fight, over the issue and it was vital that there should always be a means of substantiating the covenantal rights, as evidence that the first party had been doing nothing wrong. In cases like these it was always the wounds (identified by the healed scar) on the arms of the representatives that proved beyond any dispute that there was a covenant in place, which would protect the one party from any unlawful claim or attack by the other party. The wounds were vital.

Jesus was a man, like us, and He was our representative pleading our case, and the case of all sinners, before Father God. Through His shed

PERSONAL NOTES

blood a New Covenant was put in place between Holy God and sinful man. We have sinned but forever we can have access to the Father through the Son. We have entrance to the glories of the Heavenly Kingdom. That is the right that Jesus won for us on the cross.

One of the names of Satan is 'accuser of the brethren' and John tells us that he *'accuses them before our God day and night'* (Revelation 12:10). Satan would tell the Father about the sins of those who are called the children of God, and that they have no rights to the Kingdom of God. So what can we do, for the accusations are true: you and I have sinned and do sin, and, yes, we don't deserve all the blessings of heaven.

We can do exactly the same thing as someone who might have been wrongfully accused in ancient times – **we can look to the wounds of Jesus, our representative, as evidence that there is a covenant in place, through which sinners can receive forgiveness for their sins and, despite their sin, be given access to the courts of heaven.**

The wounds of Jesus are our guarantee. When we get to heaven and see Jesus, we, too, will be able to see His wounds and truly, they will be to us the most beautiful sight in all of heaven's glory, for it's those wounds that are our guarantee of the New Covenant. So, whenever you sense the enemy undermining your faith and challenging your right to be a Christian, just point to the wounds of Jesus and tell the enemy, "He's my guarantor and those wounds prove the point and win the case!"

SUMMARY

The disciples were struggling to believe the reports that were coming in from those who had seen the risen Lord. Then suddenly Jesus appeared in the room where they were. He showed them His wounds and spoke His peace to a group of startled and very nervous disciples. But Thomas wasn't present when Jesus had come and he wouldn't believe the testimony of the other disciples. So Jesus chose a moment, a week later, when Thomas was present and appeared to them again, especially for the sake of Thomas. He showed him His wounds and Thomas responded with those unforgettable words "My Lord and My God".

PRAYER

Thank You, Lord, that You cared enough about Thomas to specially come and show him Your wounds and that You always care about the special needs of

Your children. Thank You, Lord, too that Your wounds are, for me, my guarantee of heaven's glory, an eternal reminder that You established a New Covenant between sinful man and Holy God and that because of You the enemy has no rights to my life. Thank You that my sin is forgiven and my life is covered by Your shed blood. In Jesus' name, Amen.

PERSONAL NOTES

THE MIRACULOUS CATCH OF FISH

I love coming home! I may have had wonderful experiences whilst away but I look forward to and greatly enjoy coming home - the place of my own personal comfort and security.

Over my life, I've valued many different places as 'home'. The first, and most influential, was the place where I grew up. Here, my first experiences of life impacted my emotions and became rooted in my memories.

I was brought up in Blackburn, a former cotton spinning town in the north of England. I recently visited it with some friends and took them on a brief drive round the area in which I lived as a child. I pointed out the house I'd lived in and the room in that house where I gave my life to the Lord. I told a few stories from my childhood and saw the first school I went to.

Other places have also become special to me. I have so many memories of what God did at Ellel Grange in the early years of the ministry that it will always be a spiritual 'home' to me. I really experienced the faithfulness of God there in fulfilling the promises of His Word, often in amazing detail.

PERSONAL NOTES

JESUS RETURNS HOME

Like me, Jesus also came from the north of His country. This was 'home' for Him. Nazareth is the village where His father worked as a carpenter and He called His disciples to follow Him from the villages surrounding the Lake of Galilee. All over the region they had enjoyed amazing experiences. Who could forget the man being delivered in the synagogue at Capernaum, or the five thousand being fed, or the Gadarene demoniac being healed, or Jairus' daughter being raised from the dead? Yes, this was their 'home' – physically and spiritually.

So it's not surprising that, when the angel of the Lord gave instructions to the women who went to the tomb, he told them that Jesus was going ahead of them to Galilee and that He would meet them there (Matthew 28:7). When Jesus Himself met some of the women He said to them, *'Do not be afraid. Go and tell my brothers to go to Galilee; there they will see me'* (Matthew 28:10). Jesus wanted to go home and spend some time in the place that meant so much to Him and His disciples.

MANY MIRACULOUS SIGNS

John tells us that Jesus did many other:

> *'miraculous signs in the presence of His disciples which are not recorded in this book. But these are written that you may believe that Jesus is the Christ, the Son of God, and that by believing you may have life in his name'* (John 20:30-31).

That's the reason why John wrote his Gospel – so that you and I would have the evidence on which to make a decision to believe in Jesus and have life.

Only a tiny fraction of the stories that could have been written were actually written down. John put it this way:

> *'If every one of them were written down, I suppose that even the whole world would not have room for the books that would be written'* (John 21:25).

The things that were written down were clearly those things the Holy Spirit considered essential for people to know so they could come to faith in Jesus. They were there for this specific purpose, written down by man in obedience to God.

One thing, however, was at the top of Jesus' agenda – the restoration of Peter. He was going to have a major role in establishing the emerging church. I love Peter. He wore his heart on his sleeve, he was full of faith and action but, like most of us, his very humanity so often got in the way of his spirituality. He often made mistakes – and sometimes big ones!

During Jesus' trial, Peter's love for Jesus made him want to get as close as he possibly could to the action. But that's where he was soon noticed. For a start, he spoke with a northern accent. Peter must have been a man who stood out in a crowd, and there were people there who thought they recognised him. As we have already seen (Stage 2, Chapter 3) there were three occasions when Peter responded out of fear of the consequences by telling lies. He denied he'd had anything to do with Jesus, despite people's protestations that they'd seen him with Jesus (John 18:26).

When the cock crowed Peter remembered what Jesus had said about denying Him three times. He became a broken man and went out and wept bitterly at what he'd done. He was utterly heart-broken (Luke 22:60-62). It was vital for Jesus to find an opportunity to show Peter the love that would heal him. This giant of a man was in danger of returning to fishing for the rest of his life, spending his time wondering what might have had happened if he'd only not denied Jesus. However, Jesus had a plan!

BACK ON GALILEE

My hobby is fishing. I love the restoration that comes through being out in the wild beauty of nature. After a long, hard period of work I find that fishing helps me get my life back in balance. I especially love salmon fishing in Scotland and even hold the record for having caught the largest salmon ever, on a particular small river which isn't normally noted for large fish! It's therefore no surprise to me to find that, when the disciples had made their way back from Jerusalem to Galilee, Peter said, *"'I'm going out to fish'"* and the others said, *"'We'll go with you'"* (John 21:3).

They were expert fishermen. They probably knew the lake as well as, if not better, than anyone else in the world. If anyone could catch fish in Galilee it would have been Peter, with his spontaneous crew of experienced fishermen. On the back of his personal failure, as well as the trauma and tragedy they had lived through in Jerusalem, they returned home to the area they knew and loved and then decided to do something they were good at. It's amazing how easily we are restored when we slip back into our own area of expertise and lose ourselves in what's familiar.

But it didn't quite go according to plan! I don't think Peter was actually ready for what happened next! Having failed Jesus so miserably in Jerusalem, he now became a failure on Galilee, in his own speciality. They had fished all night, the best time for fishing, and caught absolutely nothing!

Many times I've had to own up to the fact that I'd caught nothing. It's never easy for a skilled fisherman to own the fact that he spent all that time thinking of how he was going to show off his catch to the family back home, and then to have to creep back in, with nothing to show for all the anticipation and effort.

Many times, after rising at some ridiculous hour, all excited about a great opportunity, I've had to return to the house we stay at in Scotland, thinking I'd wasted the time I could have been asleep in my bed. Peter was bringing his boat home. They'd been up all night, wasted their time, and had absolutely nothing to show for their endeavours.

A LESSON IN SUPERNATURAL FISHING!

As they were pulling towards the shore there was a stranger there whom they didn't recognise.

'Early in the morning, Jesus stood on the shore but the disciples did not realise that it was Jesus. He called out to them, '"Friends, haven't you any fish?" "No," they answered' (John 21:4-5).

Then the stranger offered some help and said, *'"Throw your net on the right side of the boat and you will find some"'* (John 21:6). Suddenly, the net, which had been empty every time they'd cast it out during the night, was alive with a large number of big fish. It was a miracle.

'The disciple whom Jesus loved said to Peter, "It is the Lord!" As soon as Peter heard him say "It is the Lord," he wrapped his outer garment around him and jumped into the water' (John 21:7).

For a few minutes chaos reigned!

Peter was wanting to go to Jesus – and took the quickest route to shore! The others were trying to bring in the boat from about a hundred yards out, towing a huge catch of fish in the net. Peter then clambered back on board the boat and helped them bring 153 large fish to shore and, amazingly, the net didn't break with the strain of such a big catch (John 21:8-11). It was one of those extraordinary moments that neither Peter nor any of the other disciples would ever forget.

When Jesus directs the fishing the result is more than interesting! I know that back in my business days there were times when I knew the Lord was directing me in a particular direction. Those times when I made decisions in accordance with what I believed Jesus was saying always proved to be the very best decisions. There were times, however, when I did it 'my way' and my bad business decisions were always 'mine', not 'His'. Just as Peter found that Jesus was a very good fisherman, I also found He was a very good businessman!

Amazingly, Jesus already had a fire going with some fish cooking and some bread. He told the disciples to bring some of their fish, too, (John 21:10) and they had breakfast together on the shore. *'None of the disciples dared ask him, "Who are you?" They knew it was the Lord'* (John 21:12). *'Jesus took the bread,'* in his own unmistakeable way, *'and gave it to them, and did the same with the fish'* (John 21:13).

JESUS RESTORES PETER

Earlier in *Journey to Freedom* we saw how Peter betrayed Jesus on three separate occasions. Now the moment had come for Peter's healing and restoration. No-one doubted that they were in the presence of the Lord and Peter had had to admit that, even in his own area of expertise, fishing, Jesus had a power and authority which exceeded his. The disciples found out that there's no area of life where the presence and power of Jesus isn't life-transforming.

After they'd eaten Jesus took Peter for a walk along the shore. Later in the story (John 21:20), Peter made a comment about the disciple who was following them, so they must have been walking together away from where the rest of the disciples were sitting together around the fire. As they walked, Jesus said to Peter, *"Simon, Son of John, do you truly love me more than these"* (John 21:15). Earlier Peter had made the somewhat arrogant claim that *"Even if all fall away on account of you, I never will"* (Matthew 26:33). Peter had invited comparison of his own love and loyalty with that of others and now Jesus was drawing Peter's attention to what he had said.

The problem for Peter was that between 'then and now' he'd failed the test in the very area where he'd claimed superiority. It's amazing how often it is that things we've said in our past can come back to us at a later date! Peter knew that his previous claims had proven to be false and he couldn't answer the question positively. So, instead, he simply replied, *"Yes, Lord, you know that I love you."* To which Jesus responded, *"Feed my lambs"* (John 21:15).

Peter had denied Jesus three times, and it was three times that Jesus challenged him with the question, *"Do you love me?"* The second time Peter responded in the same way, *"Yes, Lord, you know that I love you."* And Jesus said, *"Take care of my sheep"* (John 21:16).

Once was no problem for Peter, twice could be seen as Jesus making sure he'd understood, but to ask the question three times was an unmistakeable reference back to the number of times Peter had denied his Lord before the crucifixion. It's not surprising, therefore, that *'Peter was hurt because Jesus asked him the third time, "Do you love me?"'* The pain of Peter's denial was still within him and Jesus was bringing it to the surface so it could be healed.

Peter's response to the third time Jesus asked the question was a simple statement of fact. There was nothing he could hide from the Lord, so he said, *"Lord, you know all things; you know that I love you."* To which Jesus responded again, *"Feed my sheep"* (John 21:17).

The first time Jesus asked the question He added the phrase *"more than these"*. The second time Jesus asked if Peter *"truly"* loved Him. But the third time it was simply *"Do you love me?"* The first time Jesus was dealing with his arrogance, the second time He was challenging whether his love for Jesus really was genuine, but the third time it was clear that there was only thing that mattered, *"Do you love me?"*

And after each response from Peter, Jesus commissioned him afresh to feed His lambs, then to take care of His sheep and finally to feed His sheep.

It's the shepherd who's the leader of the sheep. It's the shepherd who takes the flock from place to place to find food and drink. He's responsible for the lambs (the young ones) and the sheep (the old ones). Jesus was truly affirming to Peter that he was being restored to a position of leadership and responsibility despite the mistakes he'd made. I've no doubt that if Jesus hadn't done this Peter would have remained a fisherman for the rest of his days. He'd already made a choice to go back to his fishing and this was a critical moment in his life. Was he going to turn again and walk in the steps of his Master?

After the third time Jesus had told Peter to feed His sheep, He went on to give Peter a warning. Following in the steps of Jesus, from this point on, wasn't going to be easy. And at the end of his life his death would not be something he would enjoy, but it would bring glory to God (John 21:18-19). Jesus was telling Peter the truth – that being obedient to Him would mean sacrifice, and in Peter's case that sacrifice would even mean the premature ending of his own life, truly taking up his cross and following in the steps of Jesus.

Peter was the only disciple who was singled out by Jesus for this level of personal challenge. For him it was the second time to be called to follow Jesus, for the next words that would fall from the lips of Jesus were simply '*"Follow me"*'. The first time he heard those words, it was as an invitation to join the group of disciples who would walk with Jesus, learn from Him and be equipped by Him (Matthew 4:19). They had the excitement of seeing the Son of God fulfil His destiny.

But this time it was different. Jesus was soon to return to heaven. For Peter a lifetime of leading the sheep and then dying for the sheep lay ahead of him – never again would he be able to contemplate the idea of 'retiring' and spending the rest of his days having a quiet life enjoying the fishing. This time, when Jesus said, '*"Follow me"*' (John 21:19), it was to a calling of apostolic leadership of the young church, establishing the Body of Christ on earth to do the works of the Kingdom until Jesus comes again.

Peter's response was an obvious '*"Yes, Lord"*' – he was back in harness – yoked together with Jesus for the rest of his days. Jesus was once again in the driving seat of his life and he was on his way to fulfilling the destiny calling that God had prepared for him.

LESSONS FROM PETER'S EXPERIENCE

1. Jesus doesn't write us off when we make mistakes – He still loves us.

2. Jesus wants to heal us from the consequences of the mistakes we've made.

3. Jesus then wants to restore us to our place of calling and destiny.

The enemy wants us to believe that, when we've made a mistake, our days of serving the Lord are over. That is one of Satan's favourite lies which he uses time and time again. We have all made mistakes, but God doesn't want us to remain trapped by the consequences of what we've done.

He wants to lift us up. He wants to help us come to Him in repentance and be forgiven, healed, and restored. And once again the Lord wants to come to each one of us, as we sense the burden of sin rolling away at the foot of the cross. He says "Come, follow me – again!" If He could restore Peter, He can restore you – be encouraged and rejoice.

SUMMARY

After Jesus had appeared to His disciples, in Jerusalem, He went on ahead to Galilee. When the disciples got back there Peter was struggling with many things, including his own denial of Jesus, and went back to his fishing. But they caught nothing until Jesus came (as a stranger) and told them where to cast their net. When they followed His instructions the net was full to overflowing and they then recognised who the stranger on the shore was. They shared breakfast together and then Jesus took Peter aside and for each time Peter had denied His Lord, Jesus asked him if he loved Him. Finally Jesus called Peter again to '"Follow me."'

PRAYER

Thank You, Lord, that You loved Peter so much that You went out of Your way to see him forgiven, healed and restored, so that he could continue to serve You and be in the centre of Your will for his life. Thank You for teaching me through this that You don't reject those who have sinned and made mistakes. I come to You afresh today and ask You to show me every area of my life where I've got it wrong, so that I too may know Your forgiveness, healing and restoration. In Jesus' name, Amen.

STAGE 5

The Great Commission for the Body of Christ

"The Great Commission must have been the most under-staffed and under-funded, but most successful, campaign in world history. Two thousand years later it is still meeting its goal!"

GO INTO ALL THE WORLD

The year was 1953. The January weather in the north of England had taken its toll on the elderly. My grandfather was dying. He had started out in life in the nineteenth century as a painter and decorator, but for most of his working life had been a cotton spinner in the mills of Lancashire. He trod the boards of the local mill for forty years and more. He'd given his life to the Lord in his early days at St Peter's Church, and he and his wife had served the Lord faithfully all their days.

There was no such thing as central heating in the small terraced house where he and Granny lived in Bolton. It was a cold winter's day when, at the age of nine, I and my older brother, were ushered into the back room, where Grandpa lay on a bed beside the blackened kitchen range, in which a coal fire burned and on which a kettle was always boiling. It was too cold for him to be upstairs. Living conditions had changed little in the nearly hundred years since the house was built. I well remember the scene. It was etched on my memory by the emotions of the moment forever.

Granny watched as we boys were taken by my Dad to the side of Grandpa's bed. I didn't fully realise that this would be the last time I would see the Grandpa I loved so much. He stretched out his hands towards us and we gave him a kiss. Beside him was his well-worn purse which he slowly opened. Often he would give my brother and me a threepenny-piece to buy some sweets at the corner shop. But this time he took out a two-shilling piece for each of us and squeezed them into our grateful hands. To us it was a small fortune – the equivalent of only ten pence today, but worth a huge amount more in those far-off days, when you could buy something worthwhile for half an old penny! And there were 48 half pennies in two shillings! It was a real sacrifice for them to give us two shillings each out of their tiny pension.

I can't remember the actual words he said, but I know they were his farewell to his two grandsons. And I do know he prayed for us both, that we would grow up to know and love Jesus. I've still got that two-shilling piece! Even though it was such a lot of money, I couldn't bring myself to spend it. Even though it was just a coin, it was a physical link with my Grandpa, a man of God whose prayers counted for the Kingdom.

Way back in the 1890s he and his brother had started a prayer meeting in Bolton for Hudson Taylor and the China Inland Mission (CIM). That prayer meeting met every month for over sixty-five years and from it a number of missionaries went out to China to serve with the CIM, including one that I know of who gave her life, martyred on the mission field.

I didn't know at the time that that would be the last time I would see Grandpa. But, when my Dad told me a few days later that Grandpa had died, I felt a huge hole in my heart. Somehow or other I knew that he was with Jesus, and one day I would see him again if I chose to follow Jesus. It wasn't long after that that I remember kneeling at my own bedside with my father, and I invited Jesus into my heart and gave my life to Him, and another generation of believers in the family had begun.

When Grandpa died it was the first time I'd encountered death close to hand. It impacted me greatly. But I'm old enough now for there to have been a number of times that I have had to say farewell to family members and close friends. What a contrast there is between saying good-bye to those who know Jesus and those who don't. With those who know Him, parting is only for a season and we have the certainty of reunion.

That was the sort of parting that Jesus was to have with His disciples.

I know my grandfather told me things that he considered important for my life. And I know there are things that one day I will want to say to my own children and my grandchildren before I finally go to be with the Lord. We read about this in the Old Testament Scriptures as well, such as when Jacob gathered his sons around him (Genesis 49:1-28). It's a spiritual instinct that God has built into humanity. While such partings are painful, to believers they are also sweet, for the hope of future certainty soothes away the pain of current sorrow.

Jesus also wanted to spend time with those who were closest to Him. He had important farewell things to say which would impact, not only the rest of their days, but the rest of time as well.

JESUS PREPARES TO GO HOME

Jesus started preparing His disciples for His departure long before He died. Much of His teaching in the latter part of John's Gospel (especially chapters 14, 15 and 16) is exactly that. The first few verses of John 14 are often used at funeral services, as the minister encourages those who are left behind by using the words of Jesus to His own disciples, *"'In my Father's house are many rooms; if it were not so I would have told you. I am going there to prepare a place for you'"* (John 14:2)

But Jesus was also able to teach His disciples once He'd risen from the dead, in the short time before He finally returned to heaven. It's what He said then that we're focussing on in the new Stage of our *Journey to Freedom*.

The different Gospel writers vary in the amount of information they give us about Jesus' post-resurrection appearances. John tells us nothing. Luke only tells us of the ascension to heaven from Bethany, Matthew gives us what is generally known as the 'Great Commission' for the church and Mark gives us a slightly different version of what Matthew says.

Although Luke doesn't tell us much at the end of his Gospel apart from details of the ascension, he includes much more at the beginning of His second book, the Acts of the Apostles. Here we have a much more detailed description of what Jesus did with His disciples in the time before His ascension to heaven. But before that, Luke tells us that after His suffering, Jesus:

PERSONAL NOTES

'showed himself to these men [the apostles] and gave many convincing proofs that he was alive. He appeared to them over a period of forty days and spoke about the Kingdom of God' (Acts 1:3).

We will come back to this later, but for now I want to concentrate on what was obviously the underlying theme of everything Jesus said to the apostles during this period of time – the commission that Jesus was giving to them. And it's Matthew who most succinctly summarises these things in words that, throughout the history of the church, have been known as the 'Great Commission', and which have been the foundational command to share the Gospel with the world for two thousand years.

THE GREAT COMMISSION

In all armies of the world there are different levels of responsibility, according to the rank of the soldier. Only an officer can give instructions, and a commissioned officer derives his or her authority from the sovereign power of the country he serves. When an officer is commissioned, he is charged with carrying out the duties and responsibilities of the position he holds. The commission describes his responsibilities and his field of operation. Jesus gave a commission to the disciples, which formed the parameters of responsibility for the church throughout its future history.

Military terminology is frequently used in the Scriptures to describe the roles and responsibilities of Christian believers. For example, Paul urges believers to be willing *'to endure hardship, like a good soldier of Jesus Christ'* (2 Timothy 2:3). And in his letter to the Ephesians, Paul uses the weaponry of a Roman soldier as a parable to describe the different pieces of equipment we need in order to *'be strong in the Lord and in his mighty power'* (Ephesians 6:10). He then urges us to *'put on the full armour of God, so that when the day of evil comes, you may be able to stand your ground'* (Ephesians 6:13) using as our primary offensive weapon *'the sword of the Spirit, which is the word of God'* (Ephesians 6:17).

On one of the occasions that the risen Lord met with His disciples in Galilee, they went to *'the mountain where Jesus had told them to go'* (Matthew 28:16). This was most likely the place where Jesus had taught the crowds in the Sermon on the Mount. When Jesus began to speak, He told them that:

"'All authority in heaven and on earth has been given to me. Therefore, go and make disciples of all nations, baptising them in the name of the Father and of the Son and of the Holy Spirit, and teaching them to obey everything I have commanded you. And surely I am with you always, to the very end of the age'" (Matthew 28:18-20).

ALL AUTHORITY

These are the words of the Great Commission. They begin with Jesus establishing why He is able to give the disciples these final instructions. All authority, in heaven and on earth was in His hands. His Father had given Him authority in heaven. And He had authority on earth, because He had never sinned and had never been overcome by Satan. Death was not, therefore, His inheritance, and the resurrection was the dynamic proof of His final victory over the enemy. He was *'the second Adam'* and took up the mantle of earthly authority for the whole of the human race. There was no other who could do this.

So, when Jesus gives instructions, we now know that we are taking orders from an authority that is higher than Satan's as the god of this world. We know, therefore, that when we are obeying Jesus, we have all the forces of heaven behind us, as we seek to fulfil on earth the commission that Jesus gave to the church.

THEREFORE GO ... TO ALL NATIONS

Because it is Jesus who has given the church the instructions, and He is the One who has all authority, we, as the soldiers in His 'army', can move forward with confidence to do the works of the Kingdom. We can know that He will empower us, His people, to do the things that He has asked us to do. Most of us will have sung at some time or other the old hymn 'Onward Christian Soldiers'!

It is this thinking that led William Booth to call the new organisation the Lord had inspired him to start, the 'Salvation Army'. He believed that, in order to achieve the objectives God had given him for a great mission to the poor, in the heart of nineteenth century London, his teams needed to be under orders. He was absolutely right and God gave him the military structure of the Salvation Army as a model. Through

PERSONAL NOTES

this amazing organisation, Salvationists have been continuing to serve the poor, the hurting and the broken in the cities of the world ever since.

We may not be members of the Salvation Army, but the instructions Jesus gave to those first disciples were from the One who had ultimate authority, and they were given as commands to those who chose to follow and serve Him. Later, we will look at what these instructions to *make disciples* actually mean. But, for now, I want to focus our attention on the fact that Jesus placed no boundaries whatsoever on our area of operation. The instruction was to *go to all nations*, meaning the whole world (Matthew 28:19). The word 'nation' means, literally, 'a people group'.

There are many nations in some countries. Each distinct tribe, or people group, is a nation according to the Scriptural definition – and Jesus doesn't want any of them to be left out! Jesus Himself has a vision, and that vision is clearly, and repeatedly, expressed in the book of Revelation on five separate occasions, that with His blood He *purchased men for God from every tribe and language and people and nation* (Revelation 5:9).

If His blood was shed for people from EVERY possible group of people, then He wanted them to take the message of salvation to them all. Jesus wanted all people to have the opportunity to hear the good news for themselves and to respond to the love of God. This love is seen in the face of Jesus Christ, His Son, and is represented at the great marriage supper of the Lamb of God (Revelation 19:9), when Jesus and the church are brought together in glory.

In Revelation 7:9-10, John describes what he saw in his vision of heaven:

'there before me was a great multitude that no one could count, from every nation, tribe, people and language, standing before the throne and in front of the Lamb. They were wearing white robes and were holding palm branches in their hands. And they cried out in a loud voice, "Salvation belongs to our God, who sits on the throne, and to the Lamb"'

When Jesus was giving the disciples their instructions, only He knew just how big the world was, and how long the Great Commission would take to fulfil. The disciples may have thought that the whole world could be covered just by them, and in a few years the task would be completed. But the vastness of the planet, and the diversity of its peoples, meant that many generations would pass before mankind would even know of all the places where there were people living!

And that brings us right up to date. It is believed that for the first time ever, through satellite imaging, we now know all the places on the planet where the nations of mankind live – we may not yet have reached them all with the Gospel, but at least we know they're there! The task is unfinished, but the goal is in sight!

THE COMMISSION IS FOR US!

Sometimes people read the Bible and distance themselves from any personal involvement in what they are reading. People could say, "well, the Great Commission was for the first disciples, it's not for us". But as we work our way through this Stage, we are going to see that we can't excuse ourselves from the action – we are all involved. We are all under orders and there is a work for each one of us to do that can be done by no other! No-one in the Body of Christ need ever be redundant!!

My Grandpa's last words were special to me alone, but the last words of Jesus were not restricted to one person, or even a group of people – they were for all believers, for all of time, till Jesus comes again.

SUMMARY

Jesus was careful to share His final words with the disciples, so that they would know what their ongoing commission was to be. According to Luke, Jesus spent up to forty days teaching them about the Kingdom of God. But His commission to the church was summarised by Matthew in words that have become known as the 'Great Commission'. This urges the Body of Christ to take the message of the Gospel to all nations – literally to the whole world – and those instructions apply as much to us today as they did to the first disciples.

PRAYER

Thank You, Lord, that You went out of Your way to speak farewell words to the family of God before returning to heaven. Help me, Lord, to understand how the Great Commission can be applied in and through my own life in the place and time in which I now live. I want to love and serve You as a 'good soldier of Jesus Christ'. In His name, Amen.

MAKE DISCIPLES

There is a huge difference between making a garden and growing a few flowers. I could grow some flowers by scattering seeds in a field and seeing what happened. When water touched the seeds they would begin to sprout and become seedlings. Then, if the roots managed to anchor themselves in the soil, the seedlings would begin to grow and eventually produce flowers and look pretty. But the plants would be unlikely to last and become a permanent feature of the landscape.

Making a garden, on the other hand requires a significant amount of work. The ground must be surveyed and the type of soil determined – for some plants grow better in particular soils. The layout of the garden needs to be carefully designed to get maximum benefit from the site. Areas of the garden must be designated for different purposes such as lawns, vegetable plots, borders, sitting areas, play areas for children, fruit and ornamental trees and perhaps many more things as well.

Where flowers and vegetables are going to be planted, the soil must be carefully prepared and all obvious weeds eradicated, for weeds will be serious competition for new plants. Then you may need to dig in fertiliser to provide added nutrients and perhaps take serious action to kill off slugs and other garden pests.

Then, when the seeds or plants you put in begin to grow, you will discover that you have produced ideal growing conditions for hundreds of weeds whose seeds are still in the soil even though you couldn't see them before. You will have a regular battle on your hands to eliminate the weeds and encourage the growth of all the good plants you have put in the garden.

BELIEVERS OR DISCIPLES?

What I have described above, by contrasting the scattering of a few seeds to grow flowers in a field, with all the work that is needed to prepare a garden for long-term use, is a fair description of the difference between someone becoming a believer in Jesus and making that believer into a true disciple. There are millions of believers in Jesus who never become disciples.

Making disciples, like making a garden, is hard work. It requires commitment and discipline to help a person make that huge transition from being someone who just believes in Jesus to someone who becomes His disciple; to someone whose life, like the garden, will have a clear purpose and be kept in good order to fulfil the purpose for which it was created.

A well-made garden provides enormous pleasure to people for many years. It offers areas for recreation and relaxation; it's beautiful to look at; it produces fragrant and colourful flowers and grows fruit and vegetables for the home; it provides shade and places of safety for birds and wildlife. A beautiful garden is a tremendous asset, that gives enormous pleasure to its owner.

In just the same way a believer in Jesus, who has become a true disciple, provides enormous pleasure to our Creator God. His or her life is like incense rising to the throne of God (2 Corinthians 2:15) bringing joy to the One who died that we might first become believers and then be trained to become disciples.

The life of a disciple is not only a blessing to the Lord; living as a disciple of Jesus is also the key to personal blessing. Christian discipleship has a purpose and is the pathway to the fulfilment of God's unique destiny for our lives. And just as a beautiful garden has to be kept free of weeds, the ground of the disciple's life has to be regularly weeded of the sins of the flesh. Otherwise these would grow up and stifle the life of the Spirit and prevent the person from realising their potential in God (Galatians 5:16-18).

When a person takes that step of faith and chooses to become a believer in Jesus, it is the beginning of a new life in Christ. But if the life of the believer is not then trained and brought under godly discipline, in order to establish godly order, then the likelihood is that the new believer may not grow and mature and enjoy the fullness of blessing that God intended. And the process of making disciples never ends – God desires to see us continually walking and growing in God's ways, just like a garden will continue to grow and mature. The more mature the garden / disciple, the more beautiful and fruitful it is.

GO AND MAKE DISCIPLES

Returning now to the Great Commission, we read these words, '"*Therefore, go and make disciples of all nations, baptising them in the name of the Father and of the Son and of the Holy Spirit*"' (Matthew 28:19). This was a clear instruction that Jesus, our Commanding Officer, was giving to the first generation of disciples.

The fact that Jesus told them to make disciples of *'all nations',* makes it very clear that Jesus did not intend the first disciples to complete the task – but it *was* their job to begin it. Jesus knew that finishing such a task in their lifetime was an impossibility – but He also knew that, for the Body of Christ, this was to be their primary objective, to harvest souls for the Kingdom of God until Jesus returns.

It's significant that Jesus didn't tell them to 'make believers' – for the fact is that none of us can ever 'make a believer'. The work of making a believer is the responsibility of the Holy Spirit. We can share the Gospel with those who do not know Jesus, but when that person comes to the point of saying Yes to Jesus and invites Him to be Lord of their life, then there is a supernatural work of grace in the life of that individual.

We can share the truths that are in the Word of God with unbelievers, but it is the work of the Spirit of God to convict a person of sin and point them to the Saviour. The Holy Spirit responds to the choices

PERSONAL NOTES

people make and, when they choose Jesus, the Spirit fills them with His presence and they are born again of the Spirit of God. A new life in Christ has begun. I was born of the flesh in 1943, but I was born of the Spirit in 1952. I have two birthdays. My physical life came to me through my father and my mother. My redeemed spiritual life came to me through the Spirit of God.

No human being can ever put life into the seeds that are in a packet, but we can water, nurture and grow those seeds so that they take their place in a garden. In just the same way, no human being can ever make a born-again believer, but we can train believers to become disciples, learning to yield to the work of the Holy Spirit in their lives so that they will take their proper place in the Body of Christ. And that instruction is implicit in the Great Commission for all generations of believers.

Down the centuries many different churches have instituted training programmes to help people make that vital transition from being a believer to being a committed disciple of Jesus Christ. One of the most effective was the Class System put in place by John Wesley. John Wesley was probably the most successful evangelist the United Kingdom has ever known. When he began to criss-cross the country on horse-back, preaching the Gospel of Salvation, wherever a crowd would gather to hear him, tens of thousands of people were born again as they heard the message of the Gospel and became believers.

But John Wesley couldn't stay around to train up the new believers and make them into disciples. He was a harvester, and the urgency of the Gospel message compelled him to move on to village after town after city, until there was hardly a community in the whole country, including Scotland, Wales and Ireland, that hadn't been touched by his preaching.

He was passionate, however, that the new converts wouldn't fall away. So he appointed a Class Leader wherever there were converts. It was his job to gather the new believers together every week for Bible study, prayer and training in righteous living. The effect was remarkable. As a methodical student at Oxford, John Wesley had acquired the nickname 'methodist'. But now his methodical approach to making disciples was really producing great fruit for the Kingdom of God.

The results across the nation were so remarkable that even secular historians had to admit that the evangelical revival under the leadership of John Wesley had transformed the nation. Eighteenth century

Britain was a far better place to live in than it had been before John Wesley took to his horse, preached the Gospel and made disciples. It was an astonishing achievement and resulted in the founding of the Methodist Church.

Over the years I have been involved in a number of evangelistic missions, but the one majorly disappointing statistic to come from these, and many other missions across the world, is that a year after the event, the majority of the new converts are nowhere near the church. **I passionately believe that the main reason for this is that so much of today's church has forgotten that once people have become believers, the main responsibility of the church is not to entertain them, but to make them into disciples.**

BAPTISM – THE FIRST STEP

You don't need to get baptised in order to be born again, but the Bible is very clear on this issue. The next step, following conversion, is to seal your commitment to the Lord in baptism, following repentance, and on confession of your own faith. In the Great Commission the first instruction from Jesus to the apostles about how to make disciples was to baptise them '*"in the name of the Father, and of the Son and of the Holy Spirit"'* (Matthew 28:19).

Baptism is not just a symbolic act; it is a statement by the person being baptised of their desire to die to self and be raised to new life. When John the Baptist preached repentance, those who responded came and were baptised in the River Jordan. The act of baptism for repentance represented a new beginning in their life. When Jesus was baptised, He did not need to repent of anything, but He was associating Himself with sinners, in fulfilment of His calling and destiny. His baptism also marked the beginning of His years of ministry.

After Pentecost, when Peter preached the first sermon of the pentecostal age, he was obedient to the Great Commission. He didn't just proclaim the truth about Jesus as he preached, but he also called people to '*"repent and be baptised, every one of you, in the name of Jesus Christ for the forgiveness of your sins"'* (Acts 2:38).

Ever since the earliest days of the church, being baptised has been considered the moment when someone becomes a member of the church.

They have taken that critical first step on their journey of discipleship. They have turned their back on their previous way of life, renouncing all other beliefs and religions, and recognising that Jesus is the only way to the Father. In obedience to their Commanding Officer (Jesus), they have publicly testified in baptism to their faith in Jesus Christ.

Spurgeon said, 'nothing is more plainly taught in the New Testament than that it is the duty of every believer in Christ to be baptised.' It is indeed a very significant step. **Baptism is not essential for Salvation but a person who is saved will desire to be obedient to the Saviour, and so, said Spurgeon 'baptism, therefore, is essential to our obedience to Christ.'**

The church my parents went to when they were young, baptised babies. So I was baptised as a baby in the traditional manner in the Church of England, as is done in many of the long-established churches. But as a teenager I realised the Scriptures said that baptism follows repentance and I couldn't repent of my sin as a baby. As a result, I decided to be baptised by immersion at the age of sixteen, believing then, as I do now, that that was what the Scriptures taught. I've never regretted being baptised as a young adult, at an age when I could make the choice for myself.

I believe also, however, that it's very important to dedicate babies to the Lord in the family of God and to pray for them. How I thank God that this is what my parents did as they presented me to the Lord as a baby. I believe it is a wonderful thing to do, as the blessings arising from the prayers of the assembled fellowship fall upon the child. I am sure there has been great blessing on my life as a result. But how I thank the Lord also that, as an adult, I realised God required obedience to His Word and that in obedience there is great blessing.

I will never forget when a man, who had been a priest for thirty-five years, suddenly realised that, while he knew all about Jesus, he didn't know Jesus personally. On one of our Healing Retreats he was born again of the Spirit of God. The following day he read his Bible with a new understanding. When he came to the Acts of the Apostles, he realised that, even though he had been baptised as a baby himself, and had baptised hundreds of babies during his career, the Word of God was telling him that he now needed to be baptised.

It was an amazing experience when I had the privilege of agreeing to his request to be baptised in our swimming pool at Ellel Grange. It proved to be a defining moment in his life – and a profound lesson to me in the importance and value of baptism as a means of sealing the redeeming work of the Spirit of God in the life of the repentant sinner.

Next, we'll look at some other consequences of the Great Commission in the discipleship journey we are all making together with *Journey to Freedom*.

SUMMARY

The Great Commission is a commandment from the lips of Jesus to the church that would bear His name. It is an instruction to make disciples, by teaching believers and training them in the things of God, so that they will grow strong as loyal soldiers of Jesus Christ. Jesus said that the first step towards becoming a disciple is to be baptised – an act which marks out the believer for the rest of his or her days as someone who has chosen to follow Jesus and to live in obedience to Him.

PRAYER

Forgive me, Lord, I pray, for all those times I have lived as a believer but have not wanted to live in obedience to You as a disciple and loyal soldier in the army of the Lord. Help me, Lord, to see those things from Your word that are important for me and how I live my life. Show me the way that I should go so that, as a disciple, I will bring joy to Your heart. In Jesus' name, Amen.

Stage 5, Chapter 3

TEACHING THEM TO OBEY

Jesus told a story of two sons (Matthew 21:28-32), one who said he would do what his father wanted, but didn't; and the other, who said he wouldn't do it, but changed his mind and did it. Both made mistakes in their attitudes and responses but the one who actually did what his father wanted was the one who was commended. Obedience, even reluctant obedience, is better than making promises and not fulfilling them.

Jesus told this story to highlight the importance of obedience as the key to blessing. Centuries earlier, when the prophet Samuel was having to deal with the rebellious King Saul, Saul protested that he had made the sacrifices that the Lord demanded, but Samuel replied by asking him:

"'Does the LORD delight in burnt offerings and sacrifices as much as in obeying the voice of the LORD? To obey is better than sacrifice'" (1 Samuel 15:22).

Samuel was explaining to Saul that no amount of religious rituals, including the sacrifice of the very best animals from his flocks, could be a substitute for obedience to God. Observance of religious duties can never be a cover for the sin of disobedience. That's why, in the Great Commission, teaching the new disciples to be obedient to their commanding officer was so important.

THE KEY TO REVIVAL

Many years ago when I was studying the history of revivals, I began to ask the Lord why it was that so many people were praying for revival in their local church, their community and even their nation, but they didn't appear to be seeing much real fruit from their intercessory labours. Over a period of time the Lord showed me that, while revival was very much on His heart for His people, most times people were praying for the wrong thing!

As I worked my way through the Scriptures, seeing all the places where God had moved in supernatural power, I began to get revelation, as the Lord showed me that simply praying for revival isn't enough. The Lord gave me three words to look up in my concordance, and then follow through in the Scriptures – first there was **vision,** then **faith** and finally **obedience.**

I saw that it was always through **vision** that God inspired His people with what He wanted them to do. Then **faith** was required to believe in the word from the Lord and, finally, that **without obedience the vision could never be fulfilled.** I suddenly saw that the first thing we need is vision from God, and that with faith and obedience it's then possible to do what's on God's heart for each one of us.

When I looked at the history of revivals, I always saw this principle at work: first there was the receiving of vision, then there was the application of faith to the vision, and finally there was the obedience to do what God was saying. And God will always bless with His presence those things that are carried out in obedience to visions that came from Him in the first place. That is the key to living in revival.

BEING OBEDIENT TO THE HEAVENLY VISION

Wherever the apostle Paul went, the reviving power of God was at work in and through him. There is a remarkable passage of Scripture in Acts

26. Here, Paul is having to defend himself before King Agrippa. His very life was at stake because of the charges that the Jewish community had brought against him in Jerusalem and Caesarea. They wanted him put to death – just as they had done with Jesus.

In his defence, Paul tells the King what happened when Jesus appeared directly to him on the road to Damascus in a dramatic vision. He explained how Jesus said:

"'I have appeared to you to appoint you as a servant and as a witness of what you have seen of me and what I will show you. I will rescue you from your own people and from the Gentiles. I am sending you to them to open their eyes and turn them from darkness to light, and from the power of Satan to God, so that they may receive forgiveness of sins and a place among those who are sanctified by faith in me'" (Acts 26:16-18).

So that was the vision. And, while there were years of preparation and training that Saul, whose name was changed to Paul, had to go through, years later it was still this vision that was driving him, even right up to his dying day. In his defence to King Agrippa, Paul spoke such important words:

"'I was not disobedient to the vision from heaven. First to those in Damascus, then to those in Jerusalem, and in all Judea, and to the Gentiles also. I preached that they should repent and turn to God and prove their repentance by their deeds'" (Acts 26:19-20).

The vision Jesus had given him meant everything to Paul, but without faith and obedience, the vision would have remained unfulfilled. God looks to mankind to do the works of the Kingdom of God on earth. He requires our co-operation and obedience. **And because Paul was not disobedient to the vision, the fruit of his life and ministry was astonishing**, bringing the reviving power of the Spirit of God throughout the region in which he travelled, and down the generations to all those who have become believers through the witness and influence of that first generation of believers. Paul's constant obedience to the leading of the Spirit brought untold blessings to the Body of Christ and the peoples of the world.

I've taken a little time at the beginning of this unit of *Journey to Freedom* to underline how, throughout Scripture, obedience to God is the outward evidence of an inner faith and how God uses vision to inspire and motivate His people.

Almost fifty years ago now, I set out to restore an old car. But after stripping the car down to its steel chassis, I discovered that the chassis was bent. And as I looked at this broken car, tears of disappointment were slowly trickling down my face. I thought "I'll never be able to restore this car now!" But as I looked, I was suddenly conscious of the presence of the Lord. It was, for me, a Damascus Road moment and I heard the voice of the Lord saying, "You could restore this broken car, but I can restore broken lives." Then He asked me a question, "Which is more important?"

It was obvious that broken lives were more important than broken cars, and God used that supernatural moment to plant in me the vision for what eventually became Ellel Ministries, through which God was going to restore many broken lives. The emotion and the inspiration of that moment have never left me – the vision is still very much alive and that experience of God speaking into my life is as fresh and as powerful today as it was then. And everything I'm still doing today, is a direct result of what God said to me on a day that I'll never forget, 19 June 1970 at about 4.00 am in the morning!

But, just as the car is still unfinished, the visionary task God had given me was also still unfinished. There are still countless people across the world whose lives have been broken through the trials and tribulations of life, and for whom there is no healing answer outside of Christ. I believe the Lord is asking this generation of believers a similar question to the one He asked Isaiah, '*"Whom shall I send? And who will go for us?"*' (Isaiah 6:8). Who will go and heal the broken-hearted?

It is certainly my personal prayer that through *Journey to Freedom*, there will be many, many people across the world who will understand, perhaps for the first time, what the Great Commission is really all about, in terms of both evangelism and healing, and in response will say "Yes, Lord, I will go. I do want to bring hope and healing to the hurting, to restore those who are grieving, to heal those who are broken-hearted and to set the captives free." For that work is right at the heart of the Great Commission and the work of making disciples.

BACK TO THE GREAT COMMISSION!

All we have looked at so far emphasises how important is the next phrase of the Great Commission's instruction to go and make disciples – *"teaching them to obey everything I have commanded you"* (Matthew 28:20). However, obedience is not something that is just for disciples – it was at the very heart of Jesus' life and ministry. For Jesus, obedience meant the cross. Paul expressed it like this, *'Jesus, being found in appearance as a man, he humbled himself and became obedient to death, even death on a cross!'* (Philippians 2:8). Jesus wasn't asking his disciples to do anything that He hadn't been willing to do Himself.

There were two great loves that controlled Jesus' life! First there was His love for His Father; and then there was His love for mankind. It was Jesus' love for His Father that caused Him to accept the commission to come to earth. It was His love for mankind that kept Him on earth to save men and women from the curse of Satan's bondage. And His obedience was always a consequence of love!

So, when Jesus said to His disciples *'"if anyone loves me, he will obey my teaching"'* (John 14:23), this was not some harsh command that He was giving to others that He wasn't willing to apply to Himself. He had already set the example and was sharing how our lives can be fruitful. *'"Whoever has my commands and obeys them, he is the one who loves me"'* (John 14:21).

When Jesus was teaching His disciples about love and obedience, He was preparing them to receive the Holy Spirit (John 14:26). Without the Holy Spirit we'll never be able to live the dynamic Christian life that He longs for us to enjoy, for the Holy Spirit is always grieved when we know what to do to bless God but choose to do something different. Obedience to God and the blessing of the Spirit always go hand in hand.

On many occasions people have asked me at the end of a meeting questions such as, "How can I be more anointed?" My response is often: "Be more obedient to what the Lord wants you to do!" For, in reality, the greatest single key to living under the anointing of the Spirit is obedience. So, when Jesus included obedience in the training manual for disciples, He was simply saying – here's the key to more anointing and more blessing!

THE BIG 'IF'!

Jesus gave us a very simple definition of what it means to be a disciple, in a verse that we have referred to before in *Journey to Freedom*, John 8:31. Here Jesus simply says that you're a disciple *'"if you hold to my teaching."'* Nothing could be simpler – at least in theory!

A person who holds to something is someone who doesn't waver in their commitment – they remain faithful and loyal whatever the circumstances. They don't change their beliefs according to who they're with, and even if it is costly to them personally, their love for the Lord means that obedience to Him is the number one priority in their lives.

Holding to the teaching of Jesus is not the same as believing it to be true. We do need to believe that it's true, but a person who holds to it also puts it into practice. I am often approached by people asking for prayer over issues in their life. They are wanting God to bless them, give them guidance, make provision for them, heal them, deliver them or any of a dozen other possible things. But so often, when I ask a few leading questions about different areas of their lives, I discover that, knowingly, they are doing things which they know are not included in the teaching of Jesus. Yet they still want Him to hear their prayers and bless them, despite the ungodly choices they are making in other areas of their lives.

Jesus then goes on to say that, when you hold to His teaching, then *'"you will know the truth and the truth will set you free"'* (John 8:32). It's so sad that so many believers are crying out to God to be set free from many, many things, and yet they are not putting themselves on the starting line of blessing, by choosing to walk in God's ways.

That's why I call this 'The Big IF.' If we want to bring our will into line with the teaching of Jesus then He will help us to do that. But if we are wanting the blessing at the same time as, in our heart, wanting to live a life that is outside His teaching, then we are giving the enemy a hook into our lives and cutting ourselves off from the stream of blessing that God longs to pour upon us.

So, what's the desire of your heart? If it is to be a true disciple, holding on to the teaching of Jesus, then be encouraged, He will help you come to that place when the application of truth in your life brings you the freedom you are crying out for. But if you are thinking you can get His blessing at the same time as walk in the pathways of the enemy, then don't be surprised if your prayers aren't answered.

THE DESIRES OF THE HEART

There is only one measure of our intentions and that is determined by the desires of our heart. And God knows what they are. I often think of the verse in Hebrews that tells us: *'the word of God is living and active. Sharper than any double-edged sword, it penetrates even to dividing soul and spirit, joints and marrow; it judges the thoughts and attitudes of the heart'* (Hebrews 4:12).

It is here in the heart that we weigh our thoughts and attitudes, or intentions, and then exercise our will to make decisions. It is at this very sensitive point of our being that we have to ask the question, "How much do I love Jesus? Do I love Him more than I love myself?"

If we get the answer to that question right, then everything else in life will fall into place. For then our love for Him will lead us to making the right, even if sometimes hard, decisions, and when we are living our lives according to the teaching of Jesus, then He has promised that we will know the truth and the truth will set us free! (John 8:32).

PERSONAL RESPONSE

May I encourage you to spend some time with the Lord just asking yourself questions such as the following:

- How serious am I about Jesus being Lord of every area of my life?
- Am I really willing and longing for Him to be Lord of all?
- Has He ever given me a heart to do something or pray for someone or something that I haven't done?
- Is there an area of my life, in which I am failing to obey Him and His voice?

Then, share with Him your answers, ask forgiveness for the times you've 'got it wrong' and ask His help to walk forward into a new future.

SUMMARY

Disciples are people who both believe in Jesus and choose to love, follow and obey Him. Jesus said that if we love Him then we should obey Him, just as He obeyed His Father because He loved Him. Obedience to the leading of the Holy Spirit is the key to blessing and the foundation stone of revival in our personal lives and in what God will do in our fellowships and community.

PRAYER

Thank You, Lord, for teaching us the truth and that in Your Word we can read about what it means to be a disciple. Help me, Lord, to want to walk in Your ways. I don't want to disappoint You by my own disobedience or miss out on the many blessings You have for those who love to obey Your Word. In Jesus' name, Amen.

ALL I TAUGHT YOU TO DO

God has given us free will. Nevertheless, there are some things about which we don't have a choice! How can this be? Doesn't free will mean exactly that, the freedom to choose what you do or don't do? As with many such conundrums, there is definitely a 'Yes' answer that's correct. But there's also a correct 'No' answer, which is of vital importance to each of us as individuals, and to the whole body of believers that we know as the church.

As we saw in Book 2 of our *Journey to Freedom*, when we were looking at how man fell from grace in the Garden of Eden, it was the gift to mankind of God's free will, that set in motion the salvation plan of Father God, that ended with the cross. Man had free will but used it to say 'Yes' to things God had said 'No' to.

What we learned from those first experiences of mankind on earth was that if we use our free will to say 'Yes' to things God has said 'No' to, there are serious consequences. God hasn't made us so that we are unable to say 'Yes' to bad things – for then we would be automatons without free will – or unable to say 'No' to good things.

The continuing decline and fall of twenty-first century man, into an amoral and immoral abyss, is a direct result of mankind saying 'Yes' to the things God has said 'No' to. All this is glaringly obvious to those whose eyes are open to the spiritual realities of this world and perhaps you are wondering why I'm taking time at this stage of *Journey to Freedom* to repeat things that we have already learned together?

Let me explain! God never takes away our capacity to exercise free will. We may serve God faithfully all our lives and then, sadly, towards the end of our days, fall into temptation and choose to sin. On more than one occasion I have had to help people, both men and women, who have fallen victim to one of Satan's traps, even after years of Christian service.

Equally there are people who serve themselves, and can even live grossly immoral lives who, at the end of their days, see the folly of their ways, use their free will to repent and find the Lord. Free will works in both directions! There *is* a way back to God from close to the gates of hell – as the criminal who was dying on the cross next to Jesus discovered – praise God!

SO WHAT HAPPENS WHEN WE BECOME A DISCIPLE OF JESUS?

When we say 'Yes' to Jesus and begin our pilgrimage of faith as one of His disciples, we are using our free will to choose life – eternal life. And that's a new life that begins here on earth and is continued through the transition of physical death, into the place we call paradise. After the resurrection of the dead at the end of time, we shall all enter into the glorious reality of God's eternal, heavenly Kingdom. Despite being sinners, God gave us the opportunity to use our free will to choose the incredible blessings that He's stored up for those who love Him. Hallelujah – what a Saviour! Such amazing grace is ours because He first loved us.

But when we start off on our journey as a disciple of Jesus, by saying 'Yes' to Him, we are at that moment signing up as a soldier of Jesus Christ. We have joined the Lord's army and are now under orders, **which means that we have voluntarily given up some of the rights that we might have claimed by virtue of having free will.**

A soldier doesn't have the freedom to remain in the armed forces of any country of the world, without saying 'Yes' to obeying the orders of those who are in authority over him. So, a soldier uses his or her free will to give up some of their free will! This is what Paul meant when he referred to Christians as being good soldiers of Jesus Christ who want to please their commanding officer (2 Timothy 2:3-4).

By saying 'Yes' to Jesus we are also saying 'No' to disobedience. As believers and disciples we do not have the freedom to say 'Yes' to the enemy's temptations, without that choice violating our commitment to Christ.

So, in the simplest of terms, our 'Yes' to living according to the ways of God means we are not allowing ourselves the freedom either to say 'Yes' to the ways of the enemy, or to say 'No' to the purposes of God. Even though we still have the capacity to make wrong choices, and enter into sin, we cannot do so without it damaging our relationship with God.

Most believers readily understand the sins they commit by saying 'Yes' to the enemy. These are usually referred to as the 'sins of commission', the things we consciously choose to do that we know are wrong. **But few believers have understood that, as far as the Lord is concerned, once we have chosen to follow Him, then our choosing not to do the things He asks us to do is just as sinful as doing those things He's told us not to do! Both are an act of rebellion – and, ultimately, rebellion is the essence of all sin.** It must be very important, therefore, for us to know exactly what Jesus has asked us to do.

SO WHAT HAS GOD ASKED US TO DO?

The teaching of Jesus is totally amazing. He manages to condense, into just a very few words, principles which the church has been continuously unpacking for two thousand years! And the Great Commission is, perhaps, the most condensed yet complete guideline that has ever been given by any leader, in any field of human endeavour or initiative, to those who would follow in his footsteps!

The final instructions of Jesus to the apostles, and through them to every generation of disciples until Jesus comes, are abundantly clear. Already we have seen:

- how the Great Commission provides the church with its mandate to go and make disciples (not believers);

- that its area of operation is to be multi-national – to all the nations (people groups) of the world without exception;
- that the church is to be made up of disciples, who are under the ultimate authority of their Commanding Officer and
- that, for them, obedience is a consequence of love.

Now we are looking at the instructions Jesus gave to the first disciples and the church thereafter to carry out in the years after He had returned to heaven and until He returns again.

Jesus uses just five words to tell us what it is He wants the church to do: *'everything I have commanded you'* (Matthew 28:20):

- *'everything'* means ALL;
- *'I'* means the person in whom is vested all authority in heaven and on earth (Matthew 28:18);
- *'have commanded'* means that the One who has all authority has given us an instruction that we can't say 'No' to, because we've said 'Yes' to Him;
- *'you'* means the disciples, those first apostles of the New Testament church.

So, to understand what the Great Commission says are the guidelines for all church activity, between the first and second comings of Jesus, we simply have to discover what instructions Jesus gave to the first set of disciples. If we know what these are, then we will know what the church should be doing, and finally what we should be doing as part of the church of Jesus Christ.

WHAT DID JESUS TELL THE DISCIPLES TO DO?

Fortunately we have a very clear record of what Jesus asked the disciples to do and what, therefore, were the foundational guidelines for the future history of the church. Matthew, Mark and Luke all record these instructions and have written them down in slightly different ways. But the message was the same in each of these Gospels – it was a message which defined what God intended the mission of the church to be for all of time. This is how Luke expressed it:

'When Jesus had called the Twelve together, he gave them power and authority to drive out all demons and to cure diseases, and he sent them out to preach the Kingdom of God and to heal the sick' (Luke 9:1-2). Mark remembered to include the wise instruction 'he sent them out two by two' (Mark 6:7) and tells us that 'they went out and preached that people should repent' (Mark 6:12). Matthew makes it clear that the commission Jesus gave to the disciples would not be easy (Matthew 10:11-42). There would be opposition from Satan, the god of this world; to take the wonderful truths of the Kingdom of God into the world would be like sending out sheep among wolves. Therefore all disciples of Jesus needed to be wise ('as serpents') to what the enemy was doing, yet remain innocent ('as doves') themselves of violating the Kingdom principles of Jesus through the power of the Holy Spirit (Matthew 10:16).

So, in essence, this is what Jesus asked the church to do. It is the declared manifesto of the church of Jesus Christ for all of time:

Preach repentance; proclaim the Kingdom of God; cast out demons and heal the sick.

This is what Jesus commissioned the first disciples to do and, through the words of the Great Commission, it is what He told those first disciples to teach the next generation of disciples to do, and the one after that, and the one after that, and the one after that … until we reach today's generation of believers, including you and me!

It was many years ago that I first discovered these truths for myself, as I searched the Scriptures to understand how I could fulfil the vision God had given me to bring healing to people. While it is so obvious to me now, when I first understood the simplicity and importance of what Jesus said, it hit me like the proverbial 'ton of bricks' to realise that there is much of the Great Commission that the church is simply not doing! I was shocked as I realised that the answer to questions about why the church so often seemed to be ineffective, lay in our corporate failure to understand all that the Great Commission contained.

Then I discovered that it wasn't a new problem! Even back in the days of Ezekiel the leaders of God's people were failing to look after the sheep and do what God required of them:

'You have not strengthened the weak or healed the sick or bound up the injured. You have not brought back the strays or searched for the lost. You *have ruled them harshly and brutally. So they were scattered because there was no shepherd and when they were scattered they became food for all the wild animals'* (Ezekiel 34:4-5).

The shepherds are those who should have been caring for the sheep. The sheep are the people of God, the wild animals are evil people and the powers of darkness who prey on the unprotected. When we first opened the doors of Ellel Grange, back in October 1986, it was as if the walking wounded flooded through the doors, desperate for the healing that Jesus had made available for His people, but which they had been unable to find inside the Body of Christ.

We were both overwhelmed and totally shocked at the depths of unhealed hurt, rejection, abuse, pain and brokenness that people had been taking to church Sunday by Sunday for years – even generations – but for which they had never been offered the answer, that Jesus provided for His children, through the Great Commission.

WELCOME – TEACH – HEAL

In those years of waiting for the work to begin, God had underlined for me Luke 9:11 as the foundational Scripture for the ministry that would later become known as Ellel Ministries. This verse says that Jesus **'welcomed the people'**, that He **'taught them about the Kingdom of God'** and that He **'healed those in need'**. Those three things, the welcome, the teaching and the healing became the foundation stones of the ministry.

I saw, in vision, that unless people are welcomed and loved they will never want to listen to the teaching. But unless they receive and understand the teaching about the Kingdom of God, they will never know what needs to be put right in their life, so that they can be healed. And without the healing they will simply have to go through the motions of being a Christian, without knowing the blessings on earth that God has reserved for His sheep. They would have to wait until they got to heaven before being set free!

But I passionately believe that Jesus wants His people to be set free NOW, so that for the rest of their days they can be freed to love and serve Him and know the joy that comes from His strength, empowering them to be a true disciple of Jesus Christ. So that they can live life to the full, developing their gifts and abilities, growing up families in the love and nurture of the Lord and fulfilling the plans and purposes of God.

HE HAS PROMISED TO BE WITH US

Right at the end of the Great Commission there is a short sentence which contains the wonderful promise that God is *'with [us] right to the very end of the age'* (Matthew 28:20). This wonderful promise is, however, often quoted and claimed out of context – which means that the conditions for the fulfilment of the promise haven't been met.

The promise is meant to be a great encouragement to the disciples of Jesus as they fulfil the Great Commission. I believe nothing gives the Lord greater pleasure and joy than seeing His children enjoying doing the things that the Father has prepared for us, and through which the sheep of His pasture are fed, healed and restored. But how does the Lord view those who would say they are disciples of Jesus, but who do not see the need for being obedient to the Great Commission that Jesus gave to His church? These are not easy things to say, for all of us are guilty. We are part of the church.

And in today's secular society, it's getting harder to speak out the truth of the Word of God, for the world has rejected God's Word as having any spiritual authority in their lives. Some of the public opposition that Jesus warned about in Matthew 10 is already here and a message of repentance is not welcomed, sometimes even inside the church, by people who don't recognise that the wrong things they are supporting or doing are sinful or, even, recognise the reality of sin at all! To own something as being sinful, you also have to own the reality of the God whose holiness is the measure through which we define what is sinful. We are truly battling for the Kingdom of God in what are, spiritually, very dark days indeed.

But if we set out to live the Great Commission, as being the foundation for Christian living, both in the fellowship of the church and in our private lives, then we can rightfully claim this wonderful promise for ourselves. He will be with us. Jesus knows exactly what it's like to feel the heat of opposition from the enemies of truth.

So, let's keep on moving forward, without fear, and let's begin the process of change, by asking the Lord to start the work of healing and restoration in each one of our lives. May we always be ready, willing and able to give a reason for the hope that we have in Jesus Christ (1 Peter 3:14-17).

SUMMARY

The final part of the Great Commission urges the apostles and their successors to do all the things that Jesus first taught His disciples to do - to proclaim the Kingdom of God, heal the sick and to cast out demons. These are the things that define what church is and if the Body of Christ does not bring salvation, hope and healing to the hurting and broken within their numbers, then we leave them to suffer the consequences of the enemy's inroads into their lives. When we do those things then He has promised to be with us until the end of the age.

PRAYER

Forgive me, Lord, for the times when I have chosen to ignore the instructions in Your word to do the things that You first taught Your disciples to do. Help me, Lord, to always be open to Your correction and healing in my own life, and to be alert in the Spirit to listen to Your voice in order to show Your love to those who are in need. In Jesus' name, Amen.

Stage 5, Chapter 5

THE ASCENSION

After a period of time in Galilee the disciples returned to the vicinity of Bethany, probably staying once more at the home of Lazarus, Mary and Martha. Jesus had been teaching them for *'a period of forty days and spoke about the Kingdom of God'* (Acts 1:3), and this included that vital time when Jesus gave them, and the whole church, the Great Commission as their foundational and guiding principle.

It was clear that Jesus was preparing the disciples for the day when He would return to heaven, for He began to give them instructions as to what they should do after He'd gone. He told them:

> '*"Do not leave Jerusalem, but wait for the gift my Father promised, which you have heard me speak about. For John baptised with water, but in a few days you will be baptised with the Holy Spirit"'* (Acts 1:4-5).

Even before His crucifixion, Jesus had told them to expect the gift of the Holy Spirit to come from the Father.

"'The Counsellor, the Holy Spirit, whom the Father will send in my name, will teach you all things and will remind you of everything I have said to you'" (John 14:26).

I often say to people, when teaching them how to read the Bible, not to worry about trying to remember everything they've read, for "if they get it in, the Holy Spirit can get it out!" If it's not gone in, the Holy Spirit can't get it out! And here Jesus is saying something very similar to the disciples. No doubt they were listening intently but were probably wondering how they would ever be able to remember everything they were hearing. It must have been a great comfort to them, when Jesus said that the Holy Spirit would remind them of everything they'd heard.

Once they'd heard what Jesus was saying, it would be permanently lodged in their memory. The Holy Spirit could then bring to mind, at the appropriate time, those things that they needed to teach to others or to write down, as they did in the four Gospels.

As I've said on other occasions, I've often found when I've been teaching or preaching, that quite suddenly Scriptures have come into my head that I haven't planned to use but which, when used, have proved to be exactly right for the occasion. The power of God's Word is truly:

'living and active. Sharper than any double-edged sword ... [penetrating] even to dividing of soul and spirit, joints and marrow, it judges the thoughts and attitudes of the heart' (Hebrews 4:12).

So, the disciples had already been prepared by Jesus for a significant moment that would come at some time in the future. No doubt they remembered what happened to He had been baptised by John and the heavens had opened. They had seen the Spirit of God descend upon Him like a dove – and then they'd heard the voice from heaven, saying, *"'You are my Son, whom I love; with you I am well-pleased'"* (Luke 3:22). They must have wondered if something like this would happen to them when what Jesus had promised actually happened.

THE ASCENSION

The disciples were about to experience a totally extraordinary moment for which nothing could have prepared them.

Jesus knew that He was about to leave, but He had promised that He would not leave them without the Comforter, the Holy Spirit. So the last words Jesus said related to the coming of the Spirit. When they were all gathered together He told them:

> *'"You will receive power when the Holy Spirit comes on you; and you will be my witnesses in Jerusalem, and in all Judea and Samaria, and to the ends of the earth"'* (Acts 1:8).

They were in *'the vicinity of Bethany'* (Luke 24:50) when *'he lifted up his hands and blessed them'* and as He did so, *'he left them and was taken up into heaven'* (Luke 24:51).

In the beginning of his next book, the Acts of the Apostles, Luke tells us that Jesus *'was taken up before their very eyes, and a cloud hid him from their sight'* (Acts 1:9). It's no surprise, therefore, that the disciples were transfixed, glued to the spot and were *'looking intently up into the sky as he was going'* (Acts 1:10).

There are many references in the Scriptures to angelic intervention. This must have been one of the most dramatic. You can imagine the scene, all the disciples who were present staring up into the sky, and not wanting to take their eyes off the spot where Jesus had disappeared from view in case they missed something! Then *'suddenly two men dressed in white stood beside them'* (Acts 1:10) and asked, what to the disciples must have been the most stupid question on the planet at that particular moment, *'"Men of Galilee, why do you stand here looking into the sky?"'* (Acts 1:11).

There was a very good reason why they were looking into the sky, and they must have wondered why these two men hadn't seen what they'd just seen – a man lifting off the ground unaided and disappearing from view into the clouds. Surely, everyone there must have seen what happened – even these two men in white!

But those two men in white were not men, they were angels. God had sent them to speak important words of encouragement to the disciples. They were words of prophetic good news that the fledgling church desperately needed to hear.

'Yes, He's gone … but, Yes, He's coming back … and one day, when He returns, He will come back in just the same way.' This is what the angels actually said, '"*This same Jesus, who has been taken from you into heaven, will come back in the same way you have seen him go into heaven*"' (Acts 1:11).

The angels were affirming to the disciples the truth of many prophetic Scriptures which tell of the coming time when Jesus will return. He will come, not as a babe in Bethlehem, but He will come to reign, in great power and glory. Even Daniel – way back in Old Testament days was seeing the return of the Messiah when he wrote:

'I looked, and there before me was one like a son of man, coming with the clouds of heaven. He approached the Ancient of Days and was led into his presence. He was given authority, glory and sovereign power; all peoples, nations and men of every language worshipped him. His dominion is an everlasting dominion that will not pass away, and his kingdom is one that will never be destroyed' (Daniel 7:13-14).

Revelation also talks about the millennial reign, when Jesus will reign on earth for 1000 years (Revelation 20:1-6).

What an encouragement it must have been for the disciples to be reminded of the fact that Jesus was coming back, just at the critical moment when they were experiencing the trauma, and almost certainly the grief, of Jesus leaving them. We will be looking more carefully at the return of Jesus when we talk about the second coming.

A NEW APOSTLE

Encouraged by the fact that they now had personal confirmation from the angels that one day Jesus was coming back, the disciples hurried back to Jerusalem to do what Jesus had told them to do – wait there until they received the gift of the Holy Spirit (Acts 1:4). And it was during these days of waiting that Peter assumed his position of responsibility as the leading apostle. The other disciples had seen what happened by the shores of Galilee, when Peter was commissioned by Jesus to feed the sheep. So it will have been natural for them to recognise Peter as their leader.

They had a job to do – elect a replacement for Judas. The Holy Spirit reminded Peter of the prophetic Scripture from the Psalms about what would happen to Judas, and also that the Scripture says, *'May another take his place of leadership'* (Acts 1:20 and Psalm 109:8).

They wisely looked for a new leader among the men who had been with them from the beginning – from John's baptism to the time when Jesus had just been taken from them. For, they said, he *'"must become a witness with us of his resurrection"'* (Acts 1:22).

Whilst it would be a great honour to be selected, it wasn't an appointment that many would want to be given! For the very word that is used here for 'witness', also means 'martyr'. And the fact is that most, if not all of, those first apostles were, sooner or later, martyred for their faith in Jesus.

There were two nominees – Joseph (called Barsabbas) and Matthias. The disciples prayed:

'"Lord, you know everyone's heart. Show us which of these two you have chosen to take over this apostolic ministry, which Judas left to go where he belongs." Then they cast lots and the lot fell upon Matthias; so he was added to the eleven apostles' (Acts 1:24-26).

The apostles were now restored to the number that Jesus had chosen and they could then wait, *'[joining'] together constantly in prayer, along with the women, and Mary the mother of Jesus, and with his brothers'* (Acts 1:14).

A TURNING POINT OF HISTORY

This was the moment when history was about to be turned upside down. It was as though a line had been drawn by God under everything that had gone before. The disciples were now waiting for something to happen – but, even though they had been told the Holy Spirit would be given to them, they had no idea what that would actually mean.

Behind closed doors they watched, waited and prayed, faithfully doing exactly what Jesus had told them to do. There must have been a nervous excitement in their spirits as they waited expectantly. We will be sharing in the excitement together as we see how the visitation of God's Spirit transformed a bunch of frightened men and women into an unstoppable army of spiritual warriors, who would, literally, turn the world upside down!

WAITING FOR GOD

But before we move on, may I share with you personally something of the preciousness and frustration of waiting for God? Most of us are not very good at waiting. We tend to be a little impatient when we know that something's going to happen, but it hasn't yet happened. We want to get on with it and move on. There have been times in my life when I have known in my spirit what God was going to do, but it seemed an eternity before He answered prayer and destiny was fulfilled.

But one thing I can say is this – those times of waiting for God have been some of the most precious times of my life. For, while waiting on God, you are also seeking after Him, and it is in those times when you seek God with everything you are, that you discover God rejoices to bless you with a rich awareness of His presence. It is during those times that I have learned the most about the nature and the character of God.

They have been times when I've soaked myself in the Word of God, looking for His guidance and direction, but discovered that God just wanted me to soak myself in His Word for His own sake. They have been times when I have discovered that not only did I desperately want and need God's company, but miracle of miracles I discovered that He wanted to enjoy my company as well. It was during those times of waiting that I learned about the richness of fellowshipping with the Lord. Just learning to trust Him, even when there didn't seem to be any reason for waiting for the vision that came from Him in the first place, to be fulfilled.

It is in those times that the walk, in human terms, can feel very lonely, but they are times when the loneliness of the earthly marathon, is compensated for a hundred times over by the richness of His presence and encouragement. For me, personally, the wait for the Spirit of God to open the door for the beginning of the work of Ellel Ministries felt as though it was going on forever. But looking back now, with the benefit of hindsight, I can say that all those years of waiting and daily praying were some of the most important days of my life – they were days when

God was dealing with deep issues in my own life and preparing me for something He knew all about, but which I didn't!

So, if you're going through a time of waiting, and wondering what's going to happen next, may I encourage you to make the most of the time and just enjoy fellowshipping with the Lord? You'll love His fellowship – He'll speak to your heart. He may need to bring some correction. He will definitely use the time to prepare and train you for what's ahead – and keep looking to Him. He will encourage you!

SUMMARY

After His resurrection Jesus spent forty days preparing, teaching and training the disciples to be leaders of the church. He told them that they were going to receive the gift of the Holy Spirit, and to wait in Jerusalem until they had received it. Then He went out with them to Bethany and the Mount of Olives, and there, after He'd reminded them of the coming of the Spirit, He ascended from earth to heaven. Two angels came and promised the disciples that He was coming back, so the men then hurried back to Jerusalem, appointed a replacement apostle for Judas and waited for what God had promised would happen next.

PRAYER

Thank You so much, Lord, for the wonderful promises in Your Word about the fact that You are going to return. Thank You so much for going to prepare a place for Your children in heaven. When there are things that You ask me to wait for, as You asked the disciples to wait in Jerusalem for the gift of the Holy Spirit, help me to be patient and to trust You, knowing that Your plans and timings are exactly right for me. In Jesus' name, Amen.

STAGE 6

Pentecost – Power for the Church

"Pentecost changed 120 fearful followers of Jesus into a band of fearless saints! The church without the Holy Spirit is like a car without gas – useless and going nowhere."

Stage 6, Chapter 1

THE SPIRIT FALLS ON THE CHURCH

There have been some highly significant moments in the history of the world that have happened in my lifetime. As with many people, I can remember exactly where I was and what I was doing at the time they happened. They were moments that changed the world.

For example, I can remember standing at the check-in desk at Toronto airport, when all the computers were suddenly closed down and flights cancelled, only minutes after the terrible events of 2001 when the twin towers were felled in New York City.

As a student I can remember walking through the streets of Oxford wondering if there was any point in doing any more studies that day, because the world might not exist in the morning. News of the great nuclear stand-off between Russia and the USA in Cuba was breaking, and we seriously thought the world was about to end.

As a child I remember exactly where I was when news of the death of King George the Sixth was announced on the radio and Princess Elizabeth was proclaimed Queen of England. I could list many other similar events, such as the collapse of the Berlin Wall and the assassination of President

PERSONAL NOTES

Kennedy, all of which are etched on my memory. And in a completely different arena I can remember exactly where I was when I was listening to the football (soccer) commentary of the World Cup Final in 1966, on the last occasion when the trophy was won by England.

And even though I wasn't alive at the outbreak of the Second World War, or the abdication of King Edward the Eighth, or the General Strike of 1926 or the death of Queen Victoria, I still feel very close to these events through hearing the first-hand accounts of my parents and my grand-parents. They were part of my upbringing and I felt as though they were part of me and my life! Our lives today are shaped and changed by the great events of the past.

AN EARTHSHAKING EVENT

Two thousand years ago there was no instant reporting of world events or the technology to carry news items around the world in seconds. It was therefore only the immediate eyewitnesses who could be impacted by what had happened. Until such news could be conveyed by word of mouth and then laboriously written down by hand, the rest of the world would be totally ignorant of the news.

So, when Jerusalem was literally shaken by a violent wind that came from heaven, it was, yes, a very local event. But, because the impact of that event changed the lives of those who were there for the rest of their days, and has continued to change lives ever since, it was significantly different from anything else that has ever happened. It was talked about so much that it became part of the corporate memory of the church and could never be forgotten, for the simple reason that it totally transformed the lives of the people in Jerusalem at the time. But what happened then has continued to happen in the lives of believers ever since!

The eyewitnesses weren't just mentally recording something they saw, as if it was something they weren't participating in. They were so involved in what was happening that afterwards they were radically changed on the inside. They would never be the same again. They could never go back to what they were like before.

THE PROMISE

The promise Jesus had given the disciples was that '*"in a few days' time you will be baptised with the Holy Spirit"*' (Acts 1:5), though none of them knew what would happen or what it fully meant. They knew what had happened when Jesus was baptised by the Holy Spirit at the beginning of His ministry, but they had no idea what Jesus had planned for them.

When Peter stood up and preached on that day (which we now know as Pentecost), he was being inspired by the Holy Spirit and given an understanding of what the disciples had experienced in the upper room. He was able to explain that Jesus had been *exalted to the right hand of God and [had] received from the father the promised Holy Spirit [which he had] poured out [on his followers]*" (Acts 2:33). The Spirit had come from the Father and had been given to the church by Jesus, the Son. This was the godly order established for receiving the Spirit by those first followers of Jesus, His disciples.

THE EVENT

After the ascension the disciples of Jesus, numbering about a hundred and twenty (Acts 1:15), had met and appointed a replacement apostle to serve instead of Judas (see previous Chapter). Together they were waiting for the promise of God to be fulfilled. They were, no doubt, fearful of the Jewish authorities and very reluctant to let their presence in Jerusalem become known.

Jesus had been crucified at Passover time and now the beginning of the Pentecost festival would already have been marked by the offering of a sheaf of barley. The Jewish feast of Pentecost, celebrating the completion of the barley harvest, took place exactly fifty days after the beginning of Passover. Jesus had been raised from the dead on the fourth or fifth day after the Passover festival had begun and He had then appeared to His disciples '*over a period of forty days and [spoken] about the Kingdom of God*' (Acts 1:3). So when Jesus ascended to heaven about forty-five days had already passed since the beginning of Passover.

From this we know that those one hundred and twenty believers were secretly waiting for a period of about five days to see how Jesus would fulfil His promise to them. It was on the day of Pentecost that God chose to release the Spirit on to believers in the same way that the Spirit had been given to Jesus at the beginning of His ministry. In Christian circles we tend to think that 'Pentecost' was a new name given to this special day. It was, however, a day that already existed in the Jewish calendar of festivals.

Just as there was a very important reason why God chose Passover to be the time when the Lamb of God would die for the sins of the world, I believe there are at least two reasons why God chose the day of Pentecost to pour out His Spirit on the church. The first is because Pentecost was a celebration of harvest, and the coming of the Spirit was to mark the beginning of the gathering in of the harvest of mankind. And the second was that Pentecost was also the day on which the Jewish people celebrated the giving of the Ten Commandments on Sinai – the day when the Law of God was given to His people. It was at Pentecost that God gave us the Spirit so that His Law could be written on our hearts.

SO WHAT HAPPENED?

The disciples were all together, presumably still in the upper room which had become their secret place of meeting, when the day of Pentecost dawned. After four or five days together they must have been wondering how much longer they were going to have to wait. No doubt some were already beginning to ask questions about what Jesus had said, wondering if they were going to be disappointed. And others would have been wondering if the next knock on the door might be the authorities coming to arrest them. They would have been days of great uncertainty.

It was in this situation that:

'Suddenly a sound like the blowing of a violent wind came from heaven and filled the whole house where they were sitting. They saw what seemed to be tongues of fire that separated and came to rest on each of them. All of them were filled with the Holy Spirit and began to speak in other tongues as the Spirit enabled them' (Acts 2:2-4).

All speculation was over. The event they had been waiting for had come to pass. The Spirit had come and they were now in the middle of an extraordinary manifestation of the presence of God, experiencing signs and wonders, which were beyond their capacity either to have generated themselves or to understand.

The unmistakeable evidence of God's presence by His Spirit overwhelmed them:

- They felt His power as the violent wind;
- They saw the manifestation of God's presence as the tongues of fire;
- They experienced God speaking through them when they spoke in tongues.

And they knew that it was God, through His Spirit, who was doing it, as the Spirit was enabling them.

They were experiencing a miracle they would talk about for the rest of their days. It was something they would immediately start to tell others about. They would tell it to their children and their grandchildren. They would describe it to other believers and preach and teach about it wherever they went. The "I was there when …" testimony of an eyewitness would carry the truth of what happened that day to all the known world. And, yes, it would become part of the corporate memory and experience of the church, talked about and written down for the rest of time, until Jesus comes again. The Spirit had come!

John the Baptist had prophesied that Jesus would *"baptise you with the Holy Spirit and with fire"* (Luke 3:16). On the day of Pentecost his prophecy was precisely fulfilled as the disciples were baptised with both the Spirit and the evidential fire of God.

This was the day the church was born. It had been conceived in the heart of God. Through the first Adam man broke relationship with God and lost his spiritual inheritance. Through the second Adam (Jesus) man's relationship with Father God was restored and his spiritual inheritance was given back. The Spirit of God is only available to those who are 'in Jesus', for it is only through Him that we can come to the Father and it is only from the Father that the Spirit comes.

There have been a few occasions in my own experience when the Spirit of God has come upon the ministry in great power. Just before a time of knowing the extraordinary presence and power of God, we have experienced violent winds, extreme and sudden storms, with thunder and lightning coming out of nowhere – just like the violent winds of Pentecost. It seems that, when the Spirit of God moves in great power, the physical realms (which were made by God) are also stirred.

THE FIRE OF GOD

In my student days I worked in a microbiological laboratory. The instruments we used had to be 100% free from all other organisms. The only way this could be easily and quickly achieved was by holding the working end of the instrument in the flame of a Bunsen burner for a few seconds. Cleansing the instrument in this way became second nature. No organism could survive the heat of the gas flame, cleansing was almost instantaneous and always effective. Fire cleansed.

On another occasion I remember preaching at a conference on the need to cleanse our homes of all ungodly things. On the following morning, people brought in hundreds of ungodly things that had been stored in their homes. The false gods were smashed by the elders of the church and everything that was consumable was burned. The flames consumed and destroyed everything. Fire destroyed.

When John the Baptist prophesied that Jesus would baptise with the Holy Spirit and with fire, he was indicating the importance of the two functions of the work of the Holy Spirit. Fire cleanses and fire destroys. So the evidence given to the church of the gift of the Holy Spirit was a visible symbol of the Spirit's presence. It came as *'tongues of fire, which separated and came to rest on each of them'* (Acts 2:3).

The gift of the Spirit was corporate to the whole body of believers who were present. They were, indeed, the whole church at that time. But it was also personal, to each believer individually. God intends the work of the Spirit to be both a cleansing and a destroying force within us. He wants us to participate with Him by giving Him permission to burn up all the dross of the enemy within us, and at the same time to cleanse us individually of the ungodliness that we can harbour in our hearts.

THE GIFT OF TONGUES

The evident presence of God will always drive believers to their knees in worship and adoration as soon as they sense they are walking on holy ground. As the disciples were baptised in the Holy Spirit, they were compelled in their hearts to worship God and discovered that out of their lips were coming words they had never learned and did not understand. They were *'declaring the wonders of God'* (Acts 2:12) in many different languages, some known and probably many unknown. One hundred and twenty believers, all worshipping God in a new language, must have been the most extraordinary experience of their lives.

In Jerusalem at that time were many *'God-fearing Jews from every nation under heaven'* (Acts 2:5). They had heard the sound of the sudden violent wind, but then they had heard the sound of a hundred and twenty people all telling of the wonders of God in different languages. They were totally bewildered by what was happening, especially by the fact that from the lips of these Galileans, who had never learned any other language than their local tongue, were coming out with words that they understood!

'"How is it,"' they asked, *'"that each of us hears them in his own native language?"'* (Acts 2:8). They were, understandably, utterly amazed by the event they were witnessing. They were there 'when it happened' and no doubt they, too, told their families, their children, their grandchildren what they had seen with their own eyes when the Spirit came in Jerusalem. Before very long they would have returned home to the many places they had come from (listed by Luke in Acts 2:8-11). They were people from almost every area of the world as it was known at that time. The Spirit had come, and the world was soon going to know about it! God had gifted His people with the means of telling the world on the day of Pentecost exactly what He wanted to say in a way that everyone could understand.

The believers were worshipping God from their hearts and what was coming out of their lips were the pure, unadulterated words of the Holy Spirit, giving worship and praise back to Father God. I have personally known of a few instances when the language given to a believer, baptised in the Holy Spirit, was understandable to the people around them. Once a man heard a speaker using a language unknown to him, but he was able to understand what was being said and translate it to a congregation, even though the speaker had never learned this language!

WHAT DOES THIS MEAN?

The people who saw and heard what was happening were *'Amazed and perplexed, so they asked one another, "What does this mean?"'* (Acts 2:12). They wanted an explanation. But not everyone who heard was impressed or excited by what was happening! As will always be the case, some made fun of them and accused them of all sorts of things, saying, *'"They have had too much wine"'* (Acts 2: 13), or put more simply *"They're drunk!"*

But what a great opportunity this gave the apostles to explain to the crowds what was going on. Peter, the leader of the new organisation that had just been born, began to answer all their questions, in one of the most comprehensive, authoritative and effective sermons ever preached! All their fear had gone, the Spirit gave them courage and they were not only born again, but now they were also empowered by the Spirit of God. The world had changed dramatically in a moment of time. Now God had poured out His Spirit on a body of believers. Far from being killed off at Calvary, the work of Jesus was about to explode!

Years ago, when trying to explain to a group of young people what it meant when the Spirit came, I wrote the following:

When the Spirit came, the church was born,
God's people shared in a bright new dawn.
They healed the sick, they taught God's word,
They sought the lost
They obeyed the Lord.
And it's all because the Spirit came
That the world will never be the same,
Because the Spirit came.

SUMMARY

After the ascension, the disciples waited in Jerusalem for the promise of the Holy Spirit's coming to be fulfilled. When the Spirit came, on the day of Pentecost, the place was shaken by a violent wind. The disciples saw tongues of fire come down on each one of them and they began to worship God in foreign languages as they spoke in tongues. The people who were in Jerusalem at the time were bewildered by all they experienced and wanted an explanation, which gave Peter the opportunity to preach the first sermon after the birth of the church!

PRAYER

Thank You, Lord, that You fulfilled Your promise to send the Holy Spirit to the disciples and in so doing brought the church to its moment of birth. Help me to fully understand what was happening then and what You want to do today. In the power of Your Spirit, come and work in and through my own life, and in and through the wider church. May the fire of the Spirit burn up the ungodly things in my life and cleanse me for service in the Body of Christ, In Jesus' name, Amen.

PETER'S FIRST SERMON

It's amazing how fifty days, and the dynamic presence of God the Holy Spirit, can change a frightened follower of Jesus into a fearless preacher of the truth! For that's exactly what happened to Peter when he was transformed from being a frightened rabbit, who would tell lies rather than be recognised for who he was, into a warrior for God who was afraid of no-one.

Whatever it was that happened to Peter when he was baptised in the Holy Spirit, it's something that we all desperately need. When the living power of the Holy Spirit came upon the disciples on the day of Pentecost, it was as if God Himself was suddenly loosed onto the streets of Jerusalem. Just as God is afraid of no-one, those one hundred and twenty believers were suddenly His fearless representatives. The fearlessness of God became their normal way of behaving. What an extraordinary transformation had taken place.

When you read the stories of how God took hold of men and women in the early church, and you see how they were unrestrained in their commitment to the truth, you realise how much today's church needs an injection of Holy Spirit's courage and bravery. In the face of a determined onslaught by the powers of darkness to eliminate living faith from public life, these are times when the people of God need to be on their knees in intercession for a fresh outpouring of the Spirit of God upon His church. Peter and all the apostles and disciples were changed men and women.

WHAT DOES THIS MEAN?

The crowds in Jerusalem were bewildered and amazed by what they were seeing and hearing. They had heard the violent wind storm hit the place where the disciples had been hiding and had then heard them praising God in tongues. They wanted answers. I've often said that one of the greatest problems with many evangelistic sermons is that the preacher is answering questions that his hearers aren't asking! It's no wonder people don't respond to the Gospel when they're not interested in what's being said.

But when Peter stood up to preach on the day of Pentecost, the people were asking all the questions and Peter was glad to answer them. They therefore listened to what was said and responded to the message. They wanted answers and were like hungry people waiting to be fed.

When people come to an Ellel Centre for a healing retreat it's usually because they have reached a critical point, often a crisis, in their lives. Some have been going to church for many years and may have heard the key points of the foundational teaching that we give on the retreats on many occasions. So, you might ask, why haven't they put the teaching into practice in their lives before?

The answer is often that, in the past, they haven't had a reason for wanting to either listen to such teaching or, more importantly, obey it. But when a person's health and wholeness is at stake, and they are now asking the right questions, it's amazing how people will then listen to the answers and hurry to put them into practice! As a result we often see major breakthroughs in people's lives, simply by their applying the truth of God's Word to their lives!

Then Peter 'stood up with the Eleven, raised his voice and addressed the crowd: "Fellow Jews and all of you who live in Jerusalem, let me explain…

these men are not drunk, as you suppose. It's only nine in the morning! No, this is what was spoken by the prophet Joel:

'In the last days, I will pour out my Spirit on all people. Your sons and daughters will prophesy, your young men will see visions and your old men will dream dreams. Even on my servants, both men and women, I will pour out my Spirit in those days and they will prophesy. I will show wonders in the heaven above and signs on the earth below, blood and fire and billows of smoke. The sun will be turned to darkness and the moon to blood before the coming of the great and glorious day of the Lord. And everyone who calls on the name of the Lord will be saved' (Acts 2:17-21).

I have quoted this prophetic passage in full because of its great importance to the Body of Christ – both then and now. God has promised His Spirit in these days to all believers – men and women, young and old, without exception. The promise was not just for those one hundred and twenty disciples but for the whole Body of Christ, of every generation until Jesus comes again and that, of course, includes you and me!

I will never forget the season in my own life when I was crying out to God for more of Himself, as I prayed into the vision God had given that eventually led to the establishment of Ellel Ministries. I had read many books and knew that there were people in my day who were experiencing the baptism of the Holy Spirit as it had been in the early days of the church. I knew from Scripture that it was only in the power of the Spirit that anyone could ever set out to do the works of the Kingdom.

I became desperate for the reality of God and night after night would cry out to Him. I learnt during that time that God loves to hear the prayer of desperation – the prayer that comes from a heart that has run out of ideas as to how to fix things for oneself. I had given up trying and had become totally dependent on God to do it His way!

Then, one night, I had fallen into a deep sleep when, suddenly, I was wide awake and, thinking the house was on fire, because I was so hot. I put out my hand to pick up the telephone to call the fire brigade! But before I could dial the numbers I realised there was no fire, although I was glowing, almost burning, from head to foot and in the midst of it all I heard the quiet, but comforting voice of God saying, "It's OK it's only Me!"

For me those words meant something. Because, as a child, if I was ever left in the house for a short time by myself, when my Mum came back home, she would open the door and call out, "It's OK it's only me." Those words meant safety – they meant that the owner of the house was in residence and I had no reason to fear.

So, when I sensed the Lord using exactly the same words to me, He was saying, "Don't worry, the owner of the house is in residence!" At that moment I knew His overwhelming presence as He baptised me with His Holy Spirit. No, I didn't see any flames, but I did feel the heat. And yes, from then on I was able to speak in tongues. But over and above these precious signs, it was the reality of knowing His presence in a deeper way than ever before that impacted and changed me.

Many, many things began to change as I experienced some of the gifts of the Holy Spirit (1 Corinthians 12:7-11). And, ever since, I have been finding out more and more about what it means to live in the dynamic reality of the presence of the Spirit of God.

PETER TELLS THEM THE TRUTH

When Peter stood up to preach, he was addressing the Jews who were in Jerusalem at that time – among them were many visitors to Jerusalem, as well as those resident in Jerusalem who knew all about how the Jewish authorities had crucified Jesus. He began to tell them exactly what had happened to Jesus. He described how Jesus had been killed by wicked men who *'had put him to death by nailing him to the Cross'* (Acts 2:23). Then he explained how God had raised Him from the dead *'because it was impossible for death to keep its hold on him'* (Acts 2:24).

He quoted more prophecies from the Psalms in which David told of these things, even *'of the resurrection of the Christ'* (Acts 2:31). All Peter's nervousness and fear had gone. He, himself, was evidence of the fact that the Holy Spirit had come, as he spoke out in an extraordinary way what the Spirit was putting into his mind and speaking through his lips.

'"God has raised this Jesus to life, and we are all witnesses of the fact. Exalted to the right hand of God, he has received from the Father the promised Holy Spirit and has poured out what you now see and hear"' (Acts 2:32-33).

And then in a powerful statement which was guaranteed to make him very unpopular with the authorities, he said, *"'Therefore, let all Israel be assured of this: God has made this Jesus, whom you crucified, both Lord and Christ'"* (Acts 2:36). You can always tell when the Holy Spirit is empowering the words of a preacher – the effect on the people, whose hearts truly are after God, is to bring them to repentance. For the Spirit will always draw attention to the truth about Jesus, and when people look at their own lives and put them beside the only measure of perfection that God has ever given us, the life of Jesus, we quickly see ourselves in a completely new light. And that's exactly what happened in Jerusalem on the day of Pentecost!

When 'the people heard this, *'they were cut to the heart and said to Peter and the other apostles, "Brothers, what shall we do?"'* (Acts 2:37). I just love it when people ask the questions to which you're longing to give an answer! I can imagine that all of heaven was looking down at this moment. Peter's sermon had reached its climax and the first men and women for whom Jesus had died, who now had the opportunity to respond to the Gospel message, were waiting to hear what Peter was going to say.

"'Repent and be baptised, every one of you, in the name of Jesus Christ for the forgiveness of your sins. And you will receive the Holy Spirit. The promise is for you and your children and for all who are far off – for all whom the Lord our God will call'" (Acts 2:38-39).

There is a distinct similarity between the words John the Baptist used to begin his ministry, the words Jesus used to begin His, and these words used by Peter at the beginning of his own ministry – repent and be baptised. Both John and Jesus said, *"'Repent, for the Kingdom of heaven is near'"* (Matthew 3:2 and 4:17). Peter didn't use the phrase about the Kingdom of heaven being near, for, by the time Peter stood up to preach, the kingdom of heaven had already come and the authority of the King was being administered, through the work of the Holy Spirit, from the throne room of God, with Jesus at the right hand of the Father.

So Peter simply said *"'Repent and be baptised' "*– baptism being an outward sign of an inner choice to repent and turn back to God. And that Gospel message hasn't changed, and never will till Jesus comes again. It is still the most urgent and important message that everyone on the planet needs to hear. For without repentance there can be no new life. Without the new life, which comes from God, there can be no empowering from on high through the baptism of the Holy Spirit. And without the Holy Spirit, the church simply becomes a powerless religious club of no eternal consequence!

And Peter emphasised that the promise of the Spirit wasn't just something that was for those first disciples, the apostles, it was a gift for everyone – for those present on that day, their children and for everyone who is 'far off', meaning everyone who will eventually hear the message, throughout the history of the church.

THE HARVEST BEGINS

We saw yesterday that the day of Pentecost was a harvest festival in the Jewish calendar. Well, when the people responded to the message that Peter preached, there was an amazing harvest of souls for the Kingdom of God. The New Covenant festival had begun, as the life which had been contained within one man, Jesus, for the period of His life and ministry, was unleashed from heaven through all believers.

As far as Satan was concerned, when Jesus was alive, he had done everything he could to prevent this one man, Jesus, from completing His mission. But now things were so much worse for Satan. Firstly Jesus was no longer dead, and secondly, all His followers were empowered by the Spirit of God that had empowered Him. The Kingdom of God was being established here on earth, in direct response to the prayer that Jesus taught the disciples to pray, *'Your Kingdom come, your will be done, on earth, as it is in heaven'* (Matthew 6:10).

And that is exactly what was happening, the Kingdom of God was being established in the lives of thousands of new believers who were being baptised. Luke tells us that on that first day of the church about three thousand souls were added their number (Acts 2:41). What a triumph! What a harvest! The Spirit of God had truly come.

Today we can look back, not just at that first day of the harvest, but at two thousand subsequent years of sowing and reaping of the Kingdom harvest. And we need to avoid any complacency about the harvest not yet gathered in and be willing to play our part in the Great Harvest that is yet to be fulfilled.

A PRAYER FOR YOU TO MAKE YOUR OWN

Today, I'm making our closing prayer a vital part of our personal pilgrimage together with God. May I suggest that you spend some personal time with God, reading His Word, confessing your sins and receiving God's forgiveness, before slowly and meaningfully praying this prayer to your Heavenly Father. And if you haven't personally ever been baptised, may I ask you to consider being obedient to what the Word of God says – *'repent and be baptised'*? I know that for many people we have prayed with over the years that this has been a major source of blessing for the rest of their lives.

Here's the prayer:

Thank You, Lord, for the new life You have given me. Without You I would be lost and without hope. I'm so grateful for the gift of salvation that I received when I first came to You as a sinner in need of a Saviour. Thank You that Jesus died on the cross for me. I stand amazed at Your love and Your mercy.

I so much want to love and serve You but recognise that without the empowering of Your Spirit I will be unable to know the fullness of Your presence or have the power to do the things that You have prepared in advance for me.

I recognise that the primary key to being baptised in the Holy Spirit is unconditional repentance before You. I come to you afresh today and invite You to show me any areas of darkness that still prevail in my life, so that I may fully repent of them and be cleansed by You.

Then, Lord, I ask that You will baptise me afresh in Your Spirit, and empower and equip me to serve You. Come with Your fire to cleanse me from within. Release through me, I pray, the gifts I need to fulfil my life's calling. Grow within me the fruit of the Spirit. Use me to be a harvester of souls for the Kingdom. In the name of Jesus, Amen.

SUMMARY

When the Spirit came the disciples were transformed. So much so that Peter had the courage to stand up and preach to the Jews who had crucified Jesus about what they had done! The heart of his message was his instruction to repent from sin and be baptised and receive the gift of the Holy Spirit which, Peter said, was for everyone. The Holy Spirit so empowered Peter that people were convicted of their sin and responded to the Gospel. Three thousand new believers were added to their number on that very first day of the church!

THE ACTS OF THE APOSTLES

Before we look at some of the things that were happening in the early church, I wonder how you are doing in today's church as we walk together through *Journey to Freedom*? I know there are many people whose lives are being challenged by what we are studying together day-by-day – including my own. I hope you're remembering to make a note of the things God is especially speaking to you about, as a personal record of your walk with Him.

The *Acts of the Apostles* is more than just the title of Luke's second book. It's an exact description of what the apostles were doing in those early days, months and years of the church. Everything was new: purity and holiness were paramount and God was with the apostles every step of the way as they emerged from the closet of the upper room into the white heat of spiritual reality.

It was one thing for Jesus, the totally sinless Son of God, to be baptised in the Holy Spirit and to be operating in the power of the Spirit. It was quite another for fallen men and women to be following in Jesus' footsteps and doing the works of the Kingdom, as redeemed, forgiven and empowered people. Their daily meetings must have been thrilling times with accounts of everything that was happening around them as they compared notes at the end of the day and told everyone else what God had done.

I know what it's like at the end of a conference or a teaching weekend in a local church. Everyone wants to get together and compare notes about all their experiences as they tell each other what God did as He blessed and healed people. They are very exciting times of fellowship and sharing. How wonderful must have been those meetings the apostles had with all the disciples!

Every day the apostles were teaching as the Holy Spirit told them what to say, they were breaking bread together and praying and *'everyone was filled with awe, as many signs and wonders were done by the apostles'* (Acts 2:43). They shared everything one with another and for an initial season they not only had the favour of God, but the favour of the people as well. *'And the Lord added to their number daily those who were being saved'* (Acts 2:47). They were unbelievably exciting and totally unforgettable days!

Occasionally I talk about some of the experiences we had at Ellel Grange in the early days of the ministry. The Spirit of God came down in power on one of our early training weekends. We were selecting people to join the regular ministry team for our Healing Retreats, but after the Sunday morning time of worship and teaching, the power and the presence of God was so real that for days it was hard to do anything else but pray for people, worship, minister to those under conviction of sin, and pray for deliverance and healing.

That weekend, especially, is etched on my memory and I know that till my dying day, the experience of being in a place where the presence of God was so tangible that everyone felt it, will inspire and encourage me to keep on going, even when the going may be really tough – as it often is!

HEALING – THE CRIPPLED BEGGAR

One day, as Peter and John entered the temple, they were asked for money by a crippled man, who regularly begged by the temple gate called 'Beautiful'. Peter and John looked straight at him and Peter told the beggar to look at them. *'So the man gave them his attention, expecting to get something from them'* (Acts 3:5).

Then Peter surprised the man (and probably himself as well) by saying:

'"Silver or gold I do not have, but what I have I give you. In the name of Jesus Christ of Nazareth, walk". Taking him by the right hand he helped him up, and instantly the man's feet and ankles became strong. He jumped to his feet and began to walk. Then he went with them into the temple courts, walking and jumping and praising God' When all the people saw him walking and praising God, they recognised him as the same man who used to sit begging at the temple gate called Beautiful, and they were filled with wonder and amazement at what had happened to him (Acts 3:6-10).

The crowds immediately gathered round Peter, John and the formerly crippled man. They wanted to know what was going on and how this amazing healing could possibly have happened. So, Peter, once again grabbed the opportunity and began to answer their questions:

'"Men of Israel, why does this surprise you? Why do you stare at us as if by our own power or godliness we had made this man walk?"' (Acts 3:12).

Then Peter stepped into his destiny as the Holy Spirit filled his mouth with truth and he told everyone there, right in the temple courts, about what they had done to Jesus, how God had raised Him from the dead and that it was through having *'"faith in the name of Jesus"'* that the man they saw and knew before them *'"was made strong"'* (Acts 3:16).

Then Peter called them once again to repent *'"so that [their] sins may be wiped out, that times of refreshing may come from the Lord"'* (Acts 3:19). And so Peter continued with his amazing sermon – it is well worth carefully reading through Acts 3:12-26. It's full of wonderful truth. Peter's courage knew no limits. To say these things in the courts of the very temple that was the seat of power of the authorities who had crucified Jesus, would certainly invite criticism – if not worse. It wasn't long in coming.

IN JAIL FOR PREACHING TRUTH!

Even while Peter was speaking, the Sadducees and the temple guard came to stop him. They seized him and John and put them in jail. But the authorities had a problem on their hands. There were now a great number of people who had heard the message and believed it – the men alone numbered five thousand (Acts 4:4)!

The next day, Peter and John were brought before the very people who had engineered the death of Jesus – Annas, Caiaphas and the high priest's family. Peter had no desire to tell lies about his association with Jesus, and when the priests asked them *'by what power or what name [he did] this'* (Acts 4:7), referring to the healing of the crippled beggar, Peter was filled with the Holy Spirit and preached another sermon – this time to the high priests themselves!

The central point of Peter's message was his courageous statement to the custodians of religious Judaism, that *'"Salvation is found in no one else, for there is no other name under heaven, given to men, whereby we must be saved"'* (Acts 4:12). By now, even the high priests were impressed:

'when they saw the courage of Peter and John and realised that they were unschooled, ordinary men. They were astonished and they took note that these men had been with Jesus. But since they could see the man who had been healed standing there with them, there was nothing they could say' (Acts 4:13-14).

This is amazing stuff. Even the priests recognised that *'these men had done an outstanding miracle'* (Acts 4:16) and the best they could do was tell them not to speak any more in the name of Jesus. Which brought the even more courageous response from Peter:

'"Judge for yourselves, whether it is right in God's sight to obey you rather than God. For we cannot help speaking about what we have seen and heard"' (Acts 4:19-20).

When Peter and John returned to all the disciples, they told them everything that had happened and there was great joy and praise and thanksgiving to God. And their joy turned to intercession for even more boldness and prayer to God for Him to perform more miracles! (Acts 4:23-30).

'After they prayed, the place where they were meeting was shaken. And they were all filled with the Holy Spirit and spoke the word of God boldly' (Acts 4:31).

There is an important principle contained within this last verse of Scripture. We can keep on being filled with the Holy Spirit! When Paul wrote to the church in Ephesus, he exhorted them to be filled with the Spirit (Ephesians 5:18). In fact, the Greek word he used for *'be filled'* actually means *'be continuously filled'!*

The reality is we're all creatures of flesh and there's always a battle within for spiritual authority in our lives. We continually need to come to Him for cleansing from all the soulish and spiritual dirt we pick up because of our fallen carnal nature. In this very visual world we are constantly being showered with ungodly images, tempted by less than wholesome entertainments or activities, and bombarded by songs whose words promote rebellion and immorality. Paul recognised that we need to be continually filled with the Spirit so that we'll always be equipped and ready for whatever the Lord may ask us to do.

HEALING AND EVANGELISM

There's a very close link between healing and evangelism. When a person is born again of the Spirit of God, it's a miracle of God's grace and mercy. And when a person is healed by the power of God, it's equally a miracle of God's grace and mercy. When people are healed, it not only transforms their lives, but it speaks right into the heart of those who see and hear about what God has done.

A healing church will always be an evangelising church. People who have been healed have a story to tell, which impacts unbelievers, who then have a reason to ask the right questions. On almost every one of the thousands of Healing Retreats that Ellel Ministries have conducted around the world, we have rejoiced to lead people to personal faith in Jesus as Lord of their lives. When Peter healed the crippled man, it set in motion a chain of events that led to many people being converted.

It's vital that we, as the Body of Christ, should always be ready – not just to give a reason for the faith we have, but ready to minister the healing love of Jesus into the hurting lambs that so often make up the flock of God!

'HOLY' CHURCH

The early church was not only a fellowship with a heart for healing; it was also a community in which they shared together their belongings and provided for the needs of each other.

'From time to time those who owned lands or houses sold them, brought the money from the sales and put it at the apostles' feet, and it was distributed to anyone as he had need' (Acts 4:34-35).

But God required honesty and integrity in the lives of those who were walking in the reality of the Holy Spirit's presence and power, for the Spirit is a 'HOLY' Spirit, and trying to compromise with God is dangerous. When Paul was giving his readers guidelines for receiving the bread and the wine in the Lord's Supper, he emphasised how important it was to examine oneself before eating the bread and taking the cup. For, he said, if you take the elements of Communion at the same time as continuing to live with unconfessed and unforgiven sin, there will be consequences, even to the extent, he said, that *'many among you are weak and sick and a number of you have fallen asleep'* (1 Corinthians 11:30), meaning that some have died as a result!

One of the members of the fellowship, in those early Pentecostal days, was Joseph (also known as Barnabas), from Cyprus. He had *'sold a field he owned and brought the money and put it at the apostles' feet'* (Acts 4:37). Another couple, Ananias and Sapphira, also had a piece of land which they sold to give to the Lord's work but they kept back part of the money for themselves. So, when Ananias put the money at the feet of the apostles, he gave the impression that it was the whole amount, which was untrue.

They were cheating God. Peter, obviously operating in the gift of discernment and having a word of knowledge, asked Ananias:

'"How is it that Satan has so filled your heart that you have lied to the Holy Spirit and have kept for yourself some of the money you received for

the land? … What made you do such a thing? You have not lied to men but to God'" (Acts 5:3-4).

Immediately, the judgement of God fell on Ananias, and he collapsed and died. Later, his wife, not knowing what had happened was asked by Peter if the money they had given was the whole amount they had received for the field. When she said *'"Yes, that is the price"'* (Acts 5:8), repeating the lie that they had obviously agreed on together, Peter asked, *'"How could you agree to test the Spirit of the Lord?"'* (Acts 5:9). Sapphira also fell down dead just as the men who had recently buried her husband came in through the door. And so it was that both Ananias and Sapphira were buried together on the same day! These were awesome days, and it's not surprising that Luke tells us *'great fear seized the whole church and all who heard about these events'* (Acts 5:11).

HOLY FEAR

Exodus 20:20 tells us that it's the fear of the Lord that will keep us from sinning. This isn't the sort of fear that you might have of a bad and vicious man. It's a fear motivated by love. It's a fear of the consequences of introducing sin to something that has been made holy by the presence of God – a fear motivated by worship, respect and honour.

If you really love someone, the last thing you will want to do is cause them pain because of your actions – you will be afraid of hurting them. Jesus put it very simply when he said, *'"If anyone loves me, he will obey my teaching"'* (John 14:23). We desperately need to have that fear in our hearts that results from our great love for the Lord.

We need to fear bringing into the holy presence of God that which we know to be unholy. Jesus hated the deception of hypocrisy, especially when people made a show of being very religious. In their hearts they were a million miles away from knowing what the loving holiness of God is really like. They were also harbouring sinful desires in their heart.

Stories such as that of Ananias and Sapphira are in the Scriptures, not because God wants us all to live in abject fear of dropping dead, but because He wants us to understand that the unholy cannot remain in His presence. If we nurture the unholy, then God will withdraw His presence from us. It was for this reason that Satan was thrown out of heaven in the first place. Ananias and Sapphira's experience stands as a warning to us, as believers, of what God thinks when we consciously say one thing, but in reality are doing another. We lose our covering and protection. However, this doesn't mean there can be no forgiveness for believers when they sin, for John was speaking to believers when he said, *'If we confess our sins, he is faithful and just and will forgive us our sins and purify us from all unrighteousness'* (1 John 1:9).

When sin and sinfulness are covered by the shed blood of Jesus then we can freely, as forgiven sinners, enter into His presence without fear. That's what Jesus died for. But when we say one thing but are really lying, in the hidden places of our lives to God, ourselves and others, we are betraying the very beliefs we say we have. We are putting ourselves into a dangerous place before God. It's for these sorts of reasons that, although many saw *'the apostles [perform] many miraculous signs and wonders among the people'* (Acts 5:12), they didn't *'dare to join them, even though they were highly regarded'* (Acts 5:13).

People who saw the good in what was being said and done, but whose hearts had not been convicted by the Holy Spirit and brought to repentance, could not bring themselves to join this extraordinary group of white-hot believers. They knew that they could not live up to the inner and outer holiness that was being demonstrated in their lives. They feared the consequences of joining them with unrepentant hearts!

'Nevertheless, more and more men and women believed in the Lord and were added to their number' (Acts 5:14). When the Holy Spirit convicts and people respond with repentant hearts, they have nothing to fear from a holy God, for their sin is covered before the Father by the shed blood of the Son. He has become their righteousness and, as forgiven sinners, they can rejoice in God's presence.

The events in the Acts of the Apostles had a dramatic effect on the people of Jerusalem as they watched in amazement at what God was doing.

'As a result people brought the sick into the streets and laid them on beds, and mats so that at least Peter's shadow might fall on some as he passed by. Crowds gathered also from the towns around Jerusalem, bringing their sick and those tormented by evil spirits, and all of them were healed' (Acts 5:15-16).

Yes, these were amazing days! But God didn't intend those days to be merely records of ancient history. I believe He longs for you and me to get hold of the message of these first few chapters of Acts so much that we won't leave any stone unturned in seeking for the reality of His presence. His presence comes through the indwelling power of the Spirit of God. This is what Jesus promised. God wants us to serve Him in the power of the Spirit, and He wants us to serve Him – because we love Him!

SUMMARY

The Acts of the Apostles is not just the title of a book. It's an accurate record of how God was working through the disciples in the early church, and an example to the church of how He still wants to work in and through His people. When people saw God at work they were convicted by the His Spirit and had an opportunity to respond to the message that was preached by the apostles. The ministry of the Gospel and the ministry of healing were never intended by the Lord to be separated. Today He's once again restoring to His church a passion for teaching and ministering the Kingdom of God, in the same way as He did at the beginning.

PRAYER

Thank You, Lord, for the amazing stories we read in Your Word, of what the early leaders of the church did in the name of Jesus and by the power of the Holy Spirit. I pray that You will restore to me a desire to see You at work in and through the Body of Christ today. I ask You to show me all the uncleanness in my heart which limits Your power. Please cleanse me so I'll be fully equipped to do the works of Your Kingdom. In Jesus' name, Amen.

Stage 6, Chapter 4

QUALIFICATIONS FOR SERVICE

Have you ever discovered that the way God does things is often very different from the way you would do them? Many years ago, close to the beginning of the work of Ellel Ministries, we planned a special weekend for selecting potential members of our Associate Ministry Team at Ellel Grange.

God had already shown us that it would be important for the people who would serve on the Ministry Team at our Healing Retreats, to be people from many different local churches, of different denominations. In this way the work would be solidly anchored in the local churches, which God was raising up the ministry to serve. So, we let people know that we were planning a special training weekend for anyone who thought they might like to be considered.

The Centre was packed for the weekend with both local people and people who had come from farther afield and were staying overnight in the building. I had planned a programme of teaching, and the core team of people who were working together to establish the ministry were also going to interview everybody over the weekend, so that we could assess together who we thought might be suitable. We were looking forward to the event and thought we had put together a very good programme.

Everything went fine until the Sunday morning, when the Lord prompted me to dispense with the teaching on aspects of personal ministry, to teach instead on spiritual warfare from the book of Nahum. It was a dramatic and unexpected change to the programme which took me by surprise as much as the people who were there. Earlier in the week the Lord had clearly spoken to me, telling me to read the book of Nahum, something I couldn't remember ever specifically doing before, other than as part of a daily reading plan.

As I read the three short chapters of Nahum, I knew the Lord was speaking to me. I was specially impacted by some words which, in the Good News translation read: *'Where the LORD walks, storms arise; the clouds are the dust raised by his feet'* (Nahum 1:3). But I had no idea that God was going to use this book over the coming weekend, or that as the Lord walked through the ministry, His feet would cause such a 'dust-storm'! Having read the book, I put it aside and prepared for all the people who were about to walk through our doors for the weekend.

When Sunday morning came, I looked at the pre-planned programme and had no real desire to teach it. I couldn't understand what was going on until I sensed that gentle but persistent voice of the Lord telling me to teach from the book of Nahum! Then, when I did so, and the Holy Spirit spoke through the words of the prophet, it was increasingly obvious that the Spirit of God was powerfully present in the room. So much so, that within a few minutes of the teaching having finished, we were completely overwhelmed by the presence of God.

It was an extraordinary experience as the Holy Spirit brought conviction of sin, baptism in the Spirit, deep deliverance and life-transforming change in many people's lives. It also brought us into a deep understanding of the spiritual realms, and of how Satan hated the ministry of healing, which was undoing so many of the strongholds he had on people's lives. There could be no going back into what I've sometimes called a 'tea and tissues' ministry, where there are lots of tears and tender loving care, but little attention to the hard spiritual realities that Jesus taught His disciples to deal with, and which we were quickly realising He still wants us to deal with today!

It became clear that this was going to be a ministry to which many of the people who had come on the weekend didn't feel called. But there were others who were so impacted and changed themselves by what God had done, that nothing would keep them from wanting to help others in the future. And so it was that God had His way of selecting the team who were able and willing to take the work forward. It was important that those who decided to walk with us in the work would be comfortable with the ministry God had brought into being. We hardly used the notes we had made in selecting the team – God had made the selection for us, in His way! And it wasn't a way we could possibly have thought of! There is a specific reason why I have told this story now, which will shortly unfold.

BACK IN JERUSALEM!

Back in Jerusalem the work of the early church was dramatically increasing in size and scope. Persecution by the Jewish authorities in no way closed them down. On the contrary, it had the opposite effect. So many people were now becoming believers in Jesus that the apostles were arrested and put in jail. But during the night an *'angel of the Lord opened the doors of the jail and brought them out'* (Acts 5:19) and told them to go and stand in the middle of the temple court *'and tell the people the full message of this new life'* (Acts 5:20). These were very dramatic days! The last place fearful believers would have wanted to preach the Gospel would have been in the middle of the temple, the powerbase of their accusers, but they joyfully obeyed what the angel had told them to do!

Meanwhile the elders of Israel, the Sanhedrin, had a rather unusual problem! They sent for the prisoners to come and stand trial, only to find that the jail was empty and their supposed prisoners were now *'standing in the temple courts teaching the people'* (Acts 5:25). So the captain of the temple guard was sent to arrest them again. He brought the apostles before the Sanhedrin to explain why they were still preaching about Jesus when they had been given *'strict orders not to teach in this name'* (Acts 5:28).

Once again Peter answered the charges, and said *'"we must obey God rather than men"'* (Acts 5:29), and again he explained how they had killed Jesus, but God had raised Him from the dead, and said *'"we are witnesses*

PERSONAL NOTES

of these things, and so is the Holy Spirit, whom God has given to those who obey him'" (Acts 5:32). As soon as they heard this, the elders wanted to put the apostles to death, but Gamaliel, a wise elder warned them that:

> *"'if their purpose or activity is of human origin, it will fail. But if it is from God, you will not be able to stop these men; you will only find yourselves fighting against God'"* (Acts 5:38-39).

It's important that we learn how to stand strong in our faith, despite what others may say or do. If they are fighting your godly actions, they are fighting God himself and they won't win!

The elders then agreed on the lesser punishment of flogging Peter and John and the apostles were once again ordered *'not to speak in the name of Jesus, and let them go'* (Acts 5:40). Flogging was a severe punishment, but the apostles rejoiced that *'they had been counted worthy of suffering disgrace for the Name'* (Acts 5:41). And despite what they had been told, *'day after day, in the temple courts and from house to house, they never stopped teaching and proclaiming the good news that Jesus is the Christ'* (Acts 5:42).

MANAGING THE CHURCH

The work of the church was growing so fast that it was already beyond the capacity of the apostles to handle everything that needed to be managed. And, as inevitably happens wherever there are human beings with vested interests, there were complaints coming to their ears that they didn't have time to deal with. Moses had had a similar problem – his time was being totally taken up with managing disputes as opposed to leading the people of God (Exodus 18:13-27).

The Grecian Jews felt that their widows were not being treated in the same way as the Hebraic Jews in the daily distribution of food. So the apostles gathered everyone together and told them that they couldn't give up the vital work of prayer and ministering the Word of God, so they were going to appoint seven men to act as managers of all the domestic issues that the growing number of believers was now involved in. People were pleased with their decision (Acts 6:2-5).

Returning now to the story I told earlier, at the beginning of the chapter, there was an obvious practical solution to the problem we had, but God wanted things done in a different way. And so it was in the early church. The obvious, practical solution would have been to identify people with practical management skills and put them in the job right away. Whilst that may sound obvious, it was wrong, for it's not what the apostles did.

A similar situation often comes up in local church leadership today when, for example, it's necessary to appoint a new treasurer for the fellowship. Often the church appoints someone because of their experience in dealing with money and figures, with little concern for anything else. But if that person doesn't have any understanding of the vision for the church, or is operating solely out of pragmatism rather than faith and spiritual wisdom, then they can become an obstacle to the work of the Spirit, as opposed to being a blessing to the fellowship.

It was issues such as this that were obviously the primary concern of the apostles when they decided to appoint seven men to manage the domestic affairs of the developing church. **They didn't look for people with a proven track record of good management. The primary qualification for service was spelled out by the apostles as men** *'who are known to be full of the Spirit and wisdom'* (Acts 6:3).

When Solomon was asked by God what he wanted at the beginning of his reign as king, he could have asked for wealth, long life, the death of his enemies or any of a hundred other things. But what Solomon chose was wisdom. God was pleased with his choice and said *'"I will give you a wise and discerning heart"'* (1 Kings 3:12). With wisdom Solomon would be able to make the right decisions that would, in turn, enable him to become wealthy and strong.

THE PRIMARY QUALIFICATIONS FOR SERVICE

It was essential for the apostles that whoever they appointed to manage the affairs of the church on their behalf, should have that gift of wisdom. The last thing the apostles wanted (or needed) was people who would make bad decisions, which would have caused the apostles even more problems than they had before. Wisdom was essential. The book of Proverbs is full of the wisdom of God. I sometimes find that spending half an hour just reading from this amazing book fills me afresh with new understanding from God about dealing with the realities of life. On occasions the advice it contains has been life changing and, even, lifesaving!

But the people the apostles were choosing not only needed to have wisdom, they needed to be full of the Holy Spirit. There was a very interesting phrase in Peter's response to the elders, who wanted to put him and the other apostles to death. He said that *"'God has given the Holy Spirit to those who obey him'"* (Acts 5:32). Obedience to the Lord is the primary responsibility of any man or woman of God.

In order to obey the Lord you first need to be able to hear the Lord and understand what He's saying, and with this in mind:

'they chose Stephen, a man full of faith and the Holy Spirit, also Philip, Procurus, Nicanor, Timon, Parmenas,, and Nicolas from Antioch. They presented these men to the apostles who prayed and laid hands on them' (Acts 6:5-6).

So, God's way of selecting people for positions of responsibility has always to be on the twin foundations of having wisdom and being full of the Holy Spirit. These are more important than any amount of practical skills, desire to help or, even, experience. Practical skills and experience are brilliant to have, but, without the Holy Spirit and God's wisdom, even the most able people can be constantly making mistakes and could, with misplaced priorities, become an obstacle to the very work we are seeking to be a part of. God turns our conventional wisdom upside down.

One day, in my business career, I sensed the Lord was giving me an idea that I could never have thought of for myself. I could either ignore it as being too way out for consideration, or follow it up, trusting that God knew best. Looking back now, I am so grateful that I had the wisdom to listen to what God was saying. It was one of the most important decisions I've ever made and even today, many years later, I am still being blessed by the fruit there has been from listening to the voice of God, as opposed to obeying the voice of practicality. God is the best businessman I have ever known!

The first lines of the great hymn written by William Cowper (1731-1800) express very clearly some of what I've been trying to say through today's teaching – *God moves in a mysterious way, his wonders to perform!*

What is certain is this. If we major on walking before God in obedience to Him and His Word, then the Holy Spirit will always feel welcome in our lives. And He will bring with Him the wisdom of God. Once people have been chosen and appointed, it's important to set them apart through the laying on of hands, as the apostles did here. We usually, also, anoint them with oil as a sign of their being set apart for service. These times are often very important opportunities for people to see and recognise the responsibilities that people have, so that they can respect and serve with them in the Body of Christ.

A SUGGESTION

Get your Bible, take a red pen and find a quiet place! Open your Bible at the book of Proverbs and work your way through this amazing book of wisdom. Every time you read something that impacts your spirit or seems relevant to your personal life, underline it in red.

When you've been right through the book (you might need more than one session, and that's OK) go back through the book meditating on everything you've underlined. And then pray about each underlined verse, asking the Spirit of God to make the wisdom of God, that's in His Word, to be the wisdom of God that's in your heart. Once you've got it in, the Holy Spirit can get it out!

Be blessed as you read – take this little exercise seriously and the lessons you learn will be a blessing to you for the rest of your days.

SUMMARY

As the early church grew in number, it also grew in its need for leaders to take up the work of managing the needs of the people. It was taking too much time away from preaching the Word, and the apostles couldn't handle everything. So they decided to appoint seven men to help with the many different needs that were arising. Rather than look for people who had the right sort of management skills, the apostles looked for those who were, first and foremost, full of the Holy Spirit and wisdom. Without these qualifications they wouldn't have been eligible for the appointment, even though they may well have been very able people. God's ways are different from ours (Isaiah 55:8-9) and it's vital we should follow Him and His ways, rather than tell God what we think He should be doing!

PERSONAL NOTES

PRAYER

Thank You, Lord, for this important lesson about who should be appointed to serve in the church. Forgive me for times in the past when I haven't taken note of the need to have wisdom and be filled with the Spirit. I want all my skills and abilities to be used for Your glory. From now on I want, above all, to have Your wisdom and be filled with Your Holy Spirit. In Jesus' name, Amen.

STEPHEN – THE FIRST MARTYR

Some Scriptures are hard to read – especially the prophecies that Jesus made about how His followers won't always be loved! He said that some would be persecuted and some, even, would become martyrs for their faith. We all tend to think that this won't happen to us and, in truth, it probably won't, but the reality is that in the twentieth century, there were more martyrs for the Christian faith than there had been in all the previous nineteen centuries put together. This is an awesome and true statistic.

CHRISTIAN MARTYRS

I was a boy of 12 when, in 1956, the Christian world was deeply shocked by the happenings in South America. News was filtering out of Ecuador of the martyrdom of five young American missionaries, who had been speared to death by Auca Indians. Their story, told in the amazing book *Through Gates of Splendour : The Five Missionary Martyrs of Ecuador* (Elisabeth Elliot, Authentic Media, 2005) tells of what happened to these five men, when the Aucas came toward them with their spears. The missionaries did not shoot back with their guns for they knew that, if they shot the Indians, they might save their own lives but they would never be able to teach the Aucas about Jesus! So they chose to let themselves be killed, leaving their wives as widows, so the Aucas might have another chance to become Christians.

The Aucas always remembered those five strange white men who had been so kind to them and had not used their guns. Some years later, when more missionaries tried again to speak to the Aucas about Jesus, they were ready to listen. Several of the men who had been involved in the killing of Jim Elliot and his friends with their spears, later became Christians. One of them gave this testimony at a meeting. He counted on his fingers and said, "I have killed twelve people with my spear! But I did that when my heart was black. Now Jesus' blood has washed my heart clean, so I don't live like that anymore. God's love has changed my life!"

Very recently the reality of how dangerous some parts of today's world are for Christians came home to me in a very real and vivid way. A lovely couple, who had met on our nine week training school at Glyndley Manor, married and went to work as missionaries in Uganda and Sudan. On one of Colin and Hedwig's mission trips, Colin was shot dead by members of the Lord's Resistance Army in Southern Sudan. He became a martyr for his faith in Jesus.

Despite the fact that the heart of their message is the love of God for sinful man, Christians have been the object of persecution and hatred throughout history, just as Jesus was. Even though the sum total of His message was to bring salvation and healing to a broken world, the world hated Him because darkness hates the light (John 1:3-9).

Jesus made it clear that hatred, wrongful anger and murder come from the same root, and that murder is an outworking of hatred in the heart. The fact is that Satan hated Jesus and hates everyone who chooses to follow Him. Satan will do everything he can to stir up hatred in the hearts of men against believers and make men do what Satan wants, just as he did in Nazareth when Jesus began to fulfil the ministry Isaiah had prophesied in Isaiah 61:1-3. There they tried to throw Jesus over a cliff and kill Him (Luke 4:28-30).

Satan can only act on earth directly through human beings, because it was to human beings that God gave dominionship over the planet. No wonder Jeremiah said that the heart is deceitful and wicked (Jeremiah 17:9). Satan uses the corruption in the heart of man as motivation for people to do his work.

Throughout Christian history, and in every generation, there have been believers who have held firmly to the truth, lived their lives by faith in Jesus, and have, in following Him, had to take up their own personal cross. Almost every day when I was at college in Oxford, I passed the brass cross in the road marking the spot where three bishops were burned at the stake for their steadfast commitment to the truth of the Word of God.

Their absolute faithfulness, in the face of terrible persecution, impacted me as a student and still impacts me today. Bishop Latimer's well-known dying words, to his close friend Bishop Ridley, were "Be of good cheer, Master Ridley, and play the man, for we shall this day light such a candle in England as I trust by God's grace shall never be put out."[1] And it's true that, where the blood of the martyrs has been shed on the land, the seed of new life has always eventually taken root.

Nowhere is this more the case than in China. The communist authorities tried to eliminate Christianity from the nation. Millions died as a result. One was a close friend of our family who had heard the call of God for China and was serving Him with Hudson Taylor's China Inland Mission. But today there are countless millions of believers in China who have grown to maturity in God in the underground church, and who are wanting to take the Gospel of Jesus Christ to the rest of the world! Here in the UK there are many Chinese churches that are bringing the Gospel to their Chinese brothers and sisters, who have come to England for training! The death of the saints in China has led to an unprecedented flowering of faith in China and beyond.

STEPHEN'S DEFENCE

Jesus was, of course, the very first martyr. He gave His life so that salvation and the gift of life may be available to everyone in this fallen and corrupt world. But the hatred displayed towards Peter and John when they healed the crippled man at the gate of the temple, was a sign that the enemy wasn't going to leave them alone either. They were flogged for telling

PERSONAL NOTES

people about Jesus and, as the authorities put it, for *'filling Jerusalem with [their] teaching'* and making *'[them] guilty of this man's blood'* (Acts 5:28).

Then seven men, *'known to be full of the Holy Spirit and wisdom'* (Acts 6:3) were chosen to help the apostles with their work. One of them, Stephen, was described as a man *'full of faith and of the Holy Spirit'* (Acts 6:5). The apostles prayed for these men with the laying on of hands and the Bible tells us:

> *'So the word of God spread. The number of disciples in Jerusalem increased rapidly, and a large number of priests became obedient to the faith'* (Acts 6:7).

You can be sure that, when priests were turning to Jesus in large numbers, the chief priests would be hastening to stamp out this movement which was now threatening to over-run the country. Stephen became the new target for their hatred. He was not only full of faith but was also *'a man full of God's grace and power, [who] did great wonders and miraculous signs among the people'* (Acts 6:8). Very quickly, it seemed, the same authorities who had plotted the death of Jesus were using the same tactics of false accusation and lies against Stephen.

> *'They secretly persuaded some men to say, "We have heard Stephen speak words of blasphemy against Moses and against God" … They produced false witnesses, who testified, "This fellow never stops speaking against this holy place and against the law"'* (Acts 6:11, 13).

By now Stephen had been brought before the Sanhedrin to answer the charges that the chief priests had concocted against him. The fact that *'his face was like the face of an angel'* (Acts 6:15) did nothing to soften their seething hatred. And when challenged with the question *"Are these charges true?"'* (Acts 7:1), Stephen launched into a totally extraordinary proclamation of the Gospel message in which he expounded the Scriptures to these supposedly learned men.

In his defence, he started with Abraham and went through the full history of God's people until the coming of Jesus. His final statement to these custodians of everything Jewish, described them as those *'"who have received the law that was put into effect by angels but have not obeyed it"'*

(Acts 7:53). It is a truly amazing sermon and I would encourage you to take the time to read it all (Acts 7:1-53).

THE DEATH OF STEPHEN

The sermon was great. The message was true. But when the Sanhedrin heard what Stephen had to say:

'they were furious and gnashed their teeth at him. But Stephen, full of the Holy Spirit, looked up to heaven and saw the glory of God, and Jesus standing at the right hand of God. "Look," he said "I see heaven open and the Son of Man standing at the right hand of God"' (Acts 7:54-56).

What an extraordinary contrast – in one and the same place Stephen was seeing through the gates of heaven and his accusers were being fuelled from the gates of hell!

They didn't even give Stephen the protection of a trial, albeit a mock one. They didn't wait to get Roman approval for his execution. They took the law into their own hands and *'dragged him out of the city and began to stone him'* (Acts 7:58), just as the crowd in Nazareth had tried to do to Jesus three years earlier.

The hearts of the priests were being exposed for what they were by the purity and power of Stephen's life and ministry. Religious spirits hate it when their falseness is exposed. And people hate it when what they are like on the inside is revealed for all to see. Pride motivates men (and women) to try and cover their own sinfulness by getting rid of the people who are bringing the exposure. This wasn't the first time that Jews had responded to the truth from God, by killing the prophets who had brought the message.

Stephen was an extraordinary man of God for, even while these evil men were stoning him, he was praying *'"Lord, do not hold this sin against them"'* (Acts 7:60), using words reminiscent of what Jesus had said from the cross, *'"Father, forgive them, for they do not know what they are doing"'* (Luke 23:34). Stephen was truly walking in the steps of His Lord and Master, Jesus Christ. He even wanted his enemies to discover the love of God.

SAUL APPROVES OF THE MURDER

Watching what was happening to Stephen was a young zealot named Saul – a very religious Jew from Tarsus, who happened to be in Jerusalem at the time. When those who were stoning Stephen stripped for action and removed their outer clothing, they left their clothes at Saul's feet for him to look after. He didn't participate in the stoning, but he was as guilty as those who had lifted and thrown the stones for, the Scripture says, Saul *gave approval for his death* (Acts 8:1).

He was there when Stephen fell on his knees and prayed, *'"Lord Jesus, receive my spirit"'* (Acts 7:59). He watched as Stephen *'fell asleep'* and died (Acts 7:60). He was, therefore, just as accountable before God as those who had killed him. The death of Stephen marked the beginning of the first great persecution of believers, which resulted in their being scattered throughout the region.

But the effect of this scattering meant that the Gospel spread much further and more quickly than it would otherwise have done. For, wherever the people went, they took their faith with them and couldn't help but talk about Jesus. And as so often happens, what Satan had meant for harm, turned out to be for the good of the Gospel!

'Godly men buried Stephen and mourned deeply for him. But Saul began to destroy the church. Going from house to house, he dragged off men and women and put them in Jail' (Acts 8:2-3).

Later, in his own testimony before King Agrippa, he said:

'"I put many of the saints in prison, and when they were put to death, I cast my vote against them … in my obsession against them, I even went to foreign cities to persecute them"' (Acts 26:10-11).

The young man Saul, the cruel-hearted Pharisee, had become the chief enemy of the saints of God. We will see later in *Journey to Freedom* what eventually happened to him.

THE SIN OF APPROVAL

Saul didn't actually do anything against Stephen. He only held the clothes of those who did. But as he said later, he owned the fact that he was as guilty as those who had done the deed. He had approved of Stephen's death. There is a profound lesson in Saul's conduct for each one of us. We may not be the perpetrators of a particular sin but, if we approve of it, then before God we are guilty of it, for God judges our hearts as well as our deeds (Hebrews 4:12-13).

On our Healing Retreats we often have to help people who have been caught in all manner of personal sins. Increasingly, these days, we find that pornography has become an addiction, even in the lives of Christian leaders. They would never, of course, indulge personally in all the perverted sexual behaviour which is photographed and filmed for other people to watch. They might even hold up their hands in disgust at such things. But if, covertly, they are looking at pornography on the internet, television or in magazines, they are like the young man Saul, who approved of Stephen's murder.

Their use of pornography means that in their hearts they approve of the conduct of those who produce it, making them passive participants in the actual sins that people indulge in, so that the pornographic material may be produced. A similar principle can be applied to many areas of life. Our approval of other people's sins brings us into the same arena of responsibility and guilt as those who are doing the deeds.

SEARCHING THE HEART

This has been an amazing stage in our *Journey to Freedom*. We have seen all the exciting and thrilling things that happened in the early days of the church. We saw how the Holy Spirit desires to bless and fill all those who want to obey God, whose desire is for purity and holiness.

As a personal exercise, may I encourage you now to take time to look afresh at your own life, to see if there are any ways in which by your actions or by what you watch (and by implication approve of) you have become like Saul – guilty through the sin of approval. What an opportunity this is to ask God to expose ungodliness in our hearts, so that He may fill us afresh with His presence and His power.

PERSONAL NOTES

SUMMARY

The believers in Jesus were hated by the authorities. They had got rid of Jesus, but now others were rising up to proclaim to the whole world what the Jews had done to Jesus, and how God had raised Him from the dead. The chief priests reacted in the same way as they had done with Jesus; they decided to get rid of the chief perpetrators of this new faith. Stephen became the first Christian martyr, but he truly demonstrated the Spirit of Jesus as he died, praying for his accusers that this sin would not be held against them. For at least one of those present on that day, the young Saul, Stephen's prayer was amazingly answered.

PRAYER

Thank You, Lord, for the amazing faith and courage of men like Stephen. Help me to live in obedience to You, so that Your Holy Spirit will always feel welcome in my life. Give me courage, Lord, so that, if I'm ever persecuted for my faith in Jesus, I won't betray Him. Help me always to do what's right as I serve You. In Jesus' name, Amen.

---

1   Bishop Latimer's words to his friend Nicholas Ridley, as they were both about to be burned as heretics for their teachings and beliefs outside Balliol College, Oxford (16 October 1555); as quoted in: Collier, William Francis, History of the British Empire (1870) p 124

STAGE 7

The Church Expands its Horizons

"Fire cannot be contained within an inflammable container. It will always break out. The Holy Spirit is the fire in believers – He will always burn His way out into the hearts of others!"

INTO AFRICA

We have now walked with Jesus through the last weeks of His life, experiencing the pain, joy and triumph of His death and resurrection, and have then been amazed at what happened to the early church, when God poured out His Spirit at Pentecost.

Most of us will already have been familiar with the outline facts of what happened to Jesus and the church, during those precious and critical days. But it has become obvious to me over the years of teaching on our schools and training courses, that understanding the daily personal significance of these truths and applying them in our lives, are a very different matter indeed. The importance of this seems to have escaped the attention of most people we've worked with in healing ministry and training courses.

People are constantly amazed to discover that understanding and applying the foundational truths of the Gospel gives a solid basis for godly living. Without it they're like a leaf blowing in the wind, without any strength to resist winds that would blow them in a wrong direction. They wouldn't have the strength to choose to walk in God's

PERSONAL NOTES

ways, when a contrary wind threatened to take them off course, such as the prevailing winds originating from their own flesh and the devil. This is often the reason why they have become vulnerable in the past to all sorts of temptations and have eventually fallen into the traps of the enemy.

When people come for personal help on a Healing Retreat, they don't just need *prayer* about their problems! They are in need of *teaching* on how to bring structure and order to their lives, whatever the immediate problem may have been that caused them to seek help. Such teaching can be difficult for them to receive and put into practice when they have, for years and years (often without realising it), done their own thing, without understanding that God is a God of order not chaos.

Just as the great artists spent years learning the disciplines of creating line and form in their drawings, before they launched into the freedom of their own personal expression, we need to spend time learning how to order our lives in God's way. Without this, people make their choices on the whim of the moment, and the picture of their lives that they create can be like the efforts of someone who picks up a paint brush for the first time, trying to create an instant masterpiece! Most such 'masterpieces' would be quickly rejected! Recently, my wife took up painting in water colours – what a difference there is between what she can paint today and what she could paint before beginning the discipline of regular learning with a skilled teacher.

The testimonies from people doing *Journey to Freedom* that bless me the most, and which are remarkably profound, are those which say something like this:

"What I'm learning about God and myself is changing the way I think, and then what I do. Before, I would just do what I thought best and then have to reap the consequences of my own wrong ways of living and wrong choices. Now God is reordering my life. My personal relationships are changing. I have a deep sense that, at last, God is in charge of my life. He is healing me in all sorts of ways. I know I've got a long way to go, but I also know that I'm going in the right direction. I'm rediscovering who I am and beginning to see once again that God has a purpose for my life!"

Testimonies like these are not just a blessing for now, they are the beginning of a new season of life through which God is giving back the years that the locust has eaten (Joel 2:25). God is now able to bless individuals, their children, grandchildren and the future generations in their families! *Journey to Freedom's* steady, solid progress, one step at a time, one day at a time, will get you to your destination in God far quicker than you realise!

The disciples and the early leaders of the church had spent three years with Jesus. In that time Jesus had taught them so much, even to the extent of His saying that it was the teaching they'd received that had made them clean (John 15:3). Without the teaching and the foundational truths that had then become part of their lives they wouldn't have been ready to jump into action when the Spirit came.

And that is what I'm passionate about! It's what *Journey to Freedom* is all about – healing, training and equipping people in the Body of Christ, so that they're ready to respond to the move of God's Spirit, whenever He speaks, and to go wherever He calls them. None of us can tell what the fruit of such obedience will be – in Philip's case it took the Gospel for the first time into the continent of Africa (Acts 8:26-40).

FIRST TO SAMARIA

Immediately after the death of Stephen:

'a great persecution broke out against the church in Jerusalem, and all except the apostles were scattered throughout Judea and Samaria ... But Saul began to destroy the church. Going from house to house, he dragged off both men and women and put them in prison' (Acts 8:1, 3).

But this didn't stop the followers of Jesus from talking about what had happened to them.

If the Christian message was merely a good idea, just one of many other good ideas, no-one would have risked their lives to keep on telling people about it. But the fact is that believers' lives had been changed by a personal encounter with the risen Lord Jesus. They had been born again of the Spirit of God. They were now different from what they had been. They now wanted to live in accordance with who they were in Christ.

Just as an elephant can only be an elephant, and a cat can only be a cat, if we are true to ourselves we can only be what we are. We cannot hide our true nature; it always shines through, particularly if there is a strong passion or desire for something. And so it was with those that had been born again at Pentecost. They simply lived out their new life, which couldn't be hindered or hidden. They couldn't pretend they were someone or something else. Becoming a Christian wasn't just a case of taking on a new way of thinking (even though knowing Jesus radically changes how we think!). No, it was a completely new life, or a spiritual heart transplant!

So, despite the opposition and risk of persecution, wherever they were scattered the believers couldn't keep quiet about who and what they now were in Jesus. Their lives couldn't help but touch the lives of the people they met. Philip went down and preached in a city in Samaria.

> *'When the crowds heard Philip and saw the miraculous signs he did, they all paid attention to what he said. With shrieks, evil spirits came out of many, and many paralytics and cripples were healed. So there was great joy in that city'* (Acts 8:6-8).

What an amazing time Philip was having. Despite the persecution, the enemy was on the run. People's lives were being transformed by the power of God. And when they saw what God was doing and heard the message of the Gospel, they responded joyfully to the good news. I don't think God ever intended healing and evangelism to be separated – the powerful demonstration of the power and presence of God in healing and deliverance convinces the soul of the truth that is being taught and convicts the spirit that is out of line with God. Repentance and salvation are the result.

DECEPTION RAISES ITS HEAD!

The apostles heard about the things that were happening in Samaria through Philip, and so they sent Peter and John to help them (Acts 8:14). When they arrived, they prayed for the many new believers (who had been saved and baptised) that they might receive the Holy Spirit. And when they *'placed their hands on them, they received the Holy Spirit'* (Acts 8:17).

A practitioner in the occult, named Simon, was so impressed with the miraculous powers that Philip was demonstrating that he had already professed faith in Jesus and had even been baptised. But when Peter and John came, he tried to buy the ability to lay hands on people so they would receive the Holy Spirit in the same way. He simply wanted the power. Peter saw straight through him, rejected his request and told him to repent of his wickedness for, he said, your heart is *"full of bitterness and captive to sin"'* (Acts 8:24).

Peter had no hesitation in dealing quickly and strongly with Simon. The desire and motive of his heart were for more power, not to love and serve Jesus. He was wanting to hook into the power of God for his own selfish purposes. This is like the temptation that was put before Jesus in the wilderness. Satan tried to persuade Jesus to change the stones into bread and have some food, when He was supposed to be fasting. When power becomes a self-serving objective, pride and the lust for power corrupt the soul.

We may not be involved in the occult as Simon was, but whenever people want to move in the power and gifts of the Spirit for the wrong reasons, they are putting themselves in a very dangerous position before God. This is why it's so important that our heart remains pure in its desires and its motives. When writing to the church in Corinth about the need for believers not to touch or be involved in anything unclean, Paul said, *'Let us purify ourselves from everything that contaminates body and soul, perfecting holiness out of reverence for God'* (2 Corinthians 7:1). John Keble (1792-1866) put this into verse when he wrote:

Still to the lowly soul, he doth Himself impart,
And for His dwelling and His throne, chooseth the pure in heart.
Lord, we thy presence seek, may ours this blessing be;
Give us a pure and lowly heart, a temple meet for thee.

AND SO TO AFRICA!

While Philip was so busy in Samaria, God spoke to him directly through the voice of an angel (Acts 8:26). I don't think it really matters whether it's God who speaks to us in the depths of our spirit, with that inner knowing of what He's saying, or the voice of an angel that plants into our spirit a message from God. What matters is that we recognise the source of the message and choose to obey it.

There are many times when I've sensed God saying something to me and, on some occasions, I've known that obeying God would result in a radical change of heart or direction. But looking back I can say with absolute confidence that the times when I did obey God always resulted in blessing; and that when I resisted what God was saying, to do my own thing, I know that I missed out on His best.

Philip didn't argue with the message, even though it meant leaving what was an extremely successful mission trip to Samaria. The message was specific: *'Go south to the road – the desert road – that goes down from Jerusalem to Gaza'* (Acts 8:26). On the face of it this was a crazy instruction! Philip was an evangelist – how can you evangelise anyone in the desert? No-one could have blamed Philip if he had chosen to ignore the voice, thinking he must have heard it wrongly! It didn't make sense – but he obeyed.

At least, it didn't make sense unless You were God, and You were wanting the good news about Jesus to get into Africa as well as the Middle East! God knew about an important Ethiopian official, who had been to Jerusalem to worship God, and who was returning home that way. He was in charge of the finances of the nation, working directly to Queen Candace. He was a very influential person. This Ethiopian had a long journey ahead of him in his chariot and was reading from the prophet Isaiah.

So God set up this most unlikely of meetings! When Philip saw the chariot coming, the Spirit told him to get close and run alongside it. Philip heard the Ethiopian reading from the book of Isaiah and asked him if he understood what he was reading. This resulted in an invitation for Philip to join him in the chariot.

The man was reading the passage which begins with *'he was led like a sheep to the slaughter, and as a lamb before the shearer is silent, so he did not open his mouth'* (Acts 8:32 and Isaiah 53:7) and, to him, it didn't make sense. So when he asked Philip what it meant Philip had a wonderful opportunity, beginning with this passage, to open up the Scriptures which told about Jesus (Acts 8:34-35).

When people ask the right questions, they really want to know the answers. It's our responsibility as believers to always be ready to give God's answer to man's questions. I get lots of people calling, emailing or writing me letters because they are trying to sell me something (like insurance) that I don't want. I never respond. But when I want to take out a new insurance policy, then I'm interested in finding answers to my questions. It's only at that moment that I want to hear from one of the many companies out there who are selling insurance. I will then listen to what they have to say! But first I have to be asking the questions.

The Ethiopian official was asking the right questions – and he wanted to hear the answers. He had been prepared by the Holy Spirit, and the Spirit had also ensured Philip was in the right place at the right time. Much of real one-to-one evangelism depends on God bringing people together in the same place at the right time and allowing the Spirit to do His work when we answer the questions!

The Ethiopian totally understood everything that Philip said. God removed the blindness from his eyes and so, when they came to some water he said, '"Look, here is water. Why shouldn't I be baptised?"' (Acts 8:36). So they got down from the chariot and Philip baptised him – what an amazing story, but it had an even more amazing ending!

As they came up out of the water, 'the Spirit of the Lord suddenly took Philip away ... and he appeared at Azotus' (Acts 8:39-40). The Ethiopian didn't see him again but went on his way rejoicing. The great transaction had taken place. The sacrifice of Jesus on the cross had been applied to the Ethiopian's life. His sinfulness had been exchanged for Christ's righteousness. And, as the Ethiopian went on his way, no doubt continuing to devour the Word of God from his scroll of Isaiah, he took with him new life.

History tells us that the oldest Christian church in Africa was established in Ethiopia. Philip's obedience led to the church being born on a different continent. The Ethiopian had the Holy Spirit as his teacher and, through him, God took the seed, planted it and it bore much fruit!

None of us know what the fruit of obedience will be. But one day, in heaven, I believe we are going to see those golden strands of destiny that linked people together, and through which new believers were brought to Jesus and entered the Kingdom of God. Heaven is going to be a pretty exciting place.

As I was writing this chapter, my daughter sent me an email to ask if I remembered someone of a certain name. She had met him at an exhibition and, having established that she was the granddaughter of

Fred Horrobin, my father, he told her what a godly influence he had been on him as a boy! It was so encouraging to hear of just one of those golden strands of destiny from my father's life that's still bearing fruit half a century later!

Why not spend a few minutes looking back on your own life and thanking God for everyone whose life influenced you for the good. Think too of the fruit there has been from your own life through blessing others.

SUMMARY

The persecution that followed the death of Stephen drove the believers to many different places. This only served to spread the Gospel. Philip went to Samaria where many people were saved, healed and delivered and there was much joy in the city. But it was here they learned the lesson of Simon the Sorcerer, whose heart motive was to seek after power, rather than one of loving and serving Jesus.

Then God told Philip to go to the road to Gaza, where he met an Ethiopian official who couldn't understand what he was reading in the book of Isaiah. Philip answered his question, the Ethiopian found faith in Jesus and was baptised by the side of the road. He then went on his way rejoicing and took the Gospel into Africa for the first time.

PRAYER

Help me, Lord, to always trust You, even when things seem to be going badly. Help me to listen to Your voice and do what You ask. Thank You that when the new believers were scattered through persecution the people stayed strong in their faith and shared the Gospel wherever they went. Thank You for the example of Philip's obedience, through which the Gospel was carried into Africa. Help me, Lord, to always be ready to answer the questions of those who are seeking You. In Jesus' name, Amen.

PAUL'S CONVERSION

There are certain moments or events in history that not only changed the lives of those who saw what was happening, but also had such a dramatic effect that they changed the world! Here are some examples.

On 28 June 1914, Archduke Ferdinand, heir to the Austro-Hungarian throne, was assassinated. This set in train a series of diplomatic events that led to the outbreak of the First World War in Europe – a conflict that took the lives of millions of innocent victims.

In 1945 the USA dropped an atomic bomb on Japan. That dramatic event finally ended the Second World War.

In the realms of science and technology there are dozens of similar events, such as Newton's sudden understanding of the laws of gravity, Pierre and Marie Curie's discovery of radiation, Einstein's explanation of relativity, and the invention of the steam engine, the motor car and the computer. All these things changed the world – sometimes very dramatically.

In the history of Christianity, after the crucifixion and resurrection of Jesus and the day of Pentecost, the dramatic and sudden conversion of

PERSONAL NOTES

the apostle Paul, must be one of the most significant and world-changing moments ever.

Saul, as he was then called, was the most unlikely of potential converts, but God needed a warrior saint with great courage and determination. He must have had his eye on this embittered zealot from the very first moment of his life. It would have been hard to find a more determined opponent of Jesus than Saul, the Pharisee. His conversion has to be the ultimate example of how the ways of God are so different from ours (Isaiah 55:8).

MURDEROUS THREATS

All the signs, wonders and miraculous events that followed the death of Stephen had no effect on Saul. He wasn't interested in finding out what it was that gave the believers in Jesus their courage and power.

'still breathing out murderous threats against the Lord's disciples, he went to the High Priest and asked him for letters to the synagogues in Damascus, so that if he found any there who belonged to the Way, whether men or women, he might take them as prisoners to Jerusalem' (Acts 9:1-2).

He was not someone believers could easily welcome – his reputation had gone before him.

In his letter to the High Priest Saul described these hated believers in Jesus as belonging to *'the Way'*. (Jesus had already referred to himself as *'the Way'* - see John 14:6.) So, even in its early days Christianity was being seen as a pilgrimage, a journey through life, following the principles that Jesus had taught and following Him throughout one's days. Christianity is not an inactive, passive religion. Knowing Jesus changes everything – everything from your ultimate destination to what you do (or don't do) on your journey to get there, *along the Way*.

THE ULTIMATE ENCOUNTER

Saul had been set apart to be God's man, but he'd shown no interest in Jesus or any inclination to respond to the message of the Gospel. Extraordinary measures were required to change the heart and direction of this man's life. His letter from the High Priest was in his pocket and he was close to his destination, Damascus, when, suddenly, his world changed, forever.

> 'A light from heaven flashed around him. He fell to the ground and heard a voice say to him, "Saul, Saul, why do you persecute me?"
>
> "Who are you, Lord?" Saul asked.
>
> "I am Jesus, whom you are persecuting," he replied. "Now get up and go into the city and you will be told what to do."' (Acts 9:3-6).

The people who were with Saul saw nothing, but they heard the voice. They were speechless as they looked at their young hero, struck down to the ground. Saul managed to get himself back on his feet but, when he tried to open his eyes after seeing the bright flashing light, he could see nothing. He was blind. Without the blindness, Saul may have tried to brush off the incident and pretend it hadn't happened – but blind, he was as useless as the blind beggars who sat at the temple gate. In a moment of time he had descended from the height of Pharisaic popularity to being a no-body, unable to see, read or write. Jesus had certainly got his attention!

There can be times in our lives as well when God uses something physical to get our attention. The promise of healing in Exodus 15:26 makes it clear that putting our lives into godly order is a key part of the healing process. And the second part of Deuteronomy 28 spells it out very clearly that breaking God's covenant can have serious physical consequences.

I know this is a difficult area for people to comprehend. For while it's true that we live in a fallen world and we're all vulnerable to the sicknesses and diseases of mankind, it's also true that there are times when God specifically uses something physical to get our attention. He may even use this to convict us of sin and bring us to repentance.

Hezekiah was a great and godly king, but in the latter part of his life he allowed pride into his heart and he 'became ill and was at the point of death' (2 Chronicles 32:24). Even though God gave him a miraculous sign in response to his prayer for healing, Hezekiah 'did not respond to the kindness shown to him; therefore the LORD's wrath was on him and Judah and Jerusalem' (2 Chronicles 32:25).

It was only after experiencing the wrath of God that Hezekiah repented of the pride in his heart. It took an early experience of God's judgement to bring him to the place of God's blessing! There are several examples of this through the Scriptures. And there have been a number of occasions in my own experience of ministering to people when God has used the difficult circumstances in a person's life to get their attention.

Whatever Saul was thinking, as he was led by hand into Damascus, God had certainly got his attention. Saul had been told by Jesus to wait for instructions and he spent three days without being able to see anything and not eating or drinking.

I was once present when a person contracted sudden, but temporary blindness. It was totally unexpected and very frightening for the person involved who had no idea whether or not she would ever be able to see again. We certainly prayed hard and I'm glad to report she eventually gained full restoration of her sight! I would love to know what Saul thought and prayed during those three days of enforced isolation, but the Scriptures are silent on what was going on in his heart as he waited for God to act, not knowing what would happen next.

God knows when we need time to process what He is doing in our lives. For Saul, these three days were necessary for him to think through what was happening and to become reconciled to such a radical change in his life. Sometimes we too need to recognise times in our own lives where God is giving us the space to process something in our hearts and minds. Saul's three days of solitude were probably just as important as the bolt of lightning and hearing the voice of God speaking. This was his decision time and it was entirely his choice whether or not to move on with God or go back to his old ways.

ANANIAS – GOD'S SPECIAL AGENT

Have you ever dreamt of living the adventurous life of a special agent? Probably not, and I doubt if Ananias lay awake in his Damascus bed, dreaming of how exciting such a life could be! And when he had a clear vision in which God spoke to him, he wasn't too thrilled with what he was being asked to do, as God's special agent.

Very occasionally in the life of most believers, there comes a moment when you know that God has spoken to you. The big question then, of course, is what you do with what God has said … and this was definitely

Ananias' problem. He knew all about Saul of Tarsus for news of Saul's determination to seek out and destroy believers in Jesus had spread quickly throughout the Christian community. He knew that Saul was on his way to Damascus with letters of authority from the chief priests in Jerusalem to arrest everyone who called on the name of Jesus (Acts 9:13-14).

God told Ananias to *'go to the house of Judas on Straight Street and ask for a man from Tarsus named Saul'* (Acts 9:11). He explained to him that Saul had been told that *'a man named Ananias would come and place his hands on him to restore his sight'* (Acts 9:12). It isn't hard to imagine how Ananias must have felt; he even started telling God what sort of a man Saul actually was, almost as if God didn't know this already.

God then explained that:

'this man is my chosen instrument to carry my name before the Gentiles and their kings and before the people of Israel. I will show him how much he must suffer for my name' (Acts 9:15-16).

I'm always amazed at the people God chooses and often how, through His choice, He demonstrates extraordinary love, mercy and forgiveness.

John Newton, for example, was a notorious infidel and slave trader. However on 10 March 1748 his ship nearly sank in a severe storm off the coast of Donegal. He was so shaken by the experience of being so close to death that he read a Bible for the rest of the journey home, became a firm believer in Jesus and later a minister of the Church of England!

Newton was certainly one of God's chosen instruments in the eighteenth century. He would have been totally amazed to know how his hymn *Amazing Grace* has today become one of the most well-known hymns ever written, the tune of which is played by Christians and non-Christians alike, with almost equal appreciation. It is the most recorded song in history with over 6000 versions so far being listed!

It was this former slave trader, who knew what he had been rescued from, who also wrote the words of one of the most beautiful and sensitive hymns ever written in the English language:

How sweet the Name of Jesus sounds
In a believer's ear!

It soothes his sorrow, heals his wounds,
And drives away his fear.
It makes the wounded spirit whole,
And calms the troubled breast;
'Tis manna to the hungry soul,
And to the weary rest.

Languishing in Damascus, blind and with no knowledge of what was going to happen next, Saul was also *'God's chosen instrument'* (Acts 9:15). He was waiting to discover what God had in store for him. He need not have feared for God's special agent was on his way. Notwithstanding his personal fear of Saul, Ananias had a greater fear of disobeying God. I can imagine him knocking on Judas' door in Straight Street, trembling somewhat as he waited to be invited in.

On entering the house, he found Saul there, exactly as God had told him, and:

'placing his hands on Saul, he said, "Brother Saul, the Lord Jesus, who appeared to you on the road as you were coming here, has sent me so that you may see again and be filled with the Holy Spirit." Immediately, something like scales fell from Saul's eyes, and he could see again. He got up and was baptised and after taking some food, regained his strength' (Acts 9:17-19).

We hear nothing more about the exploits of Ananias but the fruit of his life and ministry is still being felt today, two thousand years later. Every time anyone reads one of Paul's letters and is blessed by God through what he wrote, they should thank God for Ananias. Without his obedient intervention Saul might have spent the rest of his days blind and have never known the destiny that God had mapped out him. He was to become a special instrument of grace whom God had chosen to take the Gospel across the then known world, and finally to Rome itself.

God took all the gifting, education, and years of training that had been used to fashion and form the man Saul and transformed them by the power of His Spirit into the apostle Paul. When God takes hold of a man or a woman, there is no limit to their potential in God. It wasn't very long before some of that potential was released in Saul. Having spent several days with the disciples in Damascus, he then moved onto the streets and into the synagogues, preaching that Jesus is the Son of God (Acts 9:20).

SAUL ESCAPES

It's no wonder that the Jews were baffled. Here was a man whom they thought had come to Damascus to arrest the believers in Jesus, who was now using all his education and Pharisaical training to prove that Jesus was the Christ. What an extraordinary transformation had taken place in the heart of this former zealot. He was now a passionate preacher of the Gospel.

Saul himself became the object of wrath from the Jewish authorities who *'kept close watch on the city gates in order to kill him'* (Acts 9:24). However he managed to escape during the night in a basket that was lowered down the outside walls of the city and so he was able to return to Jerusalem, where he spoke boldly in the name of Jesus (Acts 9:25-29).

Saul was now a different man. He had had a personal, direct encounter with the risen Lord Jesus. He had been healed of his blindness and filled with the Spirit through the laying on of Ananias' hands. And now he was about to go through a special season of preparation for his life's work as the missionary apostle. His conversion truly was one of those moments that changed the history of the world.

TWO QUESTIONS

As we have looked at the conversion of Saul I have been prompted to ask two questions.

1. **Have there ever been seasons of your own life when you have known something of the wrath or judgement of God, bringing you back to a place of conviction and repentance?** If so, have you always reacted to the discipline of God in the right way? Is it possible, for example, that there are still areas of your own life where you haven't yet entered into the healing you know God wants to bring? Is He still waiting for you to respond to His love

and mercy, drawing attention to things that need His correction and encouragement?

2. **Have you ever been asked by God to be His special agent, like Ananias, and to do something specific for Him?** As you think about how God used Ananias to be an extraordinary agent for the Kingdom of God, ask yourself if you would always be willing to do what God asks you to do. It may be there are things in the past you know He's asked you to do, but which you didn't do. This is a good opportunity to bring those things before God, repent, ask for forgiveness and move on with Him – determined that from this day forward you are going to be a believer who is walking in *'the Way'*.

SUMMARY

The people God chooses for specific responsibilities in the Kingdom of God are often surprising choices by normal human standards. But God knows what He's doing. Saul was an avowed enemy of the church, but when God met him on the road, his life was turned round and he became the foremost evangelist and missionary in the early church. God used Ananias to minister healing to Saul – we must always be ready to obey God's voice and do what He asks us to do. The fruit of Ananias' obedience has changed the world!

PRAYER

I am amazed, Lord, at how You chose one of Your enemies to become the foremost missionary of the early church. Thank You, Lord, that no-one is outside the potential of Your love and that every single person has a destiny to fulfil. Help me, Lord, to be always willing to be Your special agent and, like Ananias, to have the courage to do what You ask me to do, knowing that even when the assignment seems unusual You know what You're doing! In Jesus' name, Amen.

GOOD NEWS FOR THE GENTILES TOO!

In our rapid journey through the Acts of the Apostles, I have particularly highlighted those things which can have a strategic effect on our own growth in God and our personal transformation. At each stage we have been looking out for those important spiritual principles which we can apply in our lives.

DREAMS AND VISIONS

There are several occasions now where we have seen how God can speak to people through dreams and visions. We saw how God used a vision to get Ananias' attention and then tell him to go to Straight Street to pray for Saul. It was only a short time previously, on the day of Pentecost, that Peter had quoted from the book of Joel, which said that in the last days, when God pours out His Spirit, *'your sons and daughters will prophesy, your young men will see visions and your old men will dream dreams'* (Acts 2:17).

While God creates all things in the natural realms for us to enjoy, when He gives us a dream or a vision it's not solely for our enjoyment; it has a purpose. There is usually a specific reason why He is trying to get our attention.

It could be to point us in a new direction for our lives, or to bring a measure of correction to our daily walk with Him. It might be a prophetic warning of something that's going to happen which we need to prepare for, or He could be telling us about something that's happening to someone else so that we can pray for them. These are just a few of the many possible reasons why God may want to get our attention – and dreams and visions are one of the ways that He does it.

Several times now in our *Journey to Freedom* pilgrimage I've told of occasions when God spoke to me through a vision which changed the whole direction of my life. I wouldn't be writing these notes today if, over forty years ago, God hadn't got my attention through the bent chassis of a broken car. While I could restore broken cars, God said He could restore broken lives! He got my attention immediately and, ultimately, Ellel Ministries was the result. Without the vision God gave me then, I would never have discovered what He wanted me to do with my life.

On another occasion God spoke to me through a very vivid dream about buying a shop. At that time I had no plans to open a shop – it was a totally new idea, but I recognised the presence of God speaking to me in the dream. The following morning, when driving through a local town, a shop that had been on the market for months, which I'd never noticed before, 'jumped out at me' as I drove past. I knew it was the shop from the dream. To cut a long story short, I acted that day to buy the property and thus began one of my most successful business developments. Without the dream, it would never have happened.

If it wasn't for a particular vision that God gave Peter, none of us who are Gentile (non-Jewish) believers in Jesus would ever have heard the Gospel. God can speak to us through dreams (when we are asleep) or we can have visions (when we are awake). It doesn't matter whether it is through a dream or through a vision – what matters is that we recognise His voice when God is speaking. We must then take whatever action the vision requires of us, looking to Him for the how and the when, of what happens next! The particular story we are looking at today, from the book of Acts, about Peter, could be called '*A Tale of Two Visions*'.

CORNELIUS' VISION

Cornelius was a Roman centurion – not a Jew at all. He and all his family *'were devout and God-fearing. He gave generously to those in need and prayed to God regularly'* (Acts 10:2). One day, Cornelius had a vision. *'He distinctly saw an angel of God who came to him and said, "Cornelius"'* (Acts 10:3). The angel certainly knew who he was and Cornelius knew the angel had come from God, for when he spoke, he addressed God, not the angel! *'"What is it Lord?" he asked'* (Acts 10:4).

God had got Cornelius' attention, but Cornelius had no idea why! The angel spoke again and said:

'"Your prayers and gifts to the poor have come up as a memorial offering before God. Now send men to Joppa to bring back a man named Simon who is called Peter. He is staying with Simon the tanner, whose house is by the sea"' (Acts 10:4-6).

This is a very specific word and it would not have been unreasonable for Cornelius to have thought it strange and unnecessary. But even though he didn't know why he had to do this, he did know that it was an instruction from God. And in that case, this wasn't something that could be ignored – if he didn't want to miss out on whatever the Lord was doing in his life, the message had to be obeyed. So Cornelius sent two of his servants and a devout soldier to Joppa to look for this man called Peter.

PETER'S VISION

Meanwhile Peter was staying with Simon the tanner at Joppa. He went up onto the roof of the house to pray but became hungry. Peter sounds very much like many of us – when we want to pray, we get distracted by the need for food and on our way to pray we visit the refrigerator! Then, instead of praying, we fall asleep! It does seem a rather familiar scenario!

And that's exactly what happened to Peter, while some food was being prepared for him, he fell asleep on the roof – or, at least, as the Bible says, *'he fell into a trance'* (Acts 10:10). He was having a very clear vision and, being hungry, the vision was all about food!

As well as being a believer in Jesus, Peter was also a devout Jew. In his vision God showed him all sorts of unclean animals and told him to kill them and eat them. It's not surprising that Peter objected: '*"Surely not, Lord, I have never eaten anything impure or unclean"*' (Acts 10:14).

Three times God showed him the same vision, and now Peter had a real problem. How could God be telling him to do something that was contrary to all the rules and regulations he had grown up with, and which was so much a part of who he was, as a Jew? God answered his question by saying '*"Do not call anything impure that God has made clean"*' (Acts 10:15). To underline the importance of the message God repeated the vision three times!

> '*While Peter was still thinking about the vision, the Spirit said to him, "Simon, three men are looking for you. So get up and go downstairs. Do not hesitate to go with them, for I have sent them." So Peter went down and said to the men, 'I'm the one you're looking for. Why have you come?'*' (Acts 10:19-21).

I love this story. It gives us great insight into the ways of God and how He uses visions, dreams and direct words given through the Spirit to bring about His Kingdom purposes through mankind. It's not difficult to imagine the messenger angels listening to what God is asking them to do, then doing their jobs and, finally, watching as the Father puts His plans before men for them to act upon. Having got Peter's attention through the vision, God was then able to speak directly to Peter, knowing that by now he was really listening.

When we read wonderful stories such as this, we must break through the deceptions of the enemy. He wants us to think that this sort of thing only happens to people of great importance, such as Peter. All these details appear in the Scriptures to teach us the ways of God so we can understand how He works with all His children, including you and me. He wants us to be able to recognise situations in which He is speaking to us, and to act accordingly.

The whole purpose of our studying the Scriptures like this in *Journey to Freedom* is so we can learn and understand the keys to Christian living that are clearly there in God's Word. God wants us to use these keys in our relationship with Him, and He wants to use them in His relationship with us. These lessons are for all believers, not just for the Peters of this world. Recognising the ways God speaks is fundamental to living a secure and dynamic Christian life.

At this point in the story Peter hears about Cornelius' experience (Acts 10:22) and realises there are two halves to this rather unusual story. God was orchestrating something special and, although everyone knew it, nobody knew exactly what was happening. The angels must have been smiling as they watched. Peter invited the men from Caesarea to stay the night and then they set out, taking with them some of the other believers from Joppa. A day later they were all in Caesarea and Cornelius met them at his house.

Just entering Cornelius' house was, in itself, a highly unusual event for Peter, as he explained to Cornelius:

"'You are well aware that it is against our law for a Jew to associate with a Gentile or visit him. But God has shown me that I should not call any man impure or unclean, so when I was sent for, I came without raising any objection. May I ask why you sent for me?'" (Acts 10:28-29).

Little by little Peter was being drawn into a completely new under-standing. He now realised that his vision wasn't actually about animals, it was about God's love for all people, not just the Jews. It was a vision that would transform the whole of future Christian history. But Peter didn't yet know the magnitude of the question he was asking when he said *"'why did you send for me?'"* (Acts 10:29). He was about to find out!

CORNELIUS EXPLAINS

It must have been obvious to Peter that, even though Cornelius was a Gentile, he was a true man of God. Cornelius explained his vision in detail (Acts 10:30-33), saying this was why he'd sent for Peter immediately. They were now *"all here in the presence of God to listen to everything the Lord has commanded [Peter] to tell [them]'"* (Acts 10:33).

The problem for Peter was this – he was only just finding out what it was that the Lord was commanding him to say. This was life in the Spirit, New Testament style. Peter had to listen to God at the same time as listening to Cornelius so that, when he opened his mouth it would be God who filled it with words from heaven.

As I was writing this text, I had an email from a friend who is ministering in Brazil and learning the importance of depending on the Spirit. Every day he is facing dozens of new, unplanned situations and discovering how God is in charge of the schedules and the programme. Even though his organised mind would like to be planning everything ahead, it's just not possible. He's having to lean on the Spirit of God, every step of the way, for what he says at each meeting. There's no time for more preparation, he just has to flow with what the Spirit is saying - just as Peter did in Acts 10.

Having preached a sermon at Pentecost that was prepared in heaven, Peter was now getting used to the idea that all he had had to do was open his mouth and the Lord would fill it with words that were inspired by the Spirit of God (Psalm 81:10). Here with Cornelius he was speaking words from God that he wouldn't have been able to say the day before because he wouldn't have believed them.! God had radically changed his understanding of who the Gospel was for. He now realised '"that God does not show favouritism but accepts men from every nation who fear him and do what is right"' (Acts 10:34-35).

Peter had learned that it wasn't just Jewish believers who could have a relationship with God! This may not seem surprising to us, after two thousand years of Christian history, but for Peter it was earth-shattering news. No wonder God had had to use a dramatic vision to get Peter's attention about this new understanding.

Peter then went on to preach about Jesus – everything that had happened to Him in Jerusalem, what the prophets had said about Him, and how He had healed many who had been under the power of the devil. And then, as Peter was preaching:

'the Holy Spirit came on all who heard the message. The circumcised believers who had come with Peter were astonished that the gift of the Holy Spirit had been poured out, even on the Gentiles. For they heard them speaking in tongues and praising God' (Acts 10:44-46).

This was sensational stuff. All the preconceived ideas that only Jews could have a relationship with God, and that the Gentiles could only ever be unclean, were being blown away. The experience of what God was actually doing among them was reshaping their theology and bringing it into line with the truth. As soon as Peter saw that these Gentiles were absorbing the truth about Jesus as he preached, and that they were then believing in their hearts and being filled with the Spirit, he said, *'"could anyone keep these people from being baptised with water? They have received the Holy Spirit just as we have"'* (Acts 10:47).

These uncircumcised Gentiles, who had become believers in Jesus and who had now been baptised in the Holy Spirit, were also baptised with water according to Peter's instructions. The Christian world had just changed shape and Peter had a lot of explaining to do to all the other apostles in Jerusalem. They were shocked to hear that *'Peter went into the house of uncircumcised men and ate with them'* (Acts 11:3).

So Peter went up to Jerusalem and told them the whole story from beginning to end and concluded his report by saying:

> *'"So if God gave them the same gift he gave us who believed in the Lord Jesus Christ, who was I to think that I could stand in God's way?"*
>
> *'When they heard this, [the apostles] had no further objections and praised God, saying, "So then, even to Gentiles God has granted repentance that leads to life"'* (Acts 11:17-18).

It was through the Jews that God had brought salvation into the world through His Son. But now the apostles understood that the Jews were a means of grace for the whole world! The doors for evangelism had suddenly opened on all the nations of the world. It would never be the same again. Hallelujah! All Gentile believers who've ever existed have good reason to thank God for the vision that Peter had when he went onto the roof to pray!

The Gospel is for both Gentiles and Jews and, praise God, in these days there's a growing number of Jews who are discovering that Jesus really is their Messiah. God is slowly bringing Jewish and Gentile believers together and one day, in harmony, they'll proclaim the message about Jesus to a stunned world. The world will then see how God has made them into One New Man (Ephesians 2:14-18). We truly live in exciting times.

It's a fact that Jews, Gentiles and Arab believers are all studying *Journey to Freedom*. What an incredible privilege it is to be walking together in Christ and growing closer to each other as we grow closer to Him.

SUMMARY

When Cornelius and Peter had their visions they had no idea what God was going to do. But when both were obedient to God it was as if the heavens were once more opened up and a new day dawned for the church. Peter learned that God also wanted Gentiles to come to know Jesus and be baptised in water and in the Spirit. How we thank God today that both Cornelius and Peter were obedient to the visions God gave them and that this amazing event heralded a new era of evangelism through which the Gospel was taken to all the nations of the world and not just to Jews.

PRAYER

Thank You, Lord, that You still speak to Your people today through dreams and visions. Thank You for teaching us, through this amazing story, that Your love is for all people, from all nations. Help me always to be alert to recognise those times when You speak to me through dreams and visions. Please give me the discernment to recognise those times when the enemy may be trying to deceive me with a false vision, and to test what You say against Your written Word so that I will not be deceived. In Jesus' name, Amen

THE MACEDONIAN CALL

The book of the Acts of the Apostles is one of the most thrilling Christian books ever written. It ought to be on the *New York Times* best-seller list week after week after week! So much is crammed into even one verse that the truth of all that happened during those extremely testing, but glorious, days can leave you reeling in a state of shock! You need to read the book several times – read it like you would any other book, getting into the stories and following the characters through the ups and downs of their adventures with God.

Already we've seen how the Spirit transformed a frightened group of believers into a mighty spiritual army. We've seen dramatic healings and deliverances taking place, seriously impacting the lives of those who saw God at work. We've been with Peter – in prison and then out. We've wept with the believers as they buried Stephen, the first Christian martyr. We've watched one of the greatest transformations in Christian history as Saul, the cruellest of enemies of the faith, met the risen Lord Jesus and became a mighty warrior for the Kingdom of God. And in the last chapter we saw how God used two visions to change the direction of the church for ever.

I wish we had the space in *Journey to Freedom* to go more slowly through all these amazing adventures, but we must press on and look carefully at how God directed the apostle Paul in two extraordinary and significant developments in Acts 16. But first, let's briefly fill in the gap between Acts 11 and Acts 16.

FILLING IN THE GAP

After Peter learnt that the Gospel wasn't only for the Jews, some Greeks at Antioch became believers and Barnabas was sent from Jerusalem to encourage them. Then Barnabas looked for Saul in Tarsus and brought him along to Antioch. Together they spent a whole year teaching and making disciples. It was here that the believers were first called Christians (Acts 11:26).

But back in Jerusalem the persecution was increasing, this time from a different source – King Herod. Herod had James, the brother of John, put to death with the sword and *'when he saw this pleased the Jews, he proceeded to seize Peter also'* (Acts 12:3). But God had more work for Peter and he was rescued from prison by an angel of the Lord who appeared to him in the night. The angel woke him up, the chains fell off his wrists, and he followed him out of the prison, past the sentries, with the prison door opening miraculously (Acts 12:6-11). Peter, himself, was so surprised by what had happened that, at first, he couldn't work out whether or not it was all a dream.

A little while later Herod's actions caught up with him. When he elevated himself and accepted, without correction, the crowd's adulation that his voice was the *'voice of a god, and not of a man'* (Acts 12:22), an angel was despatched by God to execute summary judgement upon him and *'he was eaten by worms and died'* (Acts 12:23)!

When people like Herod rise up in self-proclaimed glory, they will always come under God's judgement sooner or later. Just as the deaths of Ananias and Sapphira were a warning to people that God requires honesty and integrity in the heart, Herod's death warned that taking God's glory and elevating ourselves above God are acts of blasphemy. Under the law the punishment for blasphemy is death and, unless people repent of their pride, they will come under the judgement of God in this life or the next. Herod's judgement needs to serve as a warning to us all that pride and self-elevation are dangerous.

In Acts 13 and 14 we read of Paul's first great missionary journey, taking at least two years, probably between AD 46 and AD 48. Saul is now being called Paul (Acts 13:9), a name change that must have enhanced his effectiveness as an apostle to the Gentiles (1 Timothy 2:7). Saul was a very Jewish name and the Jews were a hated and despised people throughout the Roman Empire, so the change of name would have made Paul's teaching more acceptable to people, at least at the start – they might now listen to what he had to say, without first rejecting him because of his Jewish name.

In Acts 15 we learn of the great apostolic Council at Jerusalem, when the church agreed that it wasn't necessary to impose on Gentile believers all the requirements of the Jewish law (Acts 15:6-35). At end of Acts 15 Paul is sent off on a new missionary journey, with Silas as his companion, and it is here that we take up the story again in a little more detail.

PAUL'S SECOND MISSIONARY JOURNEY

By now Paul had become a seasoned evangelist. God had sent him into exile for three years (Galatians 1:18) so he could more fully understand what it was God had called him to do. As a Pharisee he had advanced in the understanding of Judaism beyond that of many Jews his own age and he had been extremely zealous for the traditions of his fathers (Galatians 1:14). He needed to be retrained by God for his real calling as an evangelist. He explained that:

> when God, who set me apart from my mother's womb and called me by his grace, was pleased to reveal his Son in me so that I might preach him among the Gentiles, my immediate response was not to consult any human being (Galatians 1:15-16).

Paul's first missionary journey had begun and ended in Syrian Antioch and had taken in places such as Derbe and Lystra, Pisidian Antioch and Pamphylia. It's worth getting a map out to see the vast territory that Paul covered in his travels – hundreds of miles, probably mostly on foot.

His second missionary journey started from Jerusalem. From there

Paul travelled north through Syria, and then west through Cilicia and parts of Galatia. The Scripture sums up these travels across huge distances in just a couple of sentences (Acts 15:41 and Acts 16:1, 2 and 4), but these were not easy journeys on a high-speed train! Wherever he went he stayed and taught the people and *'the churches were strengthened in faith and grew daily in numbers'* (Acts 16:5).

EUROPE BECKONS

There then followed one of the more unusual seasons of Paul's apostleship. The Holy Spirit closed his mouth and he was unable to teach! This must have been a period of extraordinary frustration for an activist such as Paul. He and his companions had travelled throughout Phrygia and Galatia, but they were now being *'kept by the Holy Spirit from preaching the Word in the province of Asia'* (Acts 16:6).

When they came to the border with Mysia, Paul tried to go northwards into Bithynia (Acts 16:7), but the Spirit of Jesus wouldn't allow them to go. It must have been a mystifying time for Paul and his companions. How could they possibly do the work of an evangelist if the Holy Spirit wouldn't let them go to places and speak the Good News?

So they carried on through Mysia *'and went down to Troas'*, a distance of several hundred miles, probably taking a few weeks on the road to travel the distance. It seems that they only had God's peace, the ultimate key to the guidance of God, when they kept on going and didn't stop to preach!

When God has an agenda, He will always seek to bring His people to the place where that agenda can be fulfilled. God knew that wherever Paul went and preached the Gospel, people would respond and that he would then take the time – months and even years – to stay and see a church established. But this was now a season when others would have to do that for these regions. God had a new commission for Paul. The intercessory heart of the people across the sea from Asia had touched the heart of God and He was about to answer those prayers. Paul had to be in the right place and at the right time for it to be fulfilled.

So Paul and his companions reached Troas, a port city looking west across the Aegean Sea to Macedonia, at the easterly limit of the great continent of Europe. The Aegean Sea opens up in the south to the Mediterranean Sea and in the north to the Black Sea. It divides Asia from Europe. Here in Troas, God once again used a vision to speak clear words of direction into Paul's life.

'During the night Paul had a vision of a man of Macedonia standing and begging him, "Come over to Macedonia and help us"' (Acts 16:9). This was the answer to why Paul had been prevented from preaching elsewhere. God had another special assignment for him and, in typical apostolic manner, Paul didn't waste any time. God had spoken and they were off! They got ready at once to leave for Macedonia, concluding that God had called them to preach the Gospel there (Acts 16:10).

It was Peter's vision that opened up the Gospel to the Gentiles. It was Philip's vision that took the Gospel into Africa via the Ethiopian official. And now Paul's vision was about to take the Gospel to the West. Without such a vision Paul would never have known that God had opened the door for the Gospel across the sea and into the vast continent of Europe itself.

AT PHILIPPI

So, from Troas, they took a ship that was heading west across the Aegean. They put in at the island of Samothrace en route, before landing at the port of Neapolis. They then travelled a short journey inland to Philippi, the leading city of the region and a Roman colony. Here they stayed for a while awaiting divine encounters that would open up the way for them.

Their first such encounter wasn't long in coming. On the Sabbath they *'went outside the city to the river, where they expected to find a place of prayer'* (Acts 16:13). (All the places inside the town would probably have been dedicated to pagan gods, making a hostile spiritual atmosphere for believers in the living God to meet and worship.) There Paul found a group of women, as expected, and he began to talk to them about why he was there. As he shared his message, one of the women listening was Lydia, a dealer in purple cloth from the city of Thyatira. She was already a believer in God and the Lord opened her heart to receive Paul's message.

She and her household responded immediately to the Gospel and they were all baptised in the river. Lydia then invited Paul and his companions to stay with her in her home. So, in a matter of a few hours the Lord had led Paul to a group of people who would be open to the Gospel, provided the nucleus of a new church, and given him and his companions accommodation for their stay in the city. God had gone before them and prepared the way.

Obedience to the voice of God always opens the gate on to the ways and the provision of God. Sometimes there can be years between the beginning of a sequence of events and its conclusion, but God is not only the Lord of the universe, He's also the Lord of time. Some five years before my father died, he was fishing in the north of Scotland. A young boy with his father watched excitedly, obviously longing to have a go himself. When my Dad invited the boy to come and fish on the private piece of water, the boy was thrilled and so was his father.

At the end of the day they exchanged addresses and kept in touch by sending Christmas cards to each other and sharing photos of the family. Five years later my mother and father were away on holiday when my father was suddenly taken ill and collapsed to the ground. His home-call had come. But my mother was left kneeling on the path beside my dying father. She was in a strange place and had no-one to help either my father or herself.

Suddenly she looked up and there was a man looking down at her asking if he could help. Then he looked at my Mum more closely and, totally amazed, cried out my Mum's name, "Betty!" This was the man who, five years previously, my Dad had felt prompted by the Lord to offer some fishing to his son. At the critical moment of my Mum's greatest need, God had sent a human 'angel' who knew both her and my Dad. I will never cease to thank God for His amazing provision and for the way He prompts us to do something at a certain time that has amazing ramifications later.

When Paul responded to the prompting of the Lord to go over to Macedonia, he had no idea what the consequences would be. However, through his obedience God established a body of believers in town after town after town, bringing to them the transforming life of Jesus.

SUMMARY

Paul was an amazing pioneer missionary who thought nothing of travelling huge distances to take the Gospel message throughout Asia. However, after a while he was prevented by the Holy Spirit from continuing this work (in Asia) and so he and Silas travelled on to Troas. Here God gave Paul a vision of a man from Macedonia crying out for help. Having now heard the voice of the Lord, they immediately responded and set sail, thereby taking the Gospel message into Europe for the first time.

PRAYER

Lord, I am totally amazed at the way You used Paul to take the Gospel to so many different places and then into Europe. Thank You for speaking so clearly to him and for His obedience to Your Word. Help me to realise how important it is that I listen carefully to Your voice so that I will not miss out on any of the special assignments that You have for me. In Jesus' name, Amen.

PAUL AND SILAS IN PRISON IN PHILIPPI

Even though Jesus personally overcame him at the cross, Satan is still, for the time being, the god of this world. Some people make the huge mistake of thinking that, because of Jesus' victory at Calvary, we can completely ignore the devil, as if he is an irrelevant, spent force. That is not the case. In Jesus we can overcome him, but it's only Jesus who will one day pull him down from the place of earthly authority that man gave him through the Fall.

As the spiritual ruler of planet earth (John 12:31), he has a vested interest in encouraging those powers and authorities who support him. And when his power and authority are challenged, he will always try and protect his interests. So Satan encourages evils such as the occult and sexual perversion, and opposes anything and anyone whom God is using to deliver people from evil spirits and pull down the strongholds Satan has in their lives.

I know a little about this from personal experience over the years, through our own pioneering in the area of deliverance. When people are brought to repentance and forgiveness and delivered of the powers

PERSONAL NOTES

of darkness, Satan loses authority in their lives. The deliverance ministry directly challenges Satan's position. It's not surprising, therefore, that sometimes there's a backlash from the enemy as he targets and uses people to undermine or even attack the ministry in an attempt to limit or destroy the work that God is doing.

PAUL AND SILAS FACE EVIL POWERS

Paul and Silas were staying in Lydia's house and each day they would go from there to the place of prayer. One day they were met by a slave girl who had a spirit by which she predicted the future. She earned a great deal of money for her owners by fortune-telling (Acts 16:16). The spirit in the girl obviously recognised the Spirit of God in Paul and Silas and followed them around shouting out *"these men are servants of the Most High God, who are telling you the way to be saved"* (Acts 16:17). The demon was speaking the truth!

When Jesus was confronted by a demonised man in the synagogue at Capernaum, the spirit cried out through the man *"I know who you are – the Holy One of God"* (Luke 4:34). Some people say that because demons are deceivers they always tell lies. This is not the case. This spirit in the synagogue at Capernaum was, indeed, speaking the truth. Jesus was, and is, the Holy One of God.

We have certainly found it to be the case that the evil spirits in people recognise the presence of the Holy Spirit in a believer, just as the evil spirits in the man in Capernaum knew exactly who Jesus was. This was a classic example of the demons knowing the truth about the spiritual realms and not being afraid to speak it out.

I will never forget the first time this happened to me when, in the middle of my sermon, a demonised lady in the congregation started shouting out at me, telling me to "Shut up! Shut up! Shut up!" In one way it was encouraging to know that the enemy recognised the presence and power of the Holy Spirit, but it caused a major distraction in the service, and when that happens it has to be dealt with wisely, but with authority.

In Capernaum Jesus delivered the man, and the people were amazed at what they saw happening before their very eyes. Similarly, in my own experience the people were amazed, and this incident proved to be the beginning of a very significant time of healing, in which the woman's daughter was radically healed of a lifelong asthmatic condition later in the day. The enemy raised his head, but God received the glory! But it's not always as straightforward as this, as Paul and Silas were about to find out in Philippi, especially when dealing with religious spirits.

EVEN WHEN IT'S TRUE – IT CAN BE FALSE!

There is an important passage in Deuteronomy about false prophets. Whenever a false prophet is speaking, claiming to be speaking out what the Spirit of God is saying, he may well be speaking out the words of a spirit, but it's not necessarily from the Holy Spirit. Deuteronomy 13:1-5 warns us that, even when a prophecy comes true, if the prophet encourages you to worship other gods, then *'you must not listen to the words of that prophet or dreamer'* (Deuteronomy 13:3). Scripture is warning us to be discerning.

The fact that a prophet speaks out true words doesn't necessarily mean they are coming from a true prophet. It's vital that we test prophecy, not just by the words that are said, but by the character of the prophet, and by where you'll be led if you choose to follow that prophet. Deception comes in many guises, and we must learn to test both the prophecies and the prophets if we are to avoid the danger of being deceived.

The woman they encountered in Philippi on the way to the place of prayer was a medium. She was a false prophet. She was a slave girl and was, therefore, owned by her masters who used her to make a great deal of money through fortune-telling – the occult equivalent of prophecy (Acts 16:16).

What she was saying about Paul and Silas was the absolute truth. But the vessel through whom these words were being spoken was being used by the enemy to lead people astray. So, even though what she said was true, she was still a false prophet and it was a demon who was telling her what to say.

People with religious spirits can cause a great deal of confusion – especially in the Body of Christ. What they say may seem to be OK, but the motive of their heart may be wrong, or there may be major areas of their life that are unhealed. The enemy is using that damaged part of their being to deceive both them and others. It's vital to look at the fruit that comes from a person's life, and not just to listen to what they say.

If what they say sounds all right, but there's no discernible fruit of the Spirit of God in their life, then it's right and necessary to treat their words with caution, weigh them carefully, and then reject them if there's no discernible evidence that what they are saying comes from God. And that's exactly what was happening in Philippi. The words were true, but the source of the words wasn't. If people heard Paul and Silas speak and then heard this 'true' testimony about them coming from the slave-girl, some may then have been tempted to follow her into her fortune-telling booth, thinking she was a true prophet. They would then hear false words from her lips which would bring them into deep deception and the enemy would have gained a great victory in their lives.

PAUL TAKES ACTION

One of the basic premises for deliverance is that, under normal circumstances, you don't attempt to deliver someone who doesn't want to be delivered or healed. It would be dangerous and foolish to go around trying to deliver people who, by our own discernment or judgement, are struggling with demonic holds, but without their prior acknowledgement of the problem and their submission to Jesus.

That person is giving the demon a right to be there and, unless their free will is yielded to God and co-operating with you, you will be fighting a battle that you don't normally have the authority to win. It's probably for this reason that Paul didn't make any attempt to deliver the woman at first. But, probably out of sheer frustration and because she kept this up for many days Paul finally turned around and said to the spirit, *'"In the name of Jesus I command you to come out of her!"'* The spirit immediately left her (Acts 16:18).

There were bound to be consequences of Paul's sudden and uninvited action. The woman had lost her fortune-telling demo, and she was now powerless to earn money for her owners. What Paul had done was seen as attacking the business and livelihood of the people who had always exploited her occult gift. Immediately Paul and Silas were dragged before the city authorities by the woman's owners, who said:

"'These men are Jews, and are throwing our city into an uproar by advocating customs which are unlawful for us Romans to accept or practise'" (Acts 16:20-21).

The magistrate was on the side of the townsfolk and ordered Paul and Silas to be stripped and severely flogged – which would have been no light beating. After enduring such punishment Paul and Silas would have been in physical agony, with bleeding backs and aching bodies. In this condition they were then thrown into prison, and the jailor was given strict instructions to guard them carefully. *'Upon receiving such orders, he put them in the inner cell and fastened their feet in the stocks'* (Acts 16:24).

EARTHQUAKE!

I'm not sure that I would have had the strength of spirit and courage to react as Paul and Silas did. While, no doubt, they were really hurting from the pain of being beaten, they did not lie in a broken heap, bemoaning what had happened to them. On the contrary, at midnight *'they were praying and singing hymns to God, and the other prisoners were listening to them'* (Acts 16:25).

Praise is said to be one of the most powerful spiritual activities we can ever take part in. When the Psalmist said that God inhabits the praises of His people (Psalm 22:3 KJV), he was expressing a principle that has inspired and energised God's people throughout the ages. When you read of how praise has lifted the spirits and given courage to people in jail awaiting execution for their faith, you realise what a powerful weapon it is on the lips of the saints. At Jericho the priests blowing trumpets went ahead of the army as they marched seven times round the city and the walls collapsed (Joshua 6:16-20).

Many times we have resorted to praise when facing severe battles with the enemy for the rescue of one of God's children from the control of the powers of darkness. The enemy has had to give way, and we were able to bring deliverance and healing. Praise always prepares the way for the release of God's power.

I don't think Paul and Silas were praising God in jail in order to cause an earthquake. They were praising God for who He is and, no doubt, rejoicing at the privilege of being able to share in the fellowship of His sufferings (Philippians 3:10). God encouraged them in their hearts as they sang and prayed. And as they did so, they were also ministering to the other prisoners. Then:

> 'suddenly, there was such a violent earthquake that the foundations of the prison were shaken. At once all the prison doors flew open and everybody's chains fell loose. The jailer woke up, and when he saw the prison doors open, he drew his sword and was about to kill himself because he thought the prisoners had escaped. But Paul shouted, "Don't harm yourself! We're all here!"' (Acts 16:26-28).

Now that's one of the scenes I will really want to see when I look round the video-library of heaven!

The jailer woke up to find the prison doors open and concluded all the prisoners had escaped and thought the best thing to do was to commit suicide. He was saved from doing that by Paul who reassured him that all the prisoners were there. What a traumatic event! The jailer did not know God, but now he was desperate to know Him and cried out, 'What must I do to be saved' (Acts 16:30). That question is the evangelist's dream! Paul's answer was simple, direct and life changing, 'Believe on the Lord Jesus Christ, and you will be saved – you and your household' (Acts 16:31). Then Paul taught everyone in the house about Jesus.

Finally, the jailer treated the wounds that Paul and Silas had received and then he and all his family were baptised. That must have been an extraordinary night in the home of the Philippian jailer who 'was filled with joy because he had come to believe in God – he and his whole family' (Acts 16:34). Whoever could have imagined how things would have turned out?

Satan prompted a fortune-telling woman to make a spiritual nuisance of herself, not realising he was setting in motion a series of events that would touch the lives of a Roman officer and all his family. Who knows where, in the Roman Empire, that officer would next be posted – but one thing's certain, wherever it was, he took his faith with him. God used Roman roads and Roman believers, as an amazing means of spreading the Gospel throughout Western Europe.

The next day Paul and Silas were released from prison 'and went to

Lydia's house, where they met with the brothers and encouraged them' (Acts 16:40). It would have been easy for them to be despondent at what had happened, but they knew that each step of the way they had been listening to the voice of God and doing those things that He had shown them to do. In such circumstances they had nothing to fear, for God was in charge of the consequences.

AN ENORMOUS KEY

It's no wonder that when, at a later date, Paul was writing to the church at Philippi, that had been the fruit of this first visit to the city, he told them that:

'I have learned to be content whatever the circumstances. I know what it is to be in need, and I know what it is to have plenty. I have learned the secret of being content in any and every situation, whether well fed or hungry, whether living in plenty or in want. I can do all this through him who gives me strength' (Philippians 4:11-13).

And therein is an enormous key for you and me in our *Journey to Freedom*. When we are doing those things God has asked us to do and going to those places He has told us to go, we can trust Him to be in charge of the present and the future. I can't promise that the present will always be a bed of roses, but I can promise that our obedience to Him will always produce the sweet smell of sacrificial incense, arising to the throne of grace (2 Corinthians 2:15). And He will give us the strength to do what He asks us to do.

MOVING ON

Now we must move on. It's been thrilling spending time in the book of the Acts of the Apostles, but there's more vital ground we must cover before we reach the end of our *Journey to Freedom*. May I encourage you to find some time to read through the rest of the book and to see what other life-transforming lessons the Lord teaches you as you read. It's challenging stuff!

We have now spent some time looking back at everything that

happened when Jesus came the first time. Now we are going to look forward to His next visit to planet earth – for one day He's coming back!

SUMMARY

At Philippi Paul was challenged by the presence and shouting of a fortune-teller who followed him around. Eventually he could stand it no more and took authority over the demon that gave her the power to tell fortunes and she was delivered. But then her owners had lost their means of income and they had Paul and Silas flogged and put in jail. But even here God had His way, for as Paul and Silas were praising God at midnight there was an earthquake which shook the jail from its foundations. No prisoners escaped, but the jailer and all his family were born again and baptised in the middle of the night. God used the crisis to produce great fruit for the Kingdom.

PRAYER

Thank You, Lord, for the amazing courage of Paul and Silas who took their beating and continued to praise You at midnight in the jail. Help me, Lord, in whatever circumstances I find myself as a result of following You, to always be content and trust You with the outcome, knowing that in You I can do all those things that You ask me to do, because You will be my source of strength. In Jesus' name, Amen.

STAGE 8

He's Coming Back!

"A world that disbelieves the first coming of Jesus has no reason to either fear or welcome the second coming – until it happens!"

Stage 8, Chapter 1

THE SECOND COMING

It was a very exciting day when, back in the fifties, my Mum sailed for South Africa to go and visit her family. My Dad, my brother and I stood on the dockside at Southampton and watched as the great ocean liner, the *Athlone Castle*, slowly edged her 25,567 tons out of the harbour and began her thirteen-day journey across the oceans to Cape Town.

Of course, we were going to miss her greatly, for she was our much-loved Mum, but the fact that she had a return ticket and was coming back made all the difference. Her absence was temporary and we could all look forward to the day of her return. And, yes, there were huge celebrations when a few months later we were at the docks again to welcome her back home in exactly the same way as she had gone!

JESUS IS COMING BACK!

We saw earlier in Book 6 of our *Journey to Freedom* that, when Jesus ascended to heaven in front of the disciples, they were told that He would return. Two angels, looking like men dressed in white, told them

PERSONAL NOTES

PERSONAL NOTES

that *"This same Jesus who has been taken from you into heaven, will come back in the same way you have seen him go to heaven"* (Acts 1:11).

If this had been the only time those first disciples had been told about Jesus' return, it would have been a tremendous source of encouragement to them, and to the whole of the church throughout history. But this was not the case. On numerous occasions within the Scriptures we are told not only about the Messiah's coming the first time, but also that He will return one day.

In the Old Testament alone, there are more promises about His second coming than there are about His first! Since all the promises relating to His first coming have been fulfilled, we can depend on the integrity of the prophets and the accuracy of their prophecies, knowing that one day all their other promises will be also fulfilled. Moreover, we have the promise of Jesus himself who said, *"I will come back and take you to be with me that you also may be where I am"* (John 14:3).

We are now living in the era between the first and second comings of Jesus. He came initially a baby, the Son of Man. Now God is gathering in the souls of those who love Him and have chosen to serve Him. It is the era of opportunity for the unsaved. It is the era of evangelism and harvest for the church.

During this time, those who have responded to the message of the Gospel, will die in Christ and then, at the end of time, they'll be raised again in Christ (as we will see in more detail in the next chapter). Next time Jesus will come as the King of Kings and Lord of Lords and, when that happens, everyone will see Him. Jesus Himself said they *"will see the Son of Man coming on the clouds of the sky, with power and great glory"* (Matthew 24:30).

There is a clock in heaven that only the Father can see. It is measuring the passing of the *'day of the Lord'* (Malachi 4:5). When its hands reach midnight, the era of harvest will be over. At that time, everyone whose life is anchored by faith in Christ will know that Jesus has returned to gather in the family of God for that glorious transition from time into eternity.

ESCHATOLOGY

Eschatology is the study of the End Times – the future history of the church. I don't intend to discuss within *Journey to Freedom* all the rival interpretations of Scripture and the precise beliefs which different groups have had over the years, even though they certainly make for fascinating reading. In the past many have tried to predict just when Jesus would return, but history has always proved them wrong! It surprises me enormously that anyone would even try to predict the date of such an event when Jesus himself said ' *"No one knows about that day or hour, not even the angels in heaven, nor the Son, but only the Father"'* (Matthew 24:36). If Jesus Himself doesn't know, then it is futile for us to try and work it out!

However, there are fundamentals of Christian truth concerning the second coming about which there can be little or no disagreement and which it is vital we understand and appreciate. It is the personal significance of these truths as they affect our day-to-day walk with the Lord that I intend to focus our attention on in *Journey to Freedom*.

One of the most important statements of orthodox Christian beliefs was established by the Council of Nicaea in AD 325. The Nicene Creed was the fruit of the Council's labours in which it says: 'He [Jesus] shall come again in glory to judge the living and the dead; and His kingdom shall have no end.' This profoundly simple statement is summarised in an even briefer form in the liturgy of many churches as: 'Christ has died, Christ is risen, Christ will come again.' In many ways, that's all we need to understand, for it is the knowledge of these facts that changes everything for a Christian and strongly influences what we believe and how we behave in the present time.

Christianity is not a system of morals designed for the mutual benefit of human beings that provides no personal consequence to whether or not we abide by it. Christianity is the outworking of a relationship with a Holy God through a relationship with His Son. Everything depends on that relationship. Without or outside that relationship, God and man are eternally separated (because of sin). Inside that relationship we have a destiny and a future (Jeremiah 29:11).

The News Channel I usually watch on TV often has a yellow flash-band across the screen on which it says 'Breaking News'. One day the skies will be lit up with the sign of the Son of Man (Matthew 24:30).

The 'Breaking News' of the second coming of Jesus will not need a television channel to spread the word! It will be instantly seen and understood by every human being on the planet. For those who know and love Him, it will be a time for welcoming the return of their Saviour. For those who have rejected Him, it will be a time of revelation as they come face to face with their Judge. It will be both a great and a terrible day (Joel 2:31).

THE SIGNS OF THE TIMES

Whilst we can never know exactly when Jesus is going to return, the Scriptures nevertheless encourage us to read the signs of the times. When certain events happen we must take note that the world is on a sure and certain track to the day when Jesus is coming again. For example, as we have already seen in *Journey to Freedom*, we can know that when Israel was reborn as a nation (in 1948), God's end-time prophetic agenda was beginning to unwind. And now that there is a significant body of Messianic believers growing up in the land, we can see the emergence of the 'one new man' in Christ Jesus (Ephesians 2:15, NKJV) as Jew and Gentile together jointly declare their belief in Jesus the Messiah. These are events of great prophetic significance.

As far as understanding the times and the seasons is concerned, it's vitally important that we read what Jesus Himself said – especially about His own second coming. At the beginning of Matthew 24 Jesus told the disciples that one day the temple in Jerusalem would be destroyed. This was hard for them to accept or believe. So, later, when He was alone with His disciples, they were full of questions about when it would happen; they also asked what would be the signs of His coming and of the end of the age. Jesus had obviously made it clear to them that He would return and they wanted to know more about it.

Jesus rolled the answers to all these questions into one discourse (which takes up the whole of the rest of the chapter). He told them that "*this generation will certainly not pass away until all these things have happened*" (Matthew 24:34). The Romans destroyed the temple in Jerusalem in AD 70, so it is certainly true that most of the generation to which Jesus was speaking would still be alive when that terrible event happened.

Be Not Deceived:

In answering the wider question about what signs would herald His return, Jesus begins by telling believers (not unbelievers) not to be deceived. He warns them that *'many will come in my name, claiming [they are] the Christ and deceive many'* (Matthew 24:5). The word 'Christ' means 'anointed'. But it's true that many have come with false anointings – anointings that have their origin in the powers of darkness, as opposed to the power of the Holy Spirit. People who travel the world looking for an anointing are usually chasing the end of a deceptive rainbow and can be running away from what God would have them do at home!

In our own generation many have been led away into false religions, cults that have added unique twists to Christian teaching, and they have been deceived false prophecies, signs and miracles, just as Jesus predicted (Matthew 24:5, 11 and 24). People love the sensational and Satan is a master at serving up the sensational in order to distract people from the truth.

I passionately believe in healing, deliverance and prophecy. However, I weep over the many occasions when people are seduced by shows of apparent power into thinking that this is an acceptable substitute to being a faithful disciple of the Lord Jesus. In some circles the wonderful gift of prophecy has been reduced to trying to give people directional words for their lives, when the Lord would first and foremost want us to learn to hear His directional voice for ourselves. It's so easy for people who are not grounded in truth to be tempted to follow a nice 'word', in preference to learning for themselves what it means to be a personal disciple of Jesus.

Physical Signs:

Jesus also warned that the years before He comes again will be marked by many major events, such as wars, rumours of wars, famines, earthquakes and an increase in wickedness. None of us could deny that these past hundred years have been marked by exactly what Jesus warned us about.

- Nations (people groups) have risen up against nations, with ethnic conflicts such as the terrible massacres that took place in Rwanda and all the fighting in Syria.
- We have witnessed many terrible wars – everything from global conflicts to the terrorist wars that are constantly being fought.

- Because of terrorism and suicide bombers there's nowhere on the planet where we can know we're safe from the intrusion of evil into our way of life.
- The incidence of earthquakes is rising rapidly.
- Despite advanced agricultural technology, the world still reels under news of famines that creep up on nations seemingly out of nowhere, and devastate whole populations.
- The *'fire and billows of smoke'* (Acts 2:19) that have spewed out of a volcano in Iceland brought the travelling world to its knees.

Spiritual Breakdown:

Jesus warned that there would be an *'increase in wickedness'* (Matthew 24:12). Scriptural morality is no longer an acceptable basis for making laws, and God's Word has been dismissed as irrelevant by most of the world's governments. The free availability of the most perverse of pornography on the internet and on satellite television has removed the barriers that prevented people from indulging in the 'enjoyment' of all sorts of evil.

Jesus warned that followers of Jesus will be hated by all nations because of Him and persecuted (Matthew 24:9). We're now close to that situation prevailing today in the western world. In many places it's no longer acceptable legally to proclaim that Jesus is the only Way to God and, increasingly, those who want to live their lives according to God's Word are coming up against political correctness and ungodly laws.

In many parts of the world, we now live in an all-embracing society where 'anything goes'. No-one wants to be told that what they believe and what they are doing is wrong, whatever it may be. The concept of absolute right and wrong has disappeared from society. Although most would still recognise that it's wrong to steal, sexually abuse children or commit murder, the boundaries have been severely blurred in respect of murder because of abortions and, increasingly now, the possibility of terminating the lives of the elderly.

It is in the midst of such deception and evil that Jesus said the Gospel of the Kingdom must be preached. Furthermore, when all nations (people groups) have had the opportunity to hear and believe the Gospel, the end will then come (Matthew 24:14). None of this gives us grounds for naming a date, but all of it makes us realise that the coming again of the Redeemer may be nearer than we think.

WHAT WILL HAPPEN WHEN HE COMES?

When Jesus returns those who are in faith and relationship with Him will know the joy of their redemption being finally fulfilled. For those who don't know Him and have rejected His loving provision of forgiveness from sin through the cross, only God's judgement awaits them. It will be a great and a terrible day at one and the same time. For those who are in Christ, it will be a wonderful and glorious day. For those who realise their rejection of Christ was the biggest mistake they ever made, it will be a terrible day (Malachi 4:5).

Jesus told parables at the end of Matthew 24 and in Matthew 25 illustrating how important it is for us to be ready when He comes. He talked of the two who would be working in the field and one would be in Christ and the other not (Matthew 24:36-40). He told of the wise and the foolish virgins – the foolish ones had no oil in their lamps. These five weren't ready when the Bridegroom (Jesus) came (Matthew 25:1-13) (see *Journey to Freedom, Book 5* for more details). There is only way of knowing you'll be ready when He comes and that's to be ready at all times, whether He comes or not! That way, when He comes, you know that you WILL be ready!

The Book of Revelation gives significant detail about further things that will happen when Jesus returns (Revelation 19:11-20:15). He will return, not as a baby, but as *'King of Kings and Lord of Lords'* (Revelation 19:16). He will return in triumph and will exercise on earth the authority that He has always had, and which He retained by never submitting to Satan while on earth. If Jesus had given in to Satan's temptations in the wilderness, for example, it would be Satan who would be exercising authority over Jesus and not the other way round.

Then Jesus will use His authority to capture Satan and all the powers of darkness and consign them to the Abyss, where they will be locked and sealed for a thousand years (Revelation 20:1-6). After this Jesus will reign on earth in what is known as the Millennial Reign. He will exercise authority and discipline, and during this time people will see what the world could have been like throughout history if man had not chosen to obey Satan, even though we will still have a carnal nature.

At the end of the thousand years, Satan will be released again prior to the final battle surrounding the city God loves, Jerusalem, (Revelation 20:9). Then, right at the very end, perhaps when Satan thinks he is finally going to win, the wrath and the judgement of God will be poured out and Satan will be condemned to eternal destruction (Revelation 20:10). Then, I believe, the redeemed people of God who are still on the earth will be saved and taken up with Jesus into heaven's glory (1 Thessalonians 4:17).

Clearly, none of us knows the full detail of everything that will happen, and there are certainly different interpretations of what the Scriptures say. However, but what matters above all is that we know for certain that Jesus will return and that we can totally trust Him to be our Saviour and our Redeemer through all the present and future circumstances of life!

WHAT DIFFERENCE DOES ALL THIS MAKE?

There are two answers to the question 'What differences does all this make?', opposite to each other but both correct!

- The fact that Jesus is coming again is like the icing on the cake of truth. It changes absolutely everything. We know we have a future, a glorious, redeemed and very exciting future. It gives us hope in the very core of our being!
- Yet, the fact that Jesus is coming back shouldn't change anything. For if we really love Him, we will want to obey Him anyway! But if we only choose to live according to God's Word out of fear of what will happen when He returns, then in reality we're not obeying God because we love Him and we haven't fully understood what a relationship with Him really means.

Nevertheless, there is a rightful place for holy fear. Hebrews tells us, for example, that it was *'in holy fear that Noah built the ark to save his family'* (Hebrews 11:7). We do need to have a holy fear of grieving the One we love and who loves us so much. If you really love someone you will always want to do those things that please that person and you will be 'afraid' of hurting them. That sort of fear is healthy and an important part of learning to be a disciple.

I pray that as you work through this teaching you will be so filled with love for your Saviour and be so full of thanks for the provision made for you by Father God, that you will be rejoicing to do those things that please Him – just because you love Him!

SUMMARY

When Jesus told His disciples He was coming back, He also said He was preparing a place for them. That is wonderfully good news! He's coming back for all those who've responded to the good news of the Gospel and are choosing to live as His disciples. But when He comes it will not be like His first appearing. This time the news will break across the skies and everyone will know that the Redeemer and the Judge of all the world has come. For those who recognise their Redeemer it will be an amazing day. For the others it will be a terrible day as they realise how they've not taken the time to fill their lamps with oil and be ready when He comes.

PRAYER

Thank You, Lord, that all the promises of Your first coming were faithfully fulfilled. Thank You for the encouragement this gives me that Your promise to prepare a place for Your disciples is just as true as all the other promises. I'm looking forward to the day when You come. Help me to serve You faithfully right up to that moment of Your appearing. In Jesus' name, Amen.

RAISED TO LIFE WITH HIM

From the day we are born there's only one thing in life that can be 100% guaranteed, and that's death! None of us will escape the consequences of what happened at the Fall when death entered the human race. When our spiritual relationship with God, who is Spirit, was broken (John 4:24), our human spirit became dead to God because of sin. Death (eternal separation from God) then became the inheritance of our soul, and finally our body also took on the mantle of death and now has a time limit on it!

In the early days of humanity, man still lived physically for a very long time. But as sin increased and the ongoing consequences of sin were worked out in the lives of men and women, the spiritual curse of death gained ever more authority in the physical realm. *'Three score years and ten'* (seventy – Psalm 90:10) became the basic life expectation of most human beings although there have, of course, been many exceptions who have lived much longer. With today's medical advances eighty to ninety has become the seventy to eighty of fifty years ago.

But what is death – an end or a beginning? It's both – the end of life

PERSONAL NOTES

in the physical domain and the beginning of life in eternity with God. In death we experience the gateway to life.

The nineteenth century English minister and novelist, Charles Kingsley (1819-1875), said, 'It is not darkness you are going to, for God is Light. It is not lonely, for Christ is with you. It is not unknown country, for Christ is there'. And C S Lewis, famous for the Narnia series of children's novels but a great theologian in his own right, said in a private letter to a lady who was dying, 'There are better things ahead than any we leave behind.[1]

I recently visited the place where my parents are buried. It was an opportunity to say a quiet prayer of thanksgiving to God for their lives and the inspiration they were to me. They weren't there of course – the grave was simply the temporary resting place of their dead bodies. But as I looked down at the grave I thought of the exciting moment that will one day come when, at the resurrection of the dead, there will be a mighty triumphant shout, as those who have died in Christ will rise with their new resurrection bodies to share in the glory of God.

I can almost imagine my Mum and Dad's excitement at what they know is coming soon for all those who love the Lord! Those who die in Christ truly have no reason to fear death – for they have already died in Him. They were also given new life when they were born again. Now they wait, sitting on the edge of their seats in paradise, for that moment of glorious reunion with all their loved ones. Paul wrote to the Corinthians, and to us, *'We know that the one who raised the Lord Jesus from the dead will also raise us with Jesus and present us with you in his presence'* (2 Corinthians 4:14).

Even as I write these words I can feel the excitement of the redeemed of the Lord, as if they know there's not long to wait before the final curtain of history comes down on the world as we know it. They know that this curtain is not the end – it's simply the prelude to the curtain rising on heaven's glory, and all that will mean for those who know Jesus. The more we are aware of heaven, the less we fear losing the things of earth! But all that, of course, is only for those who are blessed by being in Christ.

IS DEATH THE END FOR THOSE OUTSIDE OF CHRIST?

I don't believe there's anything in Scripture to support the idea that when people who are not 'in the Lord' die that their souls come to the end of their existence (annihilation). Nor that it's only the souls of people who die 'in the Lord' that continue their journey into eternity. Scripture supports two different destinations, but not the idea of annihilation.

Many unbelievers would welcome a theology of annihilation that says that those who've rejected God will simply be exterminated, without consequence. Such a belief, were it true, would give man unlimited license for committing sin without any connection between what is done on earth and the consequence in heaven. Tragically, this is what many believe but it's not what the Bible teaches, as we will soon see in more detail.

It's certainly not what Jesus taught. In His parable about the post-death experiences of the rich man and Lazarus, the beggar who used to sit at the rich man's gate, Jesus made this very clear. Lazarus, was taken to *'Abraham's bosom'*, meaning paradise. The rich man, however, finished up in the torment of Hades. In the story, Jesus has Abraham saying to the rich man, *"'a great chasm has been fixed so that those who want to go from here to you cannot, nor can anyone cross over from there to us'"* (Luke 16:19-31). Jesus used these powerful words to get the urgency of His message across – the soul cannot be exterminated, it is indestructible. The eternal destination of our soul is determined by the choices we make here on earth. The choice we make 'here' can't be changed 'there'*!*

The final destination of hell (Gehenna) was not prepared for mankind. Jesus said the eternal fire was *'prepared for the devil and his angels'* (Matthew 25:41). But mankind chose to follow Satan and it's as if the whole of the human race climbed on board a bus or a train that had Satan as its driver. I've travelled on many forms of transport, in many parts of the world, and I've found that all the passengers end up at the same destination as the driver!

But when Jesus died, His ultimate destination was heaven, not hell and those who travel with Him will always finish up where He is. This may sound simple, but it's the heart of the most profound statement made by Jesus when He said, *"'I am the way, and the truth and the life. No-one comes to the Father except through me'"* (John 14:6).

JESUS THE RESURRECTION FIRST-FRUITS

Jesus physically died. He chose to die, even though He was sinless and not, therefore, subject to the curse of death through the Fall. Like any other dead human being, His body had to be looked after by the living. It didn't bury itself. His body was taken down from the cross and collected from the Roman soldiers by Joseph of Arimathea.

His body was then placed in the traditional middle eastern, walk-in grave of a relatively wealthy man. A huge stone was rolled across the entrance and the grave was sealed (John 19:38-42). However, on resurrection morning, the first day of the week following His crucifixion, there was an explosion of life within the tomb. Angels rolled the stone away – although that was for the benefit of those who would want to go in and have a look, not so that Jesus could get out!

Ever since, believers have been able to say, *'Christ has indeed been raised from the dead, the first-fruits of those who have fallen asleep'* (1 Corinthians 15:20). There is no doubt that the living Lord Jesus came back into His own dead body. The physical remains of His dead body didn't stay in the tomb. His resurrection didn't take place somewhere else – it was where His body lay.

The power of God's resurrection life transformed His physical body into a spiritual, resurrection body and the physical walls of the grave were no longer an obstacle to Him. He later proved this by appearing in the midst of all the disciples, despite the door of the room being locked (John 20:19). Jesus was just as alive then as He had been before His death, but His body didn't have the physical limitations of a natural, human body any more.

Paul described Christ in His resurrection, as the 'first-fruits'. First-fruits are an early indication of what's to come later in the main harvest. Jesus told the disciples that *'the harvest is the end of the age and the harvesters are the angels'* (Matthew 13:39). The first-fruits are always the same in nature as the harvest that's to come. So we can look at Jesus' resurrection body and know that our resurrection bodies are going to be like His!

We will still look like the people we were, as Jesus did, but on the inside there will be a wonderful and glorious difference. Our body will no longer be physical in the way we currently understand physical. And we will be like Him, just as God intended us to be in the first place, without a carnal, fallen nature, prone to sin. What a glorious expectation awaits us on our resurrection morning!

• We will find out what God had intended for us in creation.

- We will discover ourselves and learn all about the people we love, who also knew the Lord.
- We will not only uncover the amazing wonders of God's Kingdom, but we'll discover the amazing depths and variety in the people that God created us to be.
- We won't have any of the inherited curses affecting us from the sins of previous generations.
- We won't have any of the bad characteristics that we learned from others as we grew up.
- We won't have any of the consequences of the mistakes we made and sins we committed – they will be forgiven and cleansed in the blood of the Lamb – for nothing impure can ever enter into heaven's glory (Revelation 21:27).
- And we definitely won't have any of the demons that plagued us from without and from within during our time on planet earth.
- **We will be like Jesus – He's our first-fruits and we're part of His harvest!**

WHAT A PROSPECT!

I don't know how God's going to do it on that final resurrection day, but I know that I can look forward to that amazing day with more than a tinge of excitement. **Our physical death is merely 'a changing room' on the way to our final destination of heaven!** And then at the final resurrection we will be changed once more.

> '*So will it be with the resurrection of the dead. The body that is sown is perishable, it is raised imperishable; it is sown in dishonour, it is raised in glory; it is sown in weakness, it is raised in power; it is sown a natural body, it is raised a spiritual body*' (1 Corinthians 15:42-44).

At the moment of physical death we will be released from the restrictions and limitations of our tired, sick, weary physical bodies and leave them behind. I only ever remember my Granny as a bed-ridden old lady who went places in a wheel-chair. I'm looking forward to watching her dance! We will enter paradise (Luke 23:43 and 2 Corinthians 12:4), the waiting room for heaven. Jesus will be there and we will know and love Him.

When John Newton (1725-1807), the writer of *Amazing Grace*, commented on this experience of entering into glory and meeting people, he said, 'When I get there, I shall see three wonders. The first wonder will be to see many there whom I did not expect to see; the second wonder will be to miss many people who I did expect to see; and the third and greatest wonder of all will be to find myself there!' What John Newton said is, I believe, so very true – there are going to be a lot of surprises. And I'm sure we will see many there who did respond to the call of God on their lives in their dying days, like the dying thief on the cross, but were never able to communicate the fact that they had given their lives to Him.

There, with all the saints of God we will become part of the great communion of saints (as the Apostle's Creed of Christian beliefs has expressed that fellowship of the heavenly realms for hundreds of years). Together in paradise we will praise and worship Him and look forward to that incredibly exciting day when:

'the trumpet will sound, the dead will be raised imperishable, and we will be changed. For the perishable must clothe itself with the imperishable, and the mortal with immortality. When the perishable has been clothed with the imperishable, and the mortal with immortality, then the saying that is written will come true, "Death has been swallowed up in victory"' (1 Corinthians 15:52-54).

I can imagine all the saints in glory rejoicing in the worship and praise of God, but at the same time constantly listening for the sound of the trumpet when they will be raised and, as Paul said *'just as we have borne the likeness of the earthly man, so shall we bear the likeness of the man from heaven'* (1 Corinthians 15:49). At that moment, Jesus said, *'He will send his angels with a loud trumpet call, and they will gather his elect from the four winds, from one end of the heavens to the other'* (Matthew 24:31).

Suddenly, paradise will be empty as in that moment that transcends time, all the dead will be resurrected as they're gathered from the graves and every place that their bodies have been lain to rest, whether they have been buried, consumed by fire, drowned in the sea or met their end in any other way. There will be a triumphant procession of the resurrected redeemed. *'Therefore, my dear brothers'* says Paul, *'stand firm.*

Let nothing move you. Always give yourselves fully to the work of the Lord, because you know that your labour in the Lord is not in vain' (1 Corinthians 15:58). There are no losers among the redeemed of the Lord – we are all on the winning side. And it's going to be glorious beyond description!

'For the Lord himself will come down from heaven with a loud command, with the voice of the archangel and with the trumpet call of God, and the dead in Christ will rise first. After that, we who are still alive and are left will be caught up together with them in the clouds to meet the Lord in the air. And so we will be with the Lord forever. Therefore, encourage each other with these words' (1 Thessalonians 4:16-18).

And that's exactly what I am praying this unit of *Journey to Freedom* will be for each one of you – a glorious encouragement in the transforming truth of the Gospel. What a Saviour, what a future we have to look forward to!

WHEN THE ROLL IS CALLED UP YONDER!

James Black (1856-1938) was a Methodist Sunday School teacher in Williamsport, Pennsylvania. One day, he was calling the roll for a youth meeting when young Bessie, the daughter of a local drunkard failed to show up. He was disappointed that she wasn't there and commented, 'Well, I trust when the roll is called up yonder, she'll be there.'

He tried to find an appropriate song to match the thought but couldn't find one in his song book and he sensed God asking him to write one. "I put away the thought" he said, "but as I opened the gate on my way home, the same thought came again so strongly that tears filled my eyes. I entered the house and sat down at the piano. The words came to me effortlessly. The tune came the same way-I dared not change a single note or word."[2] This is what he wrote:

When the trumpet of the Lord shall sound, and time shall be no more,
And the morning breaks, eternal, bright and fair;
When the saved of earth shall gather over on the other shore,
And the roll is called up yonder, I'll be there.
When the roll is called up yonder,

When the roll is called up yonder,
When the roll is called up yonder,
When the roll is called up yonder, I'll be there.

On that bright and cloudless morning when the dead in Christ shall rise,
And the glory of his resurrection share;
When his chosen ones shall gather to their home beyond the skies,
And the roll is called up yonder, I'll be there.
Let us labour for the Master from the dawn till setting sun,
Let us talk of all his wondrous love and care;
Then when all of life is over, and our work on earth is done,
And the roll is called up yonder, I'll be there.

This song was sung in the Academy award winning movie *Sergeant York*. It was also sung in my own Bible Class as a child. It was one of our favourites. I've never forgotten it – and what's more I've never forgotten the significance of the words as I realised the amazing truth that, for those who are in Christ, 'We'll be there!' Hallelujah indeed.

A SUGGESTION

Find a private place, open your Bible, find 1 Corinthians chapter 15 and read it out loud – really loud! Let the Holy Spirit inspired words of Paul be your encouragement for today. Shout it out! Sing it out! Live it out!

SUMMARY

On resurrection morning the great trumpet will sound in the heavenlies and the redeemed of the Lord will rise in triumph from the grave. Jesus was the first-fruits and all the redeemed will be the harvest on that great and glorious day. Death holds no eternal fears for those who are in Christ. We have a home to look forward to and one day Jesus is coming back for His own to take us to the place He's preparing for us. What a day of triumph that will be. Christ has died! Christ has risen! And Christ will come again - for you!

PRAYER

Lord, I am totally overwhelmed today by the wonderful provision You have made for Your children – those who have been redeemed out of the hands of the enemy and are awaiting the sound of the great trumpet. Thank You, Lord, for being the first-fruits and showing me what I can look forward to. Forgive me, Lord, for ever being afraid of death. What an exciting prospect lies ahead. I am so excited! Thank You, Thank You, Thank You. In Jesus' name, Amen.

---

[1] **Hooper, W (ed), The Collected Letters of C S Lewis, Volume 3. (HarperCollins, 2006)**

[2] Black, James, 1898, public domain

THE END OF ALL THINGS

The certainty of Jesus' coming again changes everything for the believer. In truth it changes everything for the unbeliever as well since one day those who have rejected Jesus here on earth will tragically discover how wrong they were!

For the believer, death when it comes is a welcome gateway to heaven's glory. It is not something to be feared, but a station on the journey from time to eternity. When my brother was dying that's exactly how he described the experience. By profession he was a research scientist, and even when he was living through the final stages of life on earth he was noting and recording his experiences!

On the day before he died, as his bodily systems were beginning to close down, he told me that it now felt as though he was standing on a station platform, waiting for a special train to come in that was just for him! Eventually his special train did arrive, and I was privileged to be there as he boarded the train and took his final breath here on earth. The platform was empty; my brother had gone; only his body remained.

PERSONAL NOTES

For those who are left, there is the natural human grief of parting, but when those who have died are in Christ, the grief is always tinged with the joy of knowing that eternal death has been conquered and heaven awaits. Even though the body has died, a victim of the Fall, and it's right and proper to grieve over and miss our friends and family, the good news is that the old enemy, Satan, has not been able to claim another victim beyond the grave. **The redeemed soul is freed forever from Satan and the grip of death!**

WHAT HAPPENS NEXT – FOR THE LIVING AND THE DEAD?

For those who have already died, what happens next is a glorious time of waiting in the presence of the Lord. Their journey's completed and now they are part of the worshipping community of paradise, the place to which Jesus referred on the cross, when He said to the dying criminal, *"Today you will be with me in paradise"* (Luke 23:43).

As part of the communion of saints, the family of God, I believe they are also an intercessory community whose prayers are constantly rising to the Father. They are specifically referred to by the writer of Hebrews when he says:

'Therefore, since we are surrounded by such a great cloud of witnesses, let us throw off everything that hinders and the sin that so entangles, and let us run with perseverance the race marked out for us' (Hebrews 12:1).

This certainly gives the impression that they have some knowledge of what's happening on earth, and that we are being urged on by their prayers in the ongoing race of life.

Furthermore, as Jesus' account of the rich man and Lazarus in Luke 16:19-31 makes clear, whilst here on earth the only access we have to those who have already died is through Jesus. When the rich man asked if Lazarus could be sent from *'Abraham's side'* (paradise) to warn his brothers back on earth of what awaited them after death, he was told quite categorically, *'If they will not listen to Moses and the Prophets, they will not be convinced even if someone rises from the dead'* (Luke 16:31). We cannot bridge that gulf between earth and paradise apart from through Jesus.

Those who have already died are 'in Him', and believers here on earth are also 'in him'.

It's interesting that in all the deceptive beliefs and experiences of those who dabble in spiritualism in an attempt to contact the dead, you never hear of anyone who has allegedly died warning people to repent and find Jesus before they die and it's too late! God has forbidden any such direct contact from paradise, and Satan has no interest in warning people of what will happen to them after death if they don't come to Jesus!

So the messages that allegedly come through those who dabble in the hidden world of Satan's darkness (the occult), are usually words of false comfort telling people not to worry because everything's wonderful where they are! This is all designed to create an illusion of safety. This is no different from temptations Satan constantly puts before the living, telling them no harm will come if they sin, and that everything will be OK! And that's the same old lie that Adam fell for in the Garden. History tells us differently – there was a terrible cost of believing Satan's lies, as God had rightly warned.

There can be serious consequences of dabbling in Satan's world, with things like Ouija boards and spiritualism. People are attracted by the idea of finding out things about 'the other side'. However Satan deceives people with lies and what they hear will always lead them into danger. It was forbidden in Scripture for a very good reason – it's wrong (Deuteronomy 18:9-11).

LIVING FOR GOD IN A SPIRITUALLY COMPLACENT AND HOSTILE WORLD

For those who are still living – and that includes you and me right now – we still have a race to run. As far as we know, the finishing line is not yet in sight and we have to live through whatever years are left to us, not knowing what lies ahead. However, we need to live every day of our lives as if it's our last. None of us knows the day or the hour when Jesus will return and we also don't know when our own personal home call will come.

As I was thinking about this, there was an item on the news about a terrible coach crash in which three people were killed. Earlier in the day those three were going about their normal lives – they had no idea that when they got out of bed that morning they were hastening towards their last moment of earthly existence.

Sadly, events like this happen every day, all over the world and people just accept that occasional tragedy is part of the routine of life. The thought that today could be their last day on earth doesn't bring large numbers of people to repentance. Not even huge earthquakes or a catastrophic tsunami in Asia have an impact on the beliefs of the rest of the world. People carry on living in their own sweet way as if nothing had happened, thinking these things always happen to someone else and never to them. Satan has blinded their eyes so they're unconcerned by eternity.

It's well known in history that, in times of war and great national crisis, the churches are filled with people who go to pray that God will save them and their nation. That certainly happened in the UK during the Second World War – but where were those people who went to church in wartime when peace came? A few may have found faith in Christ during the extremes of war. I have a friend, for example, who was wonderfully saved while serving in the US Forces in the Gulf War in 1990. But the vast majority of those who choose to pray in wartime, choose not to pray when the war is over – for then they think they no longer have any need of God. God has become for them like the ultimate last resort – useful in times of great emergency, but otherwise a quaint belief of a bygone age.

There's no doubt that God heard the cries from the heart of His people in England during the terrible conflict of the Second World War. Archbishop of Canterbury Dr William Temple's radio addresses and newspaper articles gave heart to the people of Britain. "Why has God preserved us?" he said. "We may, and we must, believe that He who has preserved our land in a manner so marvellous, has a purpose for us to serve in the preparation for His perfect Kingdom."[1]

If only the leaders of our nation had taken note of what their Archbishop had said! Sadly, in the years that have passed since, any respect that the nation had for the God who answered prayer has been dismissed as irrelevant to a supposedly more enlightened age. Man has taken the place of God in the hierarchy of belief. Pride and arrogance have placed man on his own throne and, not only has God been side-lined, but those who still believe in God and believe that their faith in

God should shape their life and their nation, have almost universally become the victims of political correctness and enemies of the state.

The reason I'm mentioning all this is that the western world is very quickly moving from its former traditional Christian foundation through an era of neutrality to one of increasing hostility towards believers. The west is joining all those nations which have for a long time been hostile towards the true faith. When Jesus was telling the disciples about what the times would be like in the years prior to His return He said, "'*you will be hated by all nations because of me*'" (Matthew 24:9).

The abandoning of prayer in schools, the removal of the Ten Commandments from offices of the law, the collapse of moral boundaries in society and the elevation of multi-faith beliefs are just some of the evidences of the increasingly legalised hatred and victimisation of those who believe and practise their faith. Here in the UK, for example, one of my close friends is right now, as I write this, in hospital. One of the doctors treating him is a Christian. This doctor said, "I can't be seen praying for you, I would probably lose my job." We now live in a different world to the one in which I was brought up. This is the spiritual environment of the days we are in and the End Times we are now beginning to live through.

THE END TIMES

So, what are the 'End Times'? In one sense the End Times began when Jesus came the first time and will not be concluded until He comes again! But when Christians talk about the End Times they are generally referring much more specifically to the period of time that immediately precedes the imminent coming of Jesus. But as none of us know exactly when Jesus is coming again we can't accurately describe when the End Times will be! But, as we have already seen, some of the things that are happening around us are included in Jesus' list of events that He says will take place before He comes again (Matthew 24:4-25).

There are many prophetic Scripture passages that talk about future events in addition to Matthew 24. Mark (chapter 13) and Luke (17:20-37) include similar passages in their Gospel records and the book of Revelation is full of prophetic passages about the End Times. In the Old Testament Daniel describes some of the difficult times that people will have to go through in the season immediately before the end of all things.

To analyse all these passages of Scripture thoroughly would require many weeks of study, and that's not the primary objective of *Journey to Freedom*. For those, however, who do want to look more into these things, and in much greater detail than we have the space for here, I would strongly recommend you read David Pawson's book *When Jesus Returns* (Hodder, 1995). It is a masterly analysis of all the relevant passages, and throws great light on all the different interpretations there have been of the various end-time prophetic Scriptures.

Even though we will leave it to others to take you deeper into the theology of the End Times, we can't hide the fact that Scripture does warn about difficult times ahead for those who remain faithful to Jesus. All the seven letters that Jesus wrote through John to the seven churches in Revelation 2 and 3 include words of encouragement and reward to those who overcome and endure to the end. And many of Paul's letters encourage believers to persevere through their trials. It would be comforting to think that his words were only relevant to the conditions prevailing in the first century of Christian experience. But the twentieth century had more martyrs for the faith than all the other nineteen centuries put together!

Satan has not softened his stance towards Christians just because two thousand years have passed. The reality is that, as we approach the day of Christ's return, we can expect the enemy to increase his attacks on the people of God. They are pressing on to see the Gospel preached to every people group in the world (Matthew 24:14), and Satan's days are numbered. He is like a frightened, cornered animal at its most dangerous. His available time to deceive the peoples of the world is running out, as the day of Christ's return moves ever nearer.

The Greek word for 'martyr' means a 'witness', and it's true that those who choose to witness for their faith will come under threat of persecution. But, given the choice between denying one's faith or witnessing to the truth, I pray that all of us who are journeying together through *Journey to Freedom* would be praying for the courage to be faithful under test.

So, in this present season I want to emphasise what *Journey to Freedom* has been all about since the beginning of Book 1 – equipping the saints to do the works of the Kingdom, and strengthening the Body of Christ. The most effective way we can do that is by making sure that we know our Saviour, know the spiritual ground on which we stand, know how to recognise and overcome Satan's strategies against us and know how to use the spiritual weapons that God has provided for us.

PREPARED, EQUIPPED, STRENGTHENED AND TRAINED

These four words form the basis of my personal prayer for each and every one of you who know and love the Lord. We've come a long way together since we started on our *Journey to Freedom*. Many have already given testimony to the amazing transformation there has been through applying the teaching in their lives.

Journey to Freedom is not designed to entertain, though I trust you have enjoyed the journey together so far. Neither is it designed just to be a Bible Study, giving you more information about what is in God's book. It's much more than both of these things. I remember when God first gave me the vision for writing this material, and I began to write out the titles of some of the topics we would cover, God showed me how so many believers were going out to battle, unarmed and without training. It was no surprise, therefore, that so many of them were being taken out of the warfare, wounded and in need of healing.

One of the main reasons that people are so vulnerable is that they have never understood the security of God's love. They have not learned to live in *the 'shelter of the Most High'* or *'rest in the shadow of the Almighty'*. For He is our *'refuge and fortress'* (Psalm 91:1-2). It's the security of His love that strengthens us for all that lies ahead. With Him we are like children secure under the protection of Daddy's arms.

So I'm praying that through *Journey to Freedom*:

- you will **grow in your understanding of God's love and security;**
- He will continue to **prepare you** for all the years ahead that He has in store;
- He will **equip you** with all the weapons you need to fight whatever the enemy throws at you;
- He will **nourish you** with the Word of Life and **strengthen** the backbone of your spiritual life, making it like unbreakable steel;

- He will **train you** in all the disciplines of life that will be essential for the particular calling and destiny He has for you.

SUMMARY

We are living in very testing days when opposition to the Christian faith is increasing across the world. Jesus warned us that there will be a time when all nations will hate believers and it's vital, therefore, that we are trained and equipped to be the Body of Christ. At the same time as the enemy is increasing his pressure on the church, God is raising up His people so that in every generation till Jesus comes, there will be a powerful witness to the truth of Jesus, and every people group on the planet will have heard the Gospel message. God is raising up an amazing people who will press on, against all odds, to declare through their lives into this world the wonderful message that Jesus still saves, He still heals, He still delivers and one day soon He's coming back for His own!

Prayer

Thank You, Lord, that in the Great Commission You promised to be with us always – even until the end of the age. I pray, Lord, that You will use this time of my life to prepare, equip, strengthen and train me for whatever lies ahead. I am determined to follow You all my days as a member of Your Heavenly Kingdom, serving You for the time being on earth. In Jesus' name, Amen.

---

1 Temple, William: Sermon at St Paul's Cathedral, London on Battle of Britain Sunday 1943 about the Battle of Dunkirk.

Stage 8, Chapter 4

FINAL JUDGEMENT

A major court case recently ended in London. The jury in the case unanimously agreed that the man was guilty. The trial judge then suspended the court for a season so that he could determine what the appropriate punishment should be. So the man was sent back to prison to wait for the day when his sentence would be handed down by the judge. As I write these words he knows he is guilty and is waiting to hear his punishment.

In many ways that is a very accurate description of the present condition of the whole of the human race – every single human being is tainted with sin and is, therefore, guilty. Earlier in *Journey to Freedom* we likened the condition of all human beings to that of a baby born to a mother who was already in jail. Because the mother was in jail, so was the baby.

Sin has created an unclean condition in the heart of man. This comes from the rebellion that was first in the heart of Satan which, at the Fall because of man's sin, entered the heart of all men and women. God's vision for the heavenly realms was for a kingdom made up of Himself (Father, Son and Holy Spirit) and His created beings (mankind), living and working together in the perfect harmony of a pure relationship. In this relationship we would be free to develop the creative potential that He has given us, aided by all the angelic beings.

But even before mankind was created, Satan and all the angels who joined in his rebellion, were forcibly evicted from heaven by Michael and the warrior angels. Jesus tells us how He '*"saw Satan fall like lightning from heaven"*' (Luke 10:18). God's judgement on Satan was death – meaning eternal separation from God. And, as Jesus explained in Matthew 25:41, hell was not prepared for mankind but *'for the devil and all his angels.'* The sin was 'rebellion', the judgement was 'guilty' and the punishment was 'death'. This punishment meant separation from God and eviction from heaven, with the anticipation that hell would be the final destination. So heaven was cleansed of the impurity that had entered in.

Rebellion is the source of all impurity. So, having taken such radical action to evict Satan, there's no way that God's ever going to open the doors of heaven to anything that would taint the future blessings He's stored up for Himself and the saints in the future. Scripture expresses it this way:

'Nothing impure will ever enter it, nor will anyone who does what is shameful or deceitful, but only those whose names are written in the Lamb's Book of Life' (Revelation 21:27).

There can't be any degrees of sinfulness that will be acceptable – **nothing** impure will ever enter heaven, **nothing at all.** Even the most minor act of sinful thinking, choice, or behaviour alienates us from God and removes any right for us to enter heaven. The only qualification for entry to heaven is absolute purity. That, however, became an impossible target for human beings to reach, because they all joined in Satan's rebellion. This brings us right back to the heart of the Gospel we've been studying together throughout *Journey to Freedom*.

Heaven is the home of God, but, according to Jesus, He is now preparing it for mankind to populate (John 14:2-3). This is despite the fact that there is only one man who can qualify for entry – *the* Man, Christ Jesus, who left heaven as the Son of God and then became the Son of Man.

GOD'S JUDGEMENT ON MAN'S SIN

We saw in earlier units of *Journey to Freedom* how Jesus was the only human being who had never been subject to the curse of death. Anyone who came under Satan's authority and control would automatically be under the same judgement and punishment as Satan himself. The first Adam brought the whole of mankind under the curse, judgement and punishment of death. As Paul tells us, *'Just as sin entered the world through one man, and death through sin, … in this way death came to all men, because all sinned'* (Romans 5:12). But God, in His love for mankind and His overwhelming mercy, made it possible for life from the dead to come through one man also.

Jesus was the second 'Adam' (meaning the second sinless man to walk the face of the earth). But then the first Adam sinned and death entered into humanity, but Jesus remained without sin and was not, therefore, subject to death. But God had *'sent his own Son in the likeness of man, to be a sin offering'* (Romans 8:3). God then laid upon His sinless son the sins of all mankind and pronounced Him (the guiltless one) 'guilty' and laid on Him the punishment that by rights was ours. As Isaiah prophesied, *'the punishment that brought us peace was upon him'* (Isaiah 53:5).

Jesus suffered the punishment of death that God had first pronounced upon Satan and which man inherited. He cried out from the cross, *'"My God, my God, why have you forsaken me"'* (Matthew 27:46). He tasted the separation from God which is eternal death. Judgement had been passed on sinners and the righteous punishment was now being meted out. Jesus, under the weight of man's sins descended into the abyss of eternal darkness, and cried out from His experience of hell on earth.

Many years ago I owned two black Labrador dogs. One of them was a wanderer and would jump the garden wall. For his own sake I needed to catch him in the act and punish him accordingly, so that he would relate the punishment to the 'crime' he had committed. Long after dark I waited on the other side of the wall to catch him as he jumped over. When he jumped the wall, he got such a shock as he jumped into my arms. He kicked hard against me, ran round the wall to the gate, cleared the gate in one leap and tore up the drive with me in hot pursuit.

I raced after him, managed to grab him by the collar, and gave him an appropriate beating. It was only after I'd punished him for what he'd done, I realised that I had got hold of the wrong dog, in the dark. I'd given the other dog, who was always perfectly behaved, the punishment he didn't deserve. I felt terrible as I tried to make it up to the good dog and, true to his wonderful character, he just licked my hand, looked into my eyes and seemed to say, "I understand, it's OK!"

What I had done was terrible but, as I thought about the incident, I realised that this was exactly what God had done for the sake of mankind. Judgement had fallen and He had given the punishment that was due to the guilty ones to the One who was totally innocent.

However because Jesus was totally innocent, the cords of death had no legal right to chain Him up and keep Him in hell. So, on the third day the Father stretched out His hand and raised His Son from the pit. Under the Old Covenantal Law of Moses the sins of the people were laid upon the sacrificial lamb. Under the New Covenantal grace, Jesus became the Lamb of God who took away the sins of the world. Punishment had been carried out, justice had been done.

I know this isn't the first time we've looked at the sacrifice of Jesus on the cross, but I'm doing it again so there can be no doubt about the fact that believers will only escape the righteous judgement of a holy God because the punishment has already been taken by Jesus. As Christians we look at the work of the cross from the viewpoint of judgement and mercy. It's vital to understand what happened on the cross if we're to know the peace of God, although that peace is beyond our human understanding. If we don't understand that the punishment for man's sin, including yours and mine, really has been carried for us by Jesus, then any discussion of the Final Judgement will cause us to be in fear rather than in thanksgiving.

THE END IN SIGHT

The images of the book of Revelation are only frightening for those who have not yet escaped from the curse of death and hell. For those of us who are in Christ, they are a glorious celebration and we can sing with the multitudes of the heavenly host, the angels and the redeemed of God, *'Hallelujah! For our Lord God Almighty reigns. Let us rejoice and be glad'* (Revelation 19:6-7). But let's not minimise the reality of how frightening the words of Revelation are for those who don't know the Saviour.

The picture painted by the Holy Spirit, through the pen of John, describes a special book, known as the *Lamb's Book of Life* (Revelation 20:12 and 21:27). Written in it are the names of those who have come humbly in repentance for their sin, have received forgiveness, have been born again of the Spirit of God, and are choosing to walk in the ways of God. They are the community of the redeemed, the family of God.

The faith they exercised to trust in the Saviour was accredited to them for righteousness and the righteousness of the Son of God became their covering. The blood of Jesus was the price paid for their salvation, just as the blood of the Passover lamb, on the doorposts and the lintels of their homes, was sufficient to deliver the Hebrew peoples from the curse of death in Egypt. The blood of Jesus applied to the doorway of our lives is sufficient to deliver us from the eternal curse of death, which would separate us from God forever. In Christ we are the recipients of God's merciful provision for each one of us.

We must wait to see how God unwinds the ages of history and when Jesus will come again to reign for a thousand years on earth. Then we will see what our planet looks like under the loving but disciplined reign of King Jesus (Revelation 20:1-6). And we only have a brief description of what will happen when Satan is loosed once more to deceive the nations (Revelation 20:7-8).

We do know, however, that at the very end, when the wrath of God is poured out upon the world, those who are alive at the time and are in Christ will be taken up from the earth by the Lord (1 Thessalonians 4:17) in what some people call 'the rapture'. We know that when the last trumpet sounds there will be a mighty resurrection of the dead – not just of those who have died in the Lord, but also of those who have died without having accepted God's salvation. Furthermore, we can be assured that finally Satan will receive the punishment in the lake of fire that has been reserved for him since the moment he fell from heavenly grace (Revelation 20:10).

THE FINAL JUDGEMENT

And so, at the end of all things, there is only one thing left to happen. Jesus described the events of that day in one of His most graphic parables when He said that:

'"when the Son of Man comes in his glory, he will sit on his throne in heavenly glory. All the nations will be gathered before him, and he will separate the people one from another as a shepherd separates the sheep from the goats"' (Matthew 25:31-32).

Paul tells us that:

'we must all appear before the judgement seat of Christ, that each one may receive what is due him for the things done while in the body, whether good or bad' (2 Corinthians 5:10).

John saw this awesome moment happening before *'a great white throne'* (Revelation 20:11). Heaven and earth as we know them were no more – they had *'fled from his presence and there was no place for them'* (Revelation 20:11). The books were opened, the books being the record of the life of each man and woman. *'The dead were judged according to what they had done as recorded in the books'* (Revelation 20:12).

Were it not for the fact that there was another book, this would be a terrifying time for every human being. But because of the *Lamb's Book of Life*, for those who are in Jesus this will be an awesome celebration of His great salvation (Revelation 20:12 and 21:27). But *'if anyone's name was not found written in the book of life he was thrown into the lake of fire'*, and *'the lake of fire is the second death'* (Revelation 20:14). Our first death is the physical death we die at the end of our lives on earth. But the second death is the eternal death from which there is neither escape nor return.

So the final judgement of our lives is made before the judgement throne of Christ. For those whose names are written in the *Lamb's Book of Life*, the price has already been paid for their sin and the 'slate has been wiped clean'. There is nothing to fear because there is nothing left in the record books against their name. The shed blood of Jesus has been applied to their sin and they are free – eternally and gloriously free! *'Then the King will say to those on his right:*

"Come, you who are blessed by my Father; take your inheritance, the kingdom prepared for you since the creation of the world" (Matthew 25:34).

JUDGEMENT AND REWARDS

At the Final Judgement there will be a separation of the redeemed from the lost. The lost will be those who have refused the truth of the Gospel and denied the presence and reality of God, even though God placed eternity in the heart of every man and woman (Ecclesiastes 3:11). God is not only a God of righteous judgement but also of fairness, and I don't believe any who stand before Him on that day will be able to say His judgements are unfair.

I find it fascinating to talk to young children about God – long before they have had the opportunity to hear and respond to the Gospel, they have an intuitive understanding of who He is. They have no difficulty in understanding the fact of God or of the nature of His character. It seems so obvious to them. It's built into their own nature – they are made in the image and likeness of God, so it's quite natural for them to talk to the One in whose image they are made!

But as people grow older, come under the influence of unbelievers and the powers of darkness and give licence to their carnal nature, they leave behind the wonderful simplicity of the gift of eternity that God placed in their hearts. They make their choices and they go their own way. I'm convinced that when we all stand before the throne of God everyone will know that God's judgements are right and fair. But within the realms of heaven there will be a different type of judgement, as God gives His rewards to the saints.

PRAYING FOR THE LOST

For now, let's take some time to think about all our close friends and family who do not know the Lord and who will, unless God intervenes in their lives, have to stand before the great white throne without their names being found in the *Book of Life*. That's a terrible expectation. May I encourage you to take a postcard, or something similar, put the date at the top, and then write down the names of all those people close to you, and whom the Lord puts on your heart, who don't know Him.

Then place the card somewhere where you'll see it every day – a place such as your bedside, as a bookmark in your Bible, where you brush your teeth or on the dashboard of your car. Then every time you see the card, systematically pray for the next person down the list, asking God if there's anything you should be doing to hasten the day when they come to faith in Jesus for themselves.

One man who did this systematically over the whole of his life and with extraordinary effect was George Müller (1805-1898) of Bristol. He was a Christian evangelist who built the Ashley Down orphanages and saw God meet the needs of thousands of orphaned children day after day, at the same time as introducing them to the Saviour. There was no social welfare or government help for his endeavours. He had to depend totally on God's supernatural provision.

Müller didn't grow weary as an intercessor. He wasn't discouraged by delay in the answer to his prayers for people to be converted or guided into the paths of full obedience. The year just before his death Müller spoke of two people whom he had prayed for day after day for over sixty years, and who had not to his knowledge turned to God. He said: "I have not a doubt that I shall meet them both in heaven; for my Heavenly Father would not lay upon my heart a burden of prayer for them for over threescore years, if He had not concerning them purposes of mercy."[1]

SUMMARY

All of us have joined in Satan's rebellion through the Fall, and not one of us is holy, excepting Jesus. The punishment He received, because of God's judgement on our sin, meant that those who are born again and whose names are written in the Lamb's Book of Life *have the incredible privilege of having their personal record wiped clean when they stand before Him, on that final Judgement Day. They are made whole and holy through being washed in the blood of the Lamb of God. The only expectation of those whose names are not written in the* Book of Life *is the same eternal punishment that was set aside for Satan and his angels. But heaven awaits the redeemed!*

PRAYER

Thank You, Lord, for standing in my place at Calvary, and that on Judgement Day because my name is written in Your Book of Life, I can look forward to sharing in the glories of the heavenly Kingdom. Help me, Lord, to follow George Müller's example and remain faithful throughout my life in praying for those close to me who do not yet know You. In Jesus' name, Amen.

---

1 Pierson, Arthur T, George Muller of Bristol and his Witness to a Prayer-Hearing God, 1899

HEAVEN'S GLORY

Paul was very conscious of the realities of the heavenly realms. God had shown him things that he was obviously reluctant to talk about but which had been an essential part of his preparation as an apostle. He describes how, on one occasion, the Lord gave him an insight into the spiritual realms. He describes how he *was caught up into the third heaven'* (2 Corinthians 12:2), into a place which he called paradise. There he heard things, and no doubt saw things too, about which the Lord did not permit him to speak. But it was clearly important that the Lord should give this exceptional apostle an understanding of the heavenly realms to better equip him to persevere with the particular calling there was on his life.

In 2 Corinthians 11:22-29 Paul catalogued some of the extremes of suffering he had endured as an apostle of Christ Jesus. I have no doubt that in all these horrendous experiences the vision of heaven's glory was one of the most powerful motivating factors that kept him going. He knew something of what paradise is like. His vision of heaven equipped him for life on earth.

PERSONAL NOTES

Every time a believer dies, paradise gains a precious soul! But the day is coming when the harvest in paradise (the redeemed who have died in the Lord) and the harvest on earth (those living on earth who are 'in Him') will be caught up together (see Matthew 13:43, 1 Thessalonians 4:16-17, 1 Corinthians 15:52-54). The stage will then be set for when Jesus reigns on high as Judge of all the earth, and all mankind is brought before Him and assembled before the great white throne.

I was fascinated to read how the great musician and composer, George Frideric Handel, was inspired to create the *Hallelujah Chorus* for *The Messiah*. He said, 'I saw the heavens opened, and God sitting on his great white throne.'[1] It was a vision of heaven that inspired Handel's most sublime work on earth. And I love the observation of C S Lewis when he commented that 'the Christians who did most for the present world were precisely those who thought most of the next'.[2]

A true vision and awareness of eternity motivate us to get ready for the world to come. This awareness of eternity stirs us to challenge the lost with the reality of heaven and hell. Jesus often talked about both; but those who recognise Him merely as a great teacher prefer to ignore this and choose not to believe what He was saying!

It always amazes me that scholars who study William Shakespeare can place equal value on every word he wrote, but when it comes to the teaching of Jesus they only value those words with which they agree! What an insult to the Son of God to compliment the words of His that you like, but to ignore or even rubbish what He says about heaven and hell – especially as this is the subject that He knows more about than any other person who has ever walked the surface of the earth!

WE ARE A COLONY OF HEAVEN

Paul's experience of the heavenly realms opened up for him the reality of who we are as believers. He recognised that when we're born again of the Spirit of God then:

> '*our citizenship is in heaven. And we eagerly await a Saviour from there, the Lord Jesus Christ, who, by the power that enables him to bring everything under his control, will transform our lowly bodies so that they will be like his glorious body*' (Philippians 3:20-21).

If our citizenship is in heaven but we're living on earth, then in fact we believers are like a colony of heaven living in an alien environment.

A colony is a group of citizens from one country who establish themselves in another country, and make their homes there. We're made in the image and likeness of God, and as His children we'll only feel totally at home when we're living where He is – in heaven. But for now we're a colony living in territory that currently has an alien ruler in charge. Our real home is heaven – the eternal address of those *'whose names are written in the Lamb's Book of Life'* (Revelation 21:27). That's where all the redeemed will echo the words of triumph and thanksgiving of the apostle Paul when he said, *'Thanks be to God. He gives us the victory through our Lord Jesus Christ'* (1 Corinthians 15:57).

All those whose names are not written in the Book of Life, however, will have to bear the consequences of their rejection of God's salvation. They have in fact chosen their own destination. As C S Lewis said, 'The lost enjoy for ever the horrible freedom they have demanded, and are therefore self-enslaved.'[3] Billy Graham expressed what eternity outside of heaven will be like by recognising the fact that we're made to desire and worship God. That's our very nature. He said that the experience of hell will be something worse than fire. It will be having *'a thirst for God that can't be quenched'* because it's where people will be cut off from the One they were made to relate to.

BE BLESSED BY THE TRUTH

At the beginning of the book of Revelation we find it was Jesus Himself who gave details of His revealed truth for John to write down and John *'testifies to everything he saw – that is the word of God and the testimony of Jesus Christ'* (Revelation 1:2). Jesus gives John a word of encouragement saying:

> *'"Blessed is the one who reads the words of this prophecy, and blessed are those who hear it and take to heart what is written in it, because the time is near"'* (Revelation 1:3).

The whole book of Revelation was prepared for God's people to be both an encouragement and a warning. It's an encouragement to trust and know that even though believers in the world are going to experience really tough times, if they endure to the end there will be great reward. Jesus encourages us to take the truths the book contains to heart – and not just treat them as information that we carry in our head. With our heart we can anticipate with joy all that God is preparing for His people.

But the book is also a strong warning of what's to come, so that no-one who reads these words will be without excuse. They won't be able to say they weren't told. Revelation 21:8 is very specific when it says:

'the cowardly, the unbelieving, the vile, the murderers, the sexually immoral, those who practice magic arts, the idolaters and all liars – their place will be in the fiery lake of burning sulphur. This is the second death.'

Many on that final day will want to ask God why He didn't warn them of this in advance, but He will point to the unread Bibles that lay gathering dust on their bookshelves.

The glorious good news of the Gospel doesn't exclude such people from heaven if they confess, repent, obtain forgiveness and are redeemed. Paul tells the Corinthian church that:

'that is what some of you were. But you were washed, you were sanctified, you were justified in the name of the Lord Jesus Christ and by the Spirit of our God' (1 Corinthians 6:11).

But, sadly, if people know the truth, ignore it, and remain in the practice of ungodliness, then they're placing themselves under condemnation by their own actions.

I used to own a large second-hand and antiquarian book shop. Regularly people would bring collections of books from their homes for sale. In most large family collections there was a Bible, often several Bibles. But only very rarely was it obvious that the Bibles had been read and well-used. Their owners had the truth in their hands but had never chosen to be blessed by taking it to heart.

HEAVEN BOUND

Believers often talk about going to heaven when they die but, according to the Word of God, no-one has yet entered the heaven that God has been preparing for us. Revelation tells us that no-one will enter heaven until after the day when the books are finally opened. Yes, the redeemed have been with the Lord in paradise, but paradise, as we have already seen, is more like the waiting room for heaven than heaven itself. If we want to learn more about our destiny in heaven – the ultimate destination of all believers from the time they were born again – then we need to turn to the last two chapters of the Bible, Revelation 21 and 22.

In the Gospels Jesus talks about the place that He and the Father would be preparing for the saints of God. But, in Revelation, Jesus tells John something of what heaven will actually be like. It was only after he had 'seen' the final judgement that John then saw in the Spirit what he described as **'a new heaven and a new earth**, *for the first heaven and the first earth had passed away, and there was no longer any sea'* (Revelation 21:1) (emphasis added).

After this he saw *'the Holy City,* **the new Jerusalem** *coming down out of heaven from God'* (Revelation 21:2). This was accompanied by the voice of God, declaring His original desire and intention for the creation of mankind:

> *'Now the dwelling of God is with men, and he will live with them. They will be his people, and God himself will be with them and be their God. He will wipe away every tear from their eyes. There will be no more death or mourning or crying or pain, for the old order of things has passed away'* (Revelation 21:3-5) (emphasis added).

God repeats His invitation to join Him in the new heaven and the new earth by saying:

> *'"To him who is thirsty I will give to drink without cost from the spring of the water of life. He who overcomes will inherit all this, and I will be his God and he will be my son"'* (Revelation 21:6-7).

What an incredible picture this is! Contrast it with the picture of beneficiaries of a family estate gathered around the lawyer's desk, nervously waiting to hear what they each might have inherited through the will of the one who has died. No, it's not like that with the family of God! **All** the redeemed have **all** the rights of a child of the King (John

1:12). We **all** inherit **everything** that God has prepared for us – and what's more, the One who died to make all this possible, is alive again for evermore and He's there to see us enjoying the inheritance!

The angel showed John what the new Jerusalem was going to look like – the new city that had descended from the new heaven to the new earth. Everything was magnificent, glorious and perfect (Revelation 21:9-21). The city needed no lighting:

'because the glory of God gives it light and the Lamb is its lamp. The nations will walk by its light and the kings of the earth will bring their splendour into it' (Revelation 21:23-24).

Since there is no night there the gates will never be shut and nothing impure will ever enter the city (Revelation 21:25-27). There is a *'river of the water of life'* (Revelation 22:1) flowing from the throne of God and of the Lamb, and by the river are trees that bear a fresh crop every month, the leaves of which are for the healing of the nations. In many similar expressions of the glory of God in the kingdom of heaven John describes the celestial city – the home of God and the place where those whose names are in the *Book of Life* will be welcome for eternity.

This is both our destination and our destiny. It's the place where God desires the journey of every man's life to be completed. It's also the place where we will finally discover our ultimate destiny, as we live the reality of what we were made for. We will enjoy the unique gifting and character that God gave to each and every one of His creation. It's going to be a place of huge and wonderful surprises, as we adventure with God in the enjoyment of the new heaven and the new earth.

How will all this come about? I have no idea. But it's not fanciful thinking to imagine the realities of eternal life with God in heaven. I look on the physical heavens in the night sky as we see them from planet earth. I see the amazing wonders of the created realm God has already made for His children. I see the incredible creativity that there is in the heart of man. I realise these all came from God in the first place and if this is just a sample of what He can do, I have no reason to doubt one word of what John wrote in the descriptive language of Revelation. What an incredible expectation belongs to those who choose to follow Jesus!

Perhaps John was wondering himself if what he was writing really was the truth, because right at the end of his vision he recorded the angel of God as saying to him:

> *'These words are trustworthy and true. The Lord, the God of the spirits of the prophets, sent his angel to show his servants the things that must soon take place'* (Revelation 22:6).

HEAVEN'S REWARDS

Earlier in our journey we recognised that our entrance to heaven's glory was entirely the result of God's grace and mercy. The lives of the redeemed are given as a reward to Jesus for laying down His life, whether they are those who came to Him at the end of their lives (like the thief on the cross) or those who had found the Lord near the beginning.

The reward of eternal life is entirely the fruit of what Jesus has done for us. None of us contributed anything to the salvation we received. It's entirely a result of what He did for us. Amazingly, we the redeemed are His reward! We have done nothing to merit it. Those who keep the faith are made righteous because of His shed blood, and there's also a crown of righteousness in store for them. Paul said:

> *'Now there is in store for me the crown of righteousness, which the Lord, the righteous Judge, will award to me on that day – and not only to me, but also to all who have longed for his appearing'* (2 Timothy 4:8).

There is, however, another type of reward, and when Jesus speaks to John, right at the end of his book, He tells him:

> *'Behold, I am coming soon! My reward is with me, and I will give to everyone according to what he has done'* (Revelation 22:12). For the redeemed, there will also be a judging of their lives that *'each one may receive what is due for the things done in the body'* (2 Corinthians 5:10).

The picture Paul uses to help us understand how important this is, is the testing of fire.

'The fire will test the quality of each man's work. If what he has built survives, he will receive his reward. If it is burned up, he will suffer loss; he himself will be saved, but only as one escaping through the flames' (1 Corinthians 3:13-15).

This very revealing passage refers to what we build on the foundation of Jesus Christ. He's the one and only foundation that matters and it's only what's built on Him that counts as far as eternity is concerned.

On several occasions in the Gospels Jesus talks about the rewards that are being stored up in heaven. For those who have suffered persecution and been the victim of false accusations because of Jesus, He says, *'great is your reward in heaven'* (Matthew 5:12 and Luke 6:23). Prayer is vital, but when we pray in order to impress others with our supposed godliness there's no eternal reward attached to our endeavours. However, Jesus said, when you go and pray quietly in your room, where only God can know you're praying *'then your Father, who sees what is done in secret, will reward you'* (Matthew 6:6).

When Jesus was talking to His disciples about His return, He said,

'For the Son of Man is going to come in his Father's glory with his angels, and then he will reward each person according to what he has done' (Matthew 16:27).

On another occasion He told people to *'love your enemies, do good to them . . . then your reward will be great'* (Luke 6:35). Paul sums up all these and several other Scriptures when he says,

'serve wholeheartedly, as if you were serving the Lord, not me, because you know that the Lord will reward everyone for whatever good he does, whether he is slave or free' (Ephesians 6:7-8).

There's an overwhelming testimony from the Scriptures which says that in heaven there will be rewards which are directly related to the way we've lived here on earth, and especially to what we've built in our lives on the foundation of Jesus, the one and only true foundation. There will be an award ceremony in heaven and we can look forward to entering heaven's glory and to the joy of being blessed by all that God has stored up for us.

'No eye has seen, no ear has heard, no mind has conceived what God has prepared for those who love him' (1 Corinthians 2:9). Let's keep this in mind as we seek to labour in the vineyard of the Lord, serving Him while it's still day, bringing in the harvest for eternity. Let's say 'no' to the enemy when he seeks to tempt and distract us and always say 'yes' to the voice of God when He gently whispers into our hearts by His Spirit. Heaven is a wonderful place – I'm looking forward to being there, and going on that incredible journey of discovery, finding out what my wonderful Saviour has stored up there for me and all the saints!

SUMMARY

God is preparing heaven for His children so that He can live there with them. It can't be made impure by the presence of sin, and only those whose names are in the Lamb's Book of Life *will be there. There'll be a new heaven, a new earth, and a new Jerusalem to look forward to. And it's where God is also storing up for us His rewards, which He'll give to those who've built their lives on the one and only foundation that matters – Jesus Christ.*

PRAYER

Thank You, Lord, for showing us something of what we can look forward to in heaven. I'm so grateful for my salvation and all that You're preparing for those who love You. Help me, Lord, to always be aware of the distant reality of the Heavenly Kingdom at the same time as seeking to bring heaven down to earth, as I serve You all my days in the present reality of life on earth. In Jesus' name, Amen

1   Quoted by William Barclay in his book The Ten Commandments (Collins, 1973)

2   Lewis, C S, Mere Christianity (Collins, UK ed, 2012)

3   Lewis, C S, The Joyful Christian (Macmillan, 1976)

NOW READ ON...

In Book 6 we have focussed on everything that Jesus did for us on the cross so that we could be forgiven for our sins and inherit eternal life. In Book 7 we will be taking a huge step forward in our *Journey to Freedom*. For now we are ready to look in detail at all the key areas of life and ask the important questions about our own personal healing needs.

First, we will look at God's plan for each one of us to be part of a functioning local church and then step by step we will look at how God wants to bring His wholeness into each area of our life.

Jesus' mission statement, taken from Isaiah 61:1, said that He had come to heal the broken-hearted and set the captives free. God does not want us to be continually struggling through life, unhealed from the consequences of issues that have been stumbling blocks to the fulfilment of our destiny. His plan is for each and every one of us to know and experience His healing hand on our lives.

In many ways, Book 7 is like a personal healing guide which draws on all the teaching we have learned together in Books 1-6 in order to bring us God's liberty and freedom. My prayer is that, as you work through each stage of the journey, you will enter into more and more of the healing that He has prepared for each one of us.

May I encourage you to read Book 7 carefully and prayerfully as you absorb the life-changing teaching from God's Word and apply it in your own life.

Peter Horrobin

ABOUT THE AUTHOR

Peter Horrobin is the Founder and International Director of Ellel Ministries International, which began in 1986 as a ministry of healing in the north-west of England. The work is now established in over thirty-five different countries.

After graduating from Oxford University with a degree in Chemistry, he spent a number of years in College and University lecturing, before leaving the academic environment for the world of business, where he founded a series of successful publishing and bookselling companies.

In his twenties Peter started to restore a vintage sports car (an *Alvis Speed 20*) but discovered that its chassis was bent. As he looked at the broken vehicle, wondering if it could ever be repaired, he sensed God asking him a question, *"You could restore this broken car, but I can restore broken lives. Which is more important?"* It was obvious that broken lives were more important than broken cars and so the beginnings of a vision for restoring people was birthed in his heart.

A hallmark of Peter's ministry has been his willingness to step out in faith and see God move to fulfil His promises, often in remarkable ways. His book, *Strands of Destiny*, tells many of the stories of what God has done in the past thirty years and makes an ideal companion volume to the *Journey to Freedom* Series.

In this season of their lives, Peter, and his wife Fiona are concentrating on writing so that all their knowledge and experience can be made permanently available in book form through Sovereign World Ltd.

ABOUT ELLEL MINISTRIES

www.ellel.org

OUR VISION

Ellel Ministries is a non-denominational Christian Mission Organization with a vision to resource and equip the Church by welcoming people, teaching them about the Kingdom of God and healing those in need (Luke 9:11).

OUR MISSION

Our mission is to fulfil the above vision throughout the world, as God opens the doors, in accordance with the Great Commission of Jesus and the calling of the Church to proclaim the Kingdom of God by preaching the good news, healing the broken-hearted and setting the captives free. We are, therefore, committed to evangelism, healing, deliverance, discipleship and training. The particular scriptures on which our mission is founded are **Isaiah 61:1–7; Matthew 28:18–20; Luke 9:1–2, 9:11; Ephesians 4:12; 2 Timothy 2:2.**

OUR BASIS OF FAITH

God is a Trinity. God the Father loves all people. God the Son, Jesus Christ, is Saviour and Healer, Lord and King. God the Holy Spirit indwells Christians and imparts the dynamic power by which they are enabled to continue Christ's ministry. The Bible is the divinely inspired authority in matters of faith, doctrine and conduct, and is the basis for teaching.

Ellel Ministries International
Ellel Grange
Ellel
Lancaster, LA2 0HN
United Kingdom

Further books by Peter Horrobin

STRANDS OF DESTINY

Peter Horrobin's personal account of how God envisioned him through the remains of a crashed car, to establish the healing work of Ellel Ministries at Ellel Grange, will build your faith as you journey with him through the ups and downs of what became a world-wide spiritual adventure.

Paperback 464 pages plus 48 pages of colour photographs, £14.99, ISBN 978-1-85240-835-0

FORGIVENESS – GOD'S MASTER KEY

Forgiveness is key to the restoration of our relationship with God and to healing from the consequences of hurtful, damaging human relationships. This book is one of the most outstanding and concise available on the subject of forgiveness.

Paperback 110 pages, £6.99, ISBN 978-1-85240-502-1

LIVING LIFE GOD'S WAY

Living Life God's Way is an immensely readable and practical book. In this revised and updated edition of *Living the Life – Practical Christianity for the Real World*, Peter Horrobin guides you through a landscape of hidden truths. Using real life testimonies, parables and illustrations to unlock some of the most difficult of life's issues that often make us stumble through our Christian walk. This book was written to help new Christians get established in their faith and to provide older Christians with the kind of realistic help that is needed to keep their lives on track with God.

Paperback 222 pages, £10.99, ISBN 978-1-85240-758-2

HEALING THROUGH DELIVERANCE

The Foundation and Practice of Deliverance Ministry

In this comprehensive, practical and ground-breaking volume, Peter draws on this extensive experience to set out a thorough and scriptural foundation for the healing and deliverance ministry—an integral part of fulfilling the Great Commission and a vital key to discipleship. This authoritative handbook will equip you to understand and respond to the call of God to set the captives free. A classic.

Hardback 630 pages, £24.99, ISBN 978-1-85240-498-7

HEALING FROM THE CONSEQUENCES OF ACCIDENT, SHOCK AND TRAUMA

Unhealed trauma is one of the primary reasons why some people do not easily heal from the consequences of accidents or sudden shocks. This ground-breaking book is the culmination of thirty years of experience praying for such people. This foundational teaching has been instrumental in bringing permanent healing to people all over the world.

Paperback 176 pages, £9.99, ISBN 978-1-85240-743-8

The Truth and Freedom Series

All the books in this series have been written by members of the Ellel Ministries Teams. Each one highlights a particular topic that has proved to be of significance in the lives of those who have come on our Healing Retreats. When we get God's truth into our hearts, He ministers His freedom into our lives.

Anger, How do you handle it?

Paperback, 112 pages, Paul and Liz Griffin, ISBN 978-1-85240-450-7

God's Covering, A Place of Healing

Paperback, 192 pages, David Cross, ISBN 978-1-85240-485-7

Healing from the consequences of Accident, Shock and Trauma

Paperback, 176 pages, Peter Horrobin, ISBN 978-1-85240-743-8

Hope and Healing for the Abused

Paperback, 128 pages, Paul and Liz Griffin, ISBN 978-1-85240-480-2

Intercession & Healing, Breaking Through with God

Paperback, 176 pages, Fiona Horrobin, ISBN 978-1-85240-500-7

Rescue from Rejection, Finding Security in God's Loving Acceptance

Paperback, 160 pages, Denise Cross, ISBN 978-1-85240-555-7

Soul Ties, The Unseen Bond in Relationships
Paperback, 128 pages, David Cross, ISBN 978-1-85240-597-7

Stepping Stones to the Father Heart of God
Paperback, 176 pages, Margaret Silvester, ISBN 978-1-85240-623-3

The Dangers of Alternative Ways of Healing, How to Avoid New Age Deceptions
Paperback, 176 pages, David Cross & John Berry, ISBN 978-1-85240-537-3

Trapped by Control, How to Find Freedom
Paperback, 112 pages, David Cross, ISBN 978-1-85240-501-4

ALL THESE BOOKS AND MANY MORE ARE AVAILABLE FROM SOVEREIGN WORLD.

Sovereign World Ltd

Please visit our online shop to browse our range of titles.

www.sovereignworld.com

or contact us at the headquarters address:

Sovereign World Ltd.
Ellel Grange
Bay Horse
Lancaster
Lancashire LA2 0HN
United Kingdom

Or email us at:
info@sovereignworld.com

Most books are also available in e-book format and can be purchased online.